The Unfinished Agenda

The Unfinished Agenda

Perspectives on Overcoming Hunger, Poverty, and Environmental Degradation

**Edited by Per Pinstrup-Andersen
and Rajul Pandya-Lorch**

International Food Policy Research Institute
Washington, D.C.

Library of Congress Cataloging-in-Publication Data available.

International Food Policy Research Institute
2033 K Street, NW, Washington, DC 20006-1002, USA
Telephone: +1-202-862-5600; Fax: +1-202-467-4439
www.ifpri.org

Contents

Introduction

Per Pinstrup-Andersen and Rajul Pandya-Lorch

The International Food Policy Research Institute has always held fast to the goal of generating policy information that will enable the world to feed its people sustainably, but in the early 1990s a world free of hunger and poverty looked a long way off. At that time we found that global poverty and food insecurity had fallen from their levels 20 years earlier but remained severe and persistent problems. Moreover, we were troubled to see considerable disagreement on the magnitude and nature of the world's food, agricultural, and environmental problems and no long-term vision or consensus about the steps required to feed the world, alleviate poverty, and protect the natural resource base. So in 1993, in collaboration with partners around the world, we launched an initiative called A 2020 Vision for Food, Agriculture, and the Environment, to develop a shared vision and consensus, to generate information, and to encourage debate and action on these topics. The 2020 Vision initiative undertakes these activities in pursuit of the ultimate goal of achieving a world where every person has access to sufficient food to sustain a healthy and productive life; where malnutrition is absent; and where food originates from efficient, effective, and low-cost food systems that are compatible with sustainable use of natural resources.

Today we find that some parts of the world have made great strides toward a situation of sustainable food security, others are inching toward it, and still others are moving away. This book brings together briefs and articles generated by the 2020 Vision initiative that remain highly relevant to the ongoing dialog and debate and, given the nature of the topics addressed, are likely to remain so for some time to come.

The initiative's policy briefs present state-of-the-art information on key topics related to food security, poverty alleviation, and sustainable resource management. Written by leading experts at IFPRI and around the world, these briefs draw upon a solid body of research. The initiative also publishes a periodic newsletter, *2020 News & Views*; each issue carries a lead article on an emerging or "hot" topic related to sustainable food security and based on interviews with policymakers, policy analysts, and experts. But these briefs and newsletters tend to have a short "shelf" life. Libraries usually do not catalog them, and they can easily get lost in the piles of papers on most people's desks. We have compiled them in a book as a way of making them readily available for use in policy debates and actions.

Together these pieces offer a fairly comprehensive picture of the policy issues the world must address if it is to overcome poverty, hunger, and environmental degradation. Achieving a world of sustainable food security involves policy actions in many related areas. Thus, readers will find in these pages discussions of nutrition and health problems, demographic changes, natural resources, microcredit, gender issues, globalization, and new technologies. Sub-Saharan Africa and South Asia are the sites of the world's most severe food security problems, and this book presents recent knowledge on these two specific regions.

The concluding chapter attempts to identify the most important policy actions required to achieve the 2020 Vision, based primarily on the knowledge presented in the rest of the book. At the international level, policies and institutions that guide globalization and technological progress to benefit the poor and malnourished will be of critical importance. At the national and community levels, policy action must be tailored to the particular circumstances and the intended beneficiaries should be empowered to participate in policy design and implementation. Policies to strengthen the human resource through education, primary health care, and better nutrition should be given high priority, along with policies and institutions to facilitate access by low-income people to productive resources, fair and well-functioning markets, and appropriate knowledge and technology. Good governance and an appropriate macroeconomic framework are also crucial.

Most of the briefs and articles included in this book have been left in their original form. Where deemed useful, the empirical evidence has been updated. Some of the people interviewed have moved on to other positions or occupations. However, all interviewees are identified by the position held at the time of the interviews. The rare instances when briefs were cut back or combined are noted in the source listing at the end of the book.

We wish to thank the contributors whose work has been included in this volume. We would also like to thank Heidi Fritschel for her editorial assistance.

PART 1

The Unfinished Agenda and Prospects for the Future

Chapter 1

Famine and Poverty in the 21st Century

Reported by Ellen Wilson

*The bottom line is that it is up to
governments to take action to prevent
hunger and future famine.*

When Tesfaye Getachew and his wife, Senait Gebre-Selassie, experienced a
severe drought on the heels of two years of dry weather in Ethiopia, they
had to sell off the last of their belongings to buy food. But this wasn't
enough to see them through more than a month or two because their assets were
so meager. When what little food they had ran out, Tesfaye was forced to beg. As
conditions worsened for everyone in the village because of the drought, neighbors
no longer helped each other, but fought each other for the handfuls of roots still
left in the fields. Twenty-five of the 100 families living in the village were wiped out
by cholera, which signaled the peak of the famine.

Famine. As we watch the gaunt faces on television, we wonder why does
famine happen. Should we blame the drought? Should we blame the war? Who or
what should we blame, and what can be done about it?

As researchers and policymakers work to answer these questions, they have
found that poverty, for the most part, is to blame. But poverty is complex, and its
solutions lie in its causes, which vary from locale to locale. Only after these causes
are examined can solutions be developed.

"Poverty is one of the most important unfinished tasks of this century," said
Senator Sartaj Aziz, former finance minister of Pakistan and a member of the inter-

national advisory committee for IFPRI's 2020 Vision initiative. "It is atrocious that there are still over 1 billion people living in poverty, half of them in conditions of extreme poverty, and an estimated 700 million people who lack enough food to eat."

Unfortunately, the most prevalent behavior exhibited by governments and the donor community toward poverty has been reactive—after poverty has led to famine.

"The proportion of money from the international donor community that has been made available to fight poverty has not been very significant," said Aziz. "In the late 1970s and early 1980s the problem of poverty received some attention, and many successful experiments were launched to find meaningful ways to reach the poor. However, the interest of the donor community in poverty was not sustained. In the next decade, there needs to be a much more determined effort to put these promising solutions into action on a much broader scale."

Once poverty reaches a state of famine, it is clear that there have been serious human lapses, in addition to whatever natural disasters might have occurred.

"Famine is ultimately the responsibility of governments both in its cause and in its resolution," said Patrick Webb, research fellow at IFPRI, who has written, with Joachim von Braun, several IFPRI reports on famine prevention and an IFPRI report on hunger for the World Bank's recent conference on hunger. "Famine is the final manifestation of government's failure to serve and protect its citizens. Famine also represents a breakdown in the community's ability to protect itself and its weaker members. Famine happens when governments and households fail to make the right moves and the right choices at the right moment."

There has been much debate about what the right "moves" are for governments and households in preventing poverty and, ultimately, hunger, food insecurity, and famine. According to Aziz, governments should first carry out a systematic survey to find out the causes of poverty in a particular location and then decide on how best to address these causes.

"Everything can work in the right context," said Webb. "No strategy is inherently better than another. Understanding when and where to use each tool is what matters."

According to Webb, governments and the international aid community must build up the capacity of the poor to buy food and to cope with small and large catastrophes.

The range of options includes diversifying the income base through nonfarm jobs so that families don't have to rely solely on rainfed agriculture; investing in agricultural research and transferring technology, such as drought-resistant and high-yielding crops, to farmers; allowing markets to function freely so that the buying and selling of food is not affected by artificial restrictions and political turmoil; providing some of the poor with food subsidies such as food stamps; making credit available to the poor for building up assets and purchasing needed farm supplies; investing in road building and other infrastructure because markets cannot work if there are no roads on which food can be delivered; and promoting sustainable use of the natural resource base.

According to Aziz, aid efforts also need to focus on social issues that contribute to poverty, including inadequate health care and sanitation, lack of literacy, and discrimination against segments of the population on the basis of race or ethnicity. "However, many of these solutions have not received international acceptance mainly because of the cost-benefit requirement of aid dollars," said Aziz. "How can you put a financial return on an investment in education or vocational training?"

Researchers also call on governments and the donor community to be rigorous in seeking out early warning signs of impending hunger or famine. According to Tom Zopf, director of Food Aid Management, a Washington, D.C.-based organization that seeks to improve the efficiency and effectiveness of food aid, "People have certain coping mechanisms that they use to survive through the low periods, such as using their savings, selling off assets like the family possessions or livestock, and sending family members off to the cities in search of work. These actions only make families more vulnerable to hunger, and governments must be able to track and act upon them before families and whole communities end up in refugee camps."

Researchers also point out the value in asking the community itself what needs to be done. "People need to have more control over their own resources and over the development process, be it agriculture, health, or family planning," said Zopf. "In the development community, we have many solutions, but unless the people affected tell us what the right ones are, we'll be nowhere."

In the past, according to Zopf, food aid, for the most part, did nothing to prevent the next famine or hunger in the coming years. Recently, there have been efforts to obtain long-term development benefits from emergency-relief activities, such as food-for-work programs where roads or other infrastructure are constructed or the provision of nutritional or vocational counseling in relief camps. "You need to do what you can where you can and try to get as much development mileage out of emergency aid as possible," said Zopf. "But this takes ingenuity and creativity."

Given the twin pressures of the burgeoning population and a limited natural resource base, poverty is also inextricably linked to the environment. Growing family size and deepening poverty force families to cultivate marginal lands and reduce fallow periods, which only make the next years more difficult. Although, according to Aziz, conservation of the environment is crucial, it cannot fall on the shoulders of the poor. "For example, if you ask poor farmers and pastoralists living in conditions of extreme poverty to stop cutting down trees for their fuel, then you must provide them with subsidized kerosene and stoves."

When military conflicts and political turmoil spur the onslaught of famine, what can be done? Not much except delivering emergency food aid and relief to the affected areas as soon as possible, according to researchers. "However, a past record of political instability should not be an excuse for not doing anything in a country when there is a window of opportunity," said Webb. "The international donor community should step in and reward peace and political stability with long-term development aid wherever and whenever it occurs."

Hunger is most acute now in Sub-Saharan Africa, but in terms of actual numbers, more people are hungry in Asia—in India, China, and Bangladesh. Some wonder why famine and malnutrition ever occur at all given the world's great food surpluses. According to Webb, the surpluses are in the wrong places. "When you're talking about surpluses, you're talking about Europe and North America. Though some is redistributed to the developing world through food aid, this is really a drop in the ocean compared with the need."

The bottom line is that it is up to governments to take action to prevent hunger and future famine. Amartya Sen, a leading researcher on hunger issues, has found that democracies tend to do better at preventing famines, probably because governments in democracies are charged with being responsible to the needs of the people who elected them.

"From a cynical point of view, it actually costs more to respond to emergencies, which are a constant drain on international aid dollars, than to invest properly in preventing them," said Webb. And prevention will be an essential task in the coming years as the world sees the population increase by 2.5 billion people by the year 2020.

Chapter 2

Global Food Security

A Review of the Challenges

Per Pinstrup-Andersen, Rajul Pandya-Lorch, and Mark W. Rosegrant

*The policy choices and investment decisions made will
profoundly influence the number and location of
food-insecure people in the future.*

The extent and depth of food insecurity in the developing world at the turn of a new century and millennium remains unconscionable. About 800 million people—one-sixth of the developing world's population—do not have access to sufficient food to lead healthy, productive lives. Around 280 million of these food-insecure people live in South Asia; 240 million in East Asia; 180 million in Sub-Saharan Africa; and the rest in Latin America, Middle East, and North Africa. Although progress is being made in tackling food insecurity, it is slow. And in Sub-Saharan Africa the number of food-insecure people has actually doubled since 1969–71. According to recent projections from the Food and Agriculture Organization of the United Nations (FAO), the World Food Summit goal of halving the number of food-insecure people from 800 million in 1995 to 400 million by 2015 will not be achieved until 2030 (Figure 2.1).

Results from IFPRI's revised and updated global food model, the International Model for Policy Analysis of Commodities and Trade (IMPACT), suggest that there will be similarly slow progress in reducing child malnutrition. Under the most likely or baseline scenario, 132 million children under the age of six years—one out of every four children—will be malnourished in 2020. This figure represents a decline of only 20 percent from 166 million in 1997 (Figure 2.2).

Figure 2.1 Food Insecurity in the Developing World, 1969/71–2030

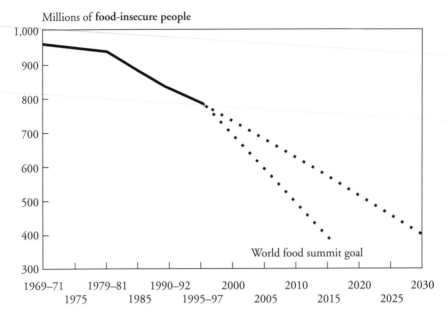

Source: Food and Agriculture Organization of the United Nations (FAO), "Agriculture: Towards 2015/30," Technical Interim Report (Rome: 2000).

Figure 2.2 Child Malnutrition in the Developing World, 1970–2020

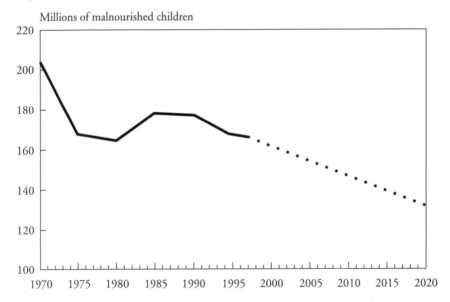

Source: 1970–95 data from Lisa Smith and Lawrence Haddad, *Overcoming Child Malnutrition in Developing Countries: Past Achievements and Future Choices*, 2020 Vision Discussion Paper 30 (Washington, D.C.: International Food Policy Research Institute, 2000); 1997–2025 projections from IFPRI IMPACT simulations, October 2000.

Figure 2.3 Poverty in the Developing World, 1987–2008

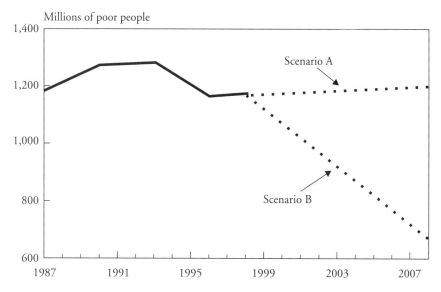

Source: World Bank, *Poverty Trends and Voices of the Poor* (Washington, D.C.: 1999).
Note: Scenario A: slow growth and rising inequality; Scenario B: Inclusive growth.

Micronutrient deficiencies remain widespread. About 2 billion people suffer from iron-deficient anemia, more than 2 billion people are at risk of iodine-deficiency disorders, and 250 million children are affected by severe vitamin A deficiency. Relatively little attention has been paid to other important but neglected micronutrients such as zinc, riboflavin, and calcium, and the global extent and consequences of their deficiencies remain unknown. The consequences of micronutrient malnutrition include higher mortality and morbidity, lower cognitive ability and work production, impaired reproduction, and forgone economic growth.

Food insecurity is closely associated with poverty. About 1.2 billion people in the developing world are absolutely poor, with only a dollar a day or less per person to meet food, shelter, and other basic needs. According to the World Bank, the number of poor people could remain unchanged over the next decade if growth remains slow and inequality increases from current levels (Scenario A in Figure 2.3). However, if countries adopt policies and interventions that foster inclusion and if all benefit equally from growth, the number of poor people could decline by 40 percent to 680 million by 2008 (Scenario B).

The majority of the world's poor live in rural areas. They depend on agriculture, either directly or indirectly, for their incomes and food security.

Figure 2.4 World Population, 1950–2020

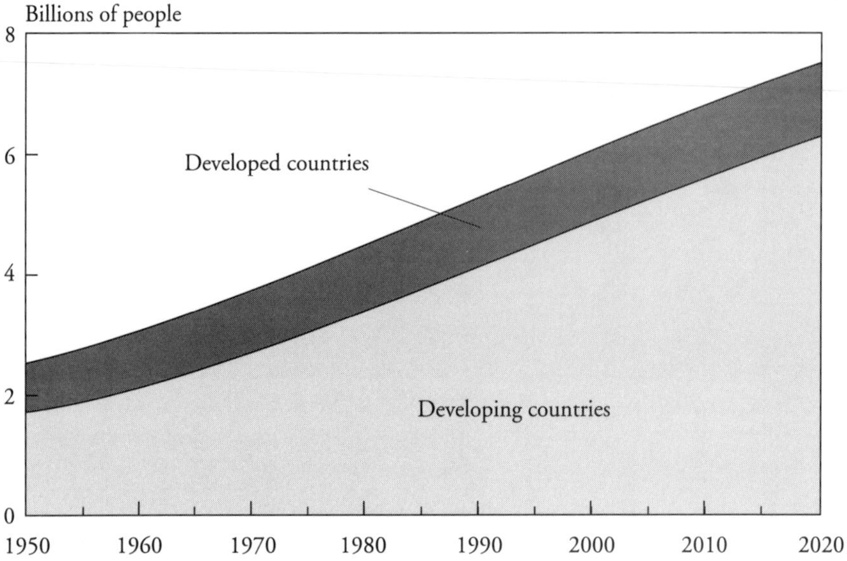

Source: United Nations, *World Population Prospects: The 1998 Revision* (New York: 1999).
Note: Medium-variant projections for 2000–2020.

During the next two decades, the world's population is projected to increase by 24 percent and to reach 7.5 billion in 2020. Virtually all of the population increase will take place in developing countries, and much of it in the urban areas (Figure 2.4). The rapid urbanization of the developing world and associated changes in lifestyles will have profound effects on food preferences and hence on demand.

Prospects for economic growth appear favorable in the developing world, with incomes projected to grow at an average of 4.7 percent annually during the next two decades (Figure 2.5). All major regions are expected to experience income increases, but Sub-Saharan Africa's average per capita income is so low that even by 2020 it is projected to remain less than a dollar a day, condemning many people in the region to persistent food insecurity.

IMPACT projects that a growing and urbanizing population with rising incomes will increase global demand for cereals by 35 percent between 1997 and 2020 to 2,497 million tons and for meat by 57 percent to 327 million tons. Almost all of the increase in demand will take place in developing countries. By 2020, developing countries as a group are forecast to demand twice as much cereals and meat as developed countries (Figure 2.6).

Figure 2.5 Projected Annual Income Growth Rates, 1997–2020

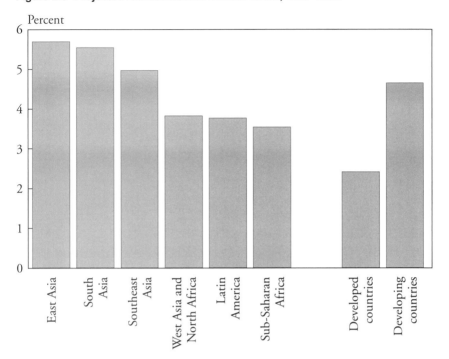

Source: IFPRI IMPACT simulations, October 2000.

Figure 2.6 Total Demand for Cereals and Meat Products, 1997–2020

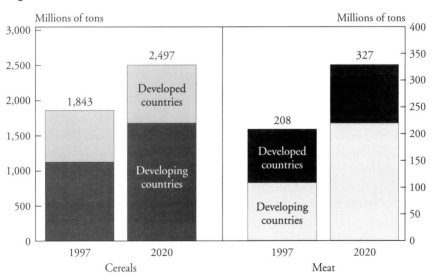

Source: IFPRI IMPACT simulations, October 2000.

Figure 2.7 Sources of Growth in Cereal Production, 1997–2020

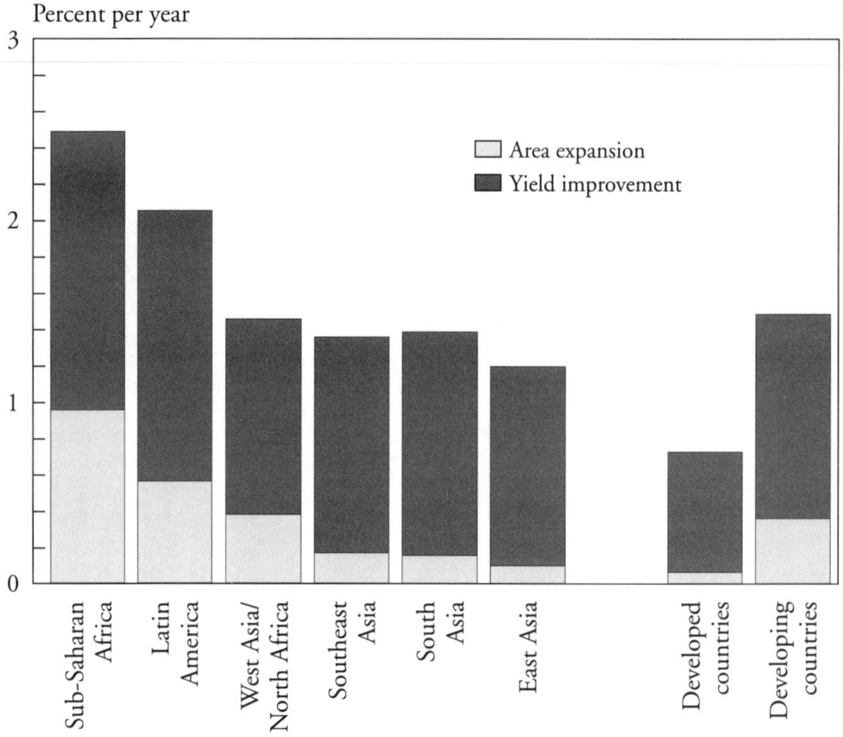

Percent per year

Source: IFPRI IMPACT simulations, October 2000.

How will farmers meet such large increases in cereal demand? Primarily through increases in productivity. Ecologically and economically sound opportunities for expanding cultivated area are limited in most developing countries and virtually nonexistent in many Asian countries. To bring about the necessary production increases, farmers will have to improve their crop yields (Figure 2.7).

Yet farmers in both developed and developing countries are experiencing slower growth in cereal yields, and this trend is projected to continue in coming decades (Figure 2.8). Contributing factors include insufficient investment in agricultural research and modern technology, inadequate extension services linking researchers and farmers, insufficient or improper use of inputs, poorly functioning markets, lack of appropriate infrastructure, and lack of timely access to credit.

As a result of the expected slowdown in crop yield increases, reduced population growth, and strong growth in demand for meat in developing countries,

Figure 2.8 Annual Growth in Cereal Yields, 1982–2020

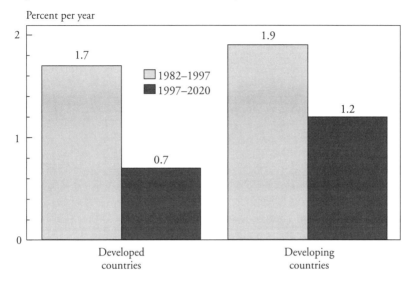

Source: IFPRI IMPACT simulations, October 2000.

food prices are projected to remain steady or fall slightly between 1997 and 2020 (Figure 2.9).

Although cereal production in the developing world is projected to increase by 45 percent between 1997 and 2020, it will not keep pace with the increase in demand. As a result, net cereal imports by developing countries are forecast to almost double over this period, with the largest absolute increase expected in East Asia and the largest relative increase in South Asia (Figure 2.10).

As noted earlier, the number of malnourished children is projected to decline from 166 million in 1997 to 132 million by 2020 in the most likely scenario. However, IMPACT projects that under certain conditions this number could drop even further to 94 million. These conditions include increases in projected income growth in developing countries; increases in crop yield growth in both developed and developing countries; increases in cultivated area and irrigated area in developing countries; improvements in health and education; and lower-than-expected population growth. Conversely, the number of malnourished children could climb to 175 million in 2020 under other conditions, such as declines in projected income growth in developing countries; declines in crop yield growth in both developed and developing countries; declines in cultivated area growth; zero growth in irrigation; reductions in health and education indicators; increases in agricultural protection

Figure 2.9 International Food Prices in Real Terms, 1997 and 2020

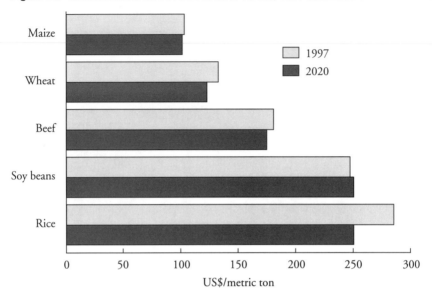

Source: IFPRI IMPACT simulations, October 2000.
Note: Beef price is per 100 kilograms.

Figure 2.10 Net Cereal Imports of Major Developing Regions, 1997 and 2020

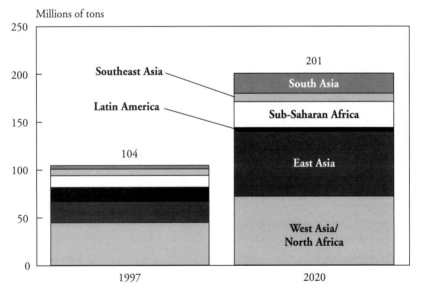

Source: IFPRI IMPACT simulations, October 2000.

in developing countries; and higher-than-expected population growth. Hence, the policy choices and investment decisions made will profoundly influence the number and location of food-insecure people in the future.

Increasing food production and productivity is essential to achieving food security, and policies that promote this goal include the following:

- developing efficient and effective markets for agricultural inputs and outputs and assuring access to land and other productive resources by the poor;

- developing and maintaining appropriate infrastructure—including transportation, storage, and marketing infrastructure—particularly in rural areas;

- facilitating timely, reasonably priced access to required plant nutrients from both organic and inorganic sources and supporting an integrated nutrient management approach that seeks to both increase agricultural production and safeguard the environment for future generations;

- removing institutional barriers to the creation and expansion of small-scale rural credit and savings institutions and making them available to small farmers, traders, transporters, and processing enterprises;

- expanding public-sector research, using the most appropriate methods, including agroecological methods, conventional research methods, and genetic engineering for the benefit of the poor and food insecure; and

- pursuing macroeconomic, trade, and sectoral policies that benefit low-income people's food security.

Making more food available is a necessary but not sufficient condition for food security. Ensuring that people have access to that food is also vital. Policies to reduce child malnutrition and improve food security by improving access to food include the following:

- investing in improving women's education and status—an IFPRI study found that improvements in women's education and status together accounted for 55 percent of the total reduction in child malnutrition in the developing world between 1970 and 1995 (Figure 2.11);

- fighting hidden hunger or micronutrient deficiencies by fortifying foods and offering vitamin supplements, encouraging diversified diets or healthier eating

Figure 2.11 Estimated Contribution of Major Determinants to Reductions in Child Malnutrition, 1970–95

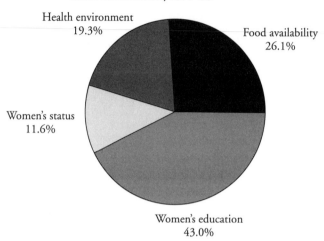

Health environment
19.3%

Food availability
26.1%

Women's status
11.6%

Women's education
43.0%

Source: Lisa Smith and Lawrence Heddad, *Overcoming Child Malnutrition in Developing Countries: Past Achievements and Future Choices,* 2020 Vision Discussion Paper 30 (Washington, D.C.: International Food Policy Research Institute, 2000).
Note: Malnourished children refers to underweight children.

habits, and breeding nutrients into staple crops through conventional plant breeding or biotechnology;

• tackling urban food insecurity by improving urban livelihoods and employment among the poor, supporting environmentally sound urban agriculture, promoting healthy physical environments and adequate caring and feeding practices, and designing more participatory and urban programs and strategies; and

• effectively addressing health risks and diseases such as HIV/AIDS, tuberculosis, malaria, and obesity that compromise food and nutrition security.

Finally, improving policies and increasing investments for food and agriculture are particularly important in Sub-Saharan Africa. This is the only region where the number of malnourished children has consistently increased since 1970, and it is the only region where it is projected to continue to increase through 2020. By then, 30 percent of the developing world's malnourished children would be residing in Sub-Saharan Africa, up from 10 percent in 1970 (Figure 2.12).

Figure 2.12 Child Malnutrition in Sub-Saharan Africa, 1970, 1997, and 2020

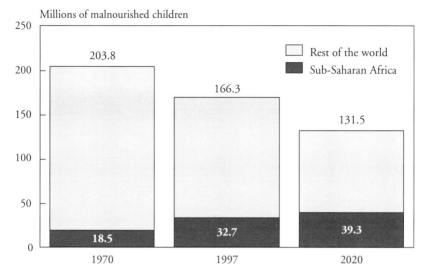

Source: Lisa Smith and Lawrence Heddad, *Overcoming Child Malnutrition in Developing Countries: Past Achievements and Future Choices,* 2000 Vision Discussion Paper 30 (Washington, D.C.: International Food Policy Research Institute, 2000); IFPRI IMPACT simulations, October 2000.

Globalization—whose key features include international trade liberalization, the opening up of economies in both developed and developing countries, and a freer flow of capital, labor, information, and technology—is a major emerging phenomenon. It has considerable potential to significantly influence food security for better or worse, but its implications and consequences are not well known or understood. It is highly unlikely that the forces of globalization can be turned back. It is imperative that we identify the domestic policy changes required in developing and developed countries to minimize negative and maximize positive effects of globalization on poor people in developing countries. In a globalizing world, new and different groups of people may be vulnerable to food insecurity, but at the same time new and different instruments and opportunities for facilitating food security may become available. The challenge is to proactively guide globalization so as to benefit poor, food-insecure people.

PART 2

Nutrition and Health: The Ultimate Goals

Chapter 3

Overcoming Child Malnutrition in Developing Countries

Past Achievements and Future Choices

Lisa C. Smith and Lawrence Haddad

*Education of women is a powerful
weapon against malnutrition.*

I n 1995, 167 million children under five years old—almost one-third of developing-country children—were malnourished. Malnutrition causes a great deal of human suffering, and it is a violation of a child's human rights. It is associated with more than half of all deaths of children worldwide. People who survive a malnourished childhood are less physically and intellectually productive and suffer from more chronic illness and disability. The costs to society are enormous. Eradicating malnutrition remains a tremendous public policy challenge. Which types of interventions will have the greatest impact in reducing child malnutrition? The study on which this brief is based uses national data for 63 countries over 1970–96 to explore this question.

Determinants of Child Nutritional Status

In order to reduce malnutrition, one must understand its causes. The *immediate* determinants of a child's nutritional status are the child's dietary intake and health. These, in turn, are influenced by three household-level *underlying* determinants: food security, adequate care for mothers and children, and a proper health environment. Finally, the underlying determinants are influenced by the *basic* determinants: the potential resources available to a country or community, and a host of political, cultural, and social factors that affect their utilization. The study focuses on the underlying determinants, using four variables to represent them: national food availability (for food security), women's education and women's status relative to men's (for both quality of care and food security), and access to safe water (for the quality of the health environment). It also explores two basic determinants, using per capita national income to capture the availability of resources in a country and democracy as an indicator of the political context that influences malnutrition.

Reductions in Child Malnutrition during 1970–95

Between 1970 and 1995, the number of malnourished children declined by 37 million, from 204 million to 167 million, while the prevalence of malnutrition (as measured by weight below the norm) in the developing world as a whole fell from 46.5 percent to 31 percent, about 15 percentage points in all (see Table 3.1). Progress in reducing malnutrition has varied greatly from one region to another. The prevalence of malnutrition has declined the fastest in South Asia (by 23 percentage points) and slowest in Sub-Saharan Africa (4 percentage points). The number of malnourished children has declined most sharply in East Asia (from 78 to 38 million). The situation is particularly troubling in Sub-Saharan Africa where the number of malnourished children has increased by 70 percent. Since 1970, the prevalence has decreased in 35 developing countries, held steady in 15, and increased in 12, with most of the countries with increases in Sub-Saharan Africa.

Table 3.1 Malnourished Children in Developing Countries, by Region, 1970, 1995, and 2020

Region	1970	1995	2020 (under the status quo)
Percent underweight			
South Asia	72.3	49.3	37.4
Sub-Saharan Africa	35.0	31.1	28.8
East Asia	39.5	22.9	12.8
Near East and North Africa	20.7	14.6	5.0
Latin America and the Caribbean	21.0	9.5	1.9
All developing countries	46.5	31.0	18.4
Number underweight (millions)			
South Asia	92.2	86.0	66.0
Sub-Saharan Africa	18.5	31.4	48.7
East Asia	77.6	38.2	21.4
Near East and North Africa	5.9	6.3	3.2
Latin America and the Caribbean	9.5	5.2	1.1
All developing countries	203.8	167.1	140.3

All four of the underlying-determinant factors the study considers are found to have made substantial contributions to the reductions in the developing-country prevalence of child malnutrition over 1970–95. Improvements in women's education have contributed by far the most, being responsible for 43 percent of the total reduction. Improvements in per capita food availability contributed about 26 percent and improvements in health environments 19 percent. The lowest contribution (12 percent) came from improvements in women's status. While this factor has a potentially strong impact, its potential has not been realized because women's status has improved little over 1970–95.

Together, women's education and relative status have contributed to more than half of the 1970–95 reduction in the prevalence of malnutrition in developing countries. Education of women is a powerful weapon against malnutrition: increased knowledge and skills enable women to earn higher incomes, and thus enhance household food security, and education improves the quality of day-to-day care women give to their children. Women's status relative to men's influences children's nutritional status through its effects on the mental and physical condition of the women themselves and through women's autonomy and ability to influence how household resources are allocated. In short, low status restricts women's capacity to act in their own and their children's best interests.

Per capita national income and democracy—the basic-determinant factors—influence the nutritional status of women only indirectly through public and private investments in the underlying factors. Increases in per capita national income have accounted for roughly 50 percent of the total reduction in child malnutrition. Democracy is a potentially powerful influence because it gives people a voice in how government resources are allocated, but democracy has not improved over the period for the developing countries as a whole. Thus no overall contribution could be measured.

Projections of Child Malnutrition to 2020

The future prevalence of child malnutrition obviously depends on the degree of effort exerted to reduce it. This study presents three scenarios based on the projected evolution of the underlying determinants of child malnutrition during 1995–2020. In the status quo, or "do-nothing-different" scenario, per capita food availability rises about 9 percent, and safe water access, female secondary school enrollment, and the female-to-male life expectancy ratio improve at the same rates as they did during 1985–95. The prevalence of underweight children falls from 31 percent in 1995 to 18 percent in 2020 (Table 3.1). About 140 million children, roughly one-fifth of developing-country children, would remain malnourished under this scenario. Under the pessimistic scenario, in which the rate of improvement in the nonfood underlying determinants is assumed to decline by 25 percent and per capita food availability to be stagnant, the predicted percentage of malnourished children under five in developing countries is 22 percent. If this scenario were to prevail, only a slight decline in the number of malnourished children would be achieved by 2020: a reduction of 12 million. In the optimistic scenario, in which the rate of improvement in the nonfood underlying determinants is assumed to increase by 25 percent and per capita food availability by 16 percent, the prevalence of child malnutrition in the year 2020 would be cut in half, falling to 15 percent (leaving 128 million children malnourished).

The projections to 2020 for the developing countries as a whole mask wide variation across the regions. Under all scenarios, South Asia will continue to be the region with the highest prevalence and numbers of malnourished children, although both will fall rapidly. Little progress in reducing the prevalence of child malnutrition will be made in Sub-Saharan Africa. Given slow rates of decrease in prevalence and large expected increases in the total number of African children under five, the number of malnourished children will increase under all scenarios, rising as high as 55 million under the pessimistic scenario. The prevalence and number of malnourished children are expected to decline the fastest in East Asia. Malnutrition will fall to very low levels in the Near East and North Africa, and will almost be eliminated in Latin America and the Caribbean.

Priorities for the Future

Even under the most optimistic of scenarios, as many as 128 million children would still be malnourished. What combinations of actions will lead to the greatest reductions in child malnutrition by 2020? Given resource constraints and knowledge of the costs of alternative interventions, how should policymakers prioritize investments to reduce child malnutrition most quickly in coming decades?

In Sub-Saharan Africa and South Asia, improvements in per capita food availability and women's education offer the best hope for future reductions in child malnutrition. In South Asia, promotion of improved status for women should also be prioritized. In East Asia, the Near East and North Africa, and Latin America and the Caribbean, women's education should be given top priority, followed by women's status relative to men's. Additional secondary priorities are food availability for East Asia and health environment improvements for Latin America and the Caribbean. To maintain the necessary resource base and political will for these investments, improvements in national income growth and democratic development must be accelerated as well.

The study finds that significant progress can be made toward reducing child malnutrition through accelerated action in sectors that have not been the traditional focus of nutrition interventions. Efforts to improve women's education, raise food supplies (or reduce population growth or both), bolster women's status, and create healthful environments should be an integral part of strategies for reducing child malnutrition in the future. These initiatives should be seen as complementary to more direct nutrition interventions, such as feeding programs and nutrition education.

Any comprehensive strategy for resolving the problem of child malnutrition must include actions to address both its underlying and basic causes. This is the key message of the study underlying this brief. If the economic resources of the developing countries, as indicated by national incomes, cannot be raised, then increased investment in health environments, women's education and relative status, and food availability will not be forthcoming. Similarly, if a democratic government is not in place, people will not be able to bring pressure on governments to have their needs met. But just having sufficient income and a democratic government are not enough. Increased national income must actually be spent on improvements in the underlying determinants, which requires knowledge of their roles in reducing child malnutrition and political commitment to do so.

Chapter 4

Health and Nutrition

Emerging and Reemerging Issues in Developing Countries

Rafael Flores

The benefits of good health and nutrition on
economic growth cannot be overstated.

A healthy and nutritionally well-fed population is indispensable for economic growth and development. Health and nutritional status affect the capacity to learn, which in turn determines productivity and economic growth. Evidence from developing countries shows that adult productivity depends to a considerable extent on the contribution health and nutrition during early childhood make to educational attainment. Studies also show that a healthy adult with a nutritionally adequate diet has a higher level of economic productivity in both own-farm production and the labor market than one who eats and keeps less well.

There are many examples of the impact of ill health, which is often tied to the vulnerabilities caused by poor nutrition, on economic outcomes. For example, in Tanzania the average cost of treatment of a single HIV/AIDS infection, including the loss of productivity, is estimated to be between 8.5 and 18 percent of per capita income. Countries with severe malaria outbreaks have an average annual economic growth rate that is 1.3 percent lower than those that do not. Tuberculosis (TB) patients are absent from work three to four months out of the year, forfeiting 20 to 35 percent of annual household income.

Causation, Risks, and Effects

While the interaction of inadequate dietary intake and disease leads to malnutrition, disability, and death, it is also clear that insufficient access to food, inappropriate caring practices, a poor environment, inadequate health services, low women's status, and poverty play a major role in catalyzing the whole process. Each of these factors can be a cause, a risk, and/or an outcome; the pathways toward and away from good health and nutrition go in multiple directions.

Take the impact of poverty on HIV/AIDS and TB. Poverty increases the exposure to, as well as the impact of, HIV/AIDS. It diminishes the perceived value of avoiding HIV/AIDS ("we will die soon anyway"), increases the relative costs of preventing and treating the illness, and worsens the impact of weakened immunity because it commingles with a more hostile bacterial and viral environment. Under these circumstances, TB reemerges rather easily, augmenting the negative impact of poverty. Poverty and TB in tandem increase the already deleterious impact of HIV/AIDS on family, friends, community, and state.

Looking at the causal process in reverse, HIV/AIDS and tuberculosis increase poverty in the short to medium run by stripping assets—human, social, financial, physical, natural, informational, and political. Asset rundown leaves individuals, families, and communities more exposed to future health and nutrition shocks. In the meantime, public health resources are increasingly diverted away from prevention and rural primary care to the treatment of HIV/AIDS-infected individuals.

The Global Burden of Disease

The 1996 World Health Organization study of the global burden of disease predicts that deaths from communicable diseases, maternal and perinatal conditions, and nutritional deficiencies (Group I) are expected to decline by more than half, from 34 percent of all deaths due to disease in 1990 to 15 percent in 2020. The projected decrease reflects the overall improvements in Group I conditions brought about by increased income, greater literacy, and progress in the development of antimicrobials and vaccines. The major exception to this trend is HIV/AIDS, for which global mortality is rising rapidly, from 300,000 deaths in 1990 to 2.7 million in 1999.

While Group I conditions as a whole are expected to decline, deaths from noncommunicable diseases (Group II) are expected to rise from 55 percent of all deaths due to disease in 1990 to 73 percent in 2020. In the developing world Group II deaths are expected to climb from 47 percent of all deaths due to disease to almost 70 percent.

HIV/AIDS, Tuberculosis, and Malaria

Today, approximately 36 million individuals are living with HIV/AIDS. Sub-Saharan Africa is the region most affected by this disease. Most, if not all, of the 25 million people in Sub-Saharan Africa infected with HIV/AIDS will have died by the year 2020, in addition to the 13.7 million Africans already claimed by the epidemic. HIV/AIDS is also spreading dramatically in Asia, which will overtake Sub-Saharan Africa in absolute numbers before 2010. HIV/AIDS has contributed dramatically to exorbitant health care costs, labor shortages, a declining asset base, breakdown of social bonds, loss of livestock, and reliance on crops that are easier to produce but less nutritious and economically valuable. All of these effects contribute to food and nutrition insecurity.

TB is the leading infectious killer of young and middle-aged adults in the world. It causes 26 percent of avoidable deaths in the developing world. TB and HIV/AIDS often conjoin to destroy lives. TB kills 30 percent of AIDS victims in Africa and Asia, and HIV accelerates the progression to active TB by up to one hundredfold. The burden of TB is expected to increase, with 80 million deaths over the next three decades. TB's negative impact on the social fabric of families and their nutrition security is enormous.

Malaria is a major health problem in parts of Asia, Latin America, the Middle East, and the Pacific. However, Africa faces the greatest burden of the disease. Each year 300 to 500 million people become ill with malaria and 1.5 to 2.7 million people die. Ninety percent of this mortality is in Africa, in children under the age of 5. Pregnant women are also severely affected, and so are their developing fetuses. Malaria is on the increase due to insecticide resistance, antimalarial drug resistance, and environmental changes. Because malaria often strikes during harvest time, it can threaten food security and agricultural production.

Intrauterine Growth Retardation, Cardiovascular and Endocrine Diseases, and Obesity

IUGR refers to fetal growth that has been constrained in the uterus. It results in newborns that have not attained their full growth potential and are already malnourished at birth. Recent estimates suggest that about 11 percent of newborns, or 12.6 million infants, suffer from low birth weight at term (the IUGR proxy). Low birth weight at term is especially common in South Central Asia, where 21 percent of newborns are affected. Low birth weight at term is also common in Middle and West Africa.

The "Barker hypothesis," which remains controversial, is founded on the concept that maternal dietary imbalances at critical periods of fetal development affect fetal structure and metabolism in ways that predispose the individual to later cardiovascular and endocrine diseases. This hypothesis may have major implications for public health, especially in developing countries. This is because in the developing world a high proportion of births occur in the birth-weight range with the highest risk of developing adult disease. In addition, the prevalence of risk factors, such as obesity, that might lead to high blood pressure, cardiovascular disease, non-insulin-dependent diabetes, and some cancers is increasing rapidly in some developing countries.

Obesity remains rare in Sub-Saharan Africa and South Asia. But in the more developed countries of Latin America, the Middle East/North Africa, and Central Eastern Europe/Commonwealth of Independent States, obesity in women and children is as common as it is in the United States. Some countries with high levels of obesity still report significant rates of childhood stunting and nutritional deficiencies. The existence of a dual nutrition agenda of obesity and undernutrition presents a difficult challenge because resources are limited.

Aging, Health, and Nutrition

The percentage of the world's population over 60 years old in 1980 was 8.5 percent. It now stands at 11 percent, or 613 million people. By 2020 there will be 1 billion elderly, with 71 percent living in developing countries. The elderly will be susceptible to the health problems traditionally associated with low-income societies, including infections and accidents, and their diet and nutritional status will interact with these conditions. Infections that traditionally produced mortality in early life, such as malaria, TB, respiratory infections, or diarrhea, may reemerge in the lives of the elderly in developing countries.

Neglected Micronutrients

Poorer populations usually consume few animal products, so their intakes of vitamin A, iron, zinc, riboflavin, vitamin B-12, vitamin B-6, and calcium are inadequate. Poor diets may also contain few fruits and a limited variety of vegetables and, therefore, low amounts of beta-carotene, folic acid, and vitamin C. Failure to address the problem of these neglected micronutrients means that a high proportion of the world's population—especially infants, children, women of reproductive age, and the elderly—will continue to suffer the illnesses and debilities associated with this form of malnutrition.

Conclusion

A positive relationship exists between health and nutrition and economic productivity. The benefits of good health and nutrition on economic growth cannot be overstated. But to harness these benefits, the interactions of risk, causation, and consequences among poverty, food insecurity, health, and nutrition need to be understood.

Chapter 5

Fighting Hidden Hunger

Reported by Heidi Fritschel

*No single solution is likely to solve
the micronutrients problem.*

In the early 1980s, researchers from the Johns Hopkins University School of Hygiene and Public Health studying vitamin A consumption and blindness in Indonesia noticed that children with mild night blindness and dry eyes—symptoms of vitamin A deficiency—appeared to be at a higher risk of dying in the next three to four months. To follow up, they studied 30,000 children in 450 villages on the island of Sumatra, giving children in half of the villages a large dose of vitamin A every six months and children in the other villages nothing. The findings were so dramatic that nutritionists could scarcely believe them.

"We found that two cents' worth of vitamin A twice a year brought down mortality rates by more than 30 percent. It generated a lot of skepticism, but other studies replicated it, and they confirmed the findings," says Keith West, an associate professor at Johns Hopkins. A lack of vitamin A, it was clear, could be lethal.

This discovery contributed to a fundamental shift in the focus of nutrition projects in developing countries. With respect to diet, instead of being concerned only with whether people were getting enough energy, development practitioners began to also concern themselves about whether people were getting enough micronutrients—the vitamins and minerals that help the body function. In the last decade or so, progress has been made—iodine and vitamin A deficiencies are on the decline—but there is a long way to go. Researchers in a number of fields are working on improving old ways of combating poor nutrition and on developing new methods of delivering nutrients to the people who need them. Their successes could lead to healthier, more productive lives for billions of people.

The Price of Poverty

In industrial countries micronutrients are everywhere. Dozens of foods, like milk, flour, and breakfast cereal, are fortified, and multivitamin supplements are readily available. And most people can afford to eat a varied diet that includes naturally occurring sources of micronutrients.

In developing countries, however, the problem of micronutrient deficiencies is huge. Although data are scarce, available estimates are cause for alarm. More than half of pregnant women and school-age children suffer from iron deficiency anemia, as do more than 40 percent of nonpregnant women and preschool children. Some 100–250 million preschool children alone are affected by severe vitamin A deficiency. And 740 million people are affected by goiter, a symptom of iodine deficiency.

The costs of these deficiencies in terms of lives lost, forgone economic growth, and poor quality of life are staggering. According to Rebecca Stoltzfus, associate professor at the Johns Hopkins University School of Hygiene and Public Health, iron deficiency anemia in children impedes mental and physical development, damages the cardiovascular system, and can lead to death. In women of reproductive age, it can cause preterm births and contribute to maternal mortality during delivery. Susan Horton, professor of public health and economics at the University of Toronto, has found that anemia causes 65,000 maternal deaths a year in low-income countries in Asia. She estimates that iodine deficiency causes losses of adult productivity equal to 3.3 percent of gross domestic product (GDP) in Pakistan, and a group of economists at the Administrative Staff College of India estimates that in India iron deficiency causes losses equal to 1.25 percent of GDP.

Iron and vitamin A deficiencies are often linked to poverty. "Poor people frequently cannot get access to a sufficient quantity and variety of high-quality foods that are rich in nutrients," says Rafael Flores, an IFPRI research fellow.

Loading Nutrients into Foods

The biggest global micronutrient success story is probably the fortification of salt with iodine. Iodine deficiency leads to mental impairment, even at mild levels. "If you did nothing about iodine deficiency, many schoolchildren would be performing at a level close to mental retardation," says Werner Schultink, senior adviser on micronutriuents at UNICEF. Fortunately, adding iodine to salt is a cheap process, and 70 percent of the world's population now consumes iodized salt, according to Schultink.

The appeal of fortification is that it does not require people to change their eating behavior. It does require, however, getting nutrients into the foods they already eat. Most Latin American countries have mandatory fortification of flour, says Venkatesh Mannar, executive director of the Micronutrient Initiative, which organizes and supports micronutrient programs worldwide. "The advantage of wheat flour is that you can add several nutrients, including vitamin D, B vitamins, folic acid, and iron. But the choice of vehicle for fortification is very limited in many countries." A food to be fortified must be available to and consumed by the entire population, and it must be "fortifiable."

The greatest micronutrient deficiencies tend to be in South Asia, where rice is a staple. "One problem is you can't cheaply fortify rice," says Horton. "You could coat the grain, but people wash rice. Or you can break down the grain, fortify it, and reconstitute it, but this is 10 times more expensive than fortifying wheat flour, and people tend to pick out the broken grains."

"The other big issue, equally important," Horton explains, "is that because rice is processed in so many places, often by small processing plants, it is very difficult to use as a fortification vehicle." Because of these difficulties, some Asian countries are beginning to fortify other local staples, like soy sauce in China, fish sauce in Viet Nam, and noodles in Thailand.

The Micronutrient Initiative is leading a project to fortify salt with iron as well as iodine. "It's quite a challenge getting both iron and iodine in salt because they compete with each other," says Mannar. "Our solution was to encapsulate each iron and iodine molecule." The new double-fortified salt is about to be tested in a few countries.

Vitamin Pills for All?

A range of efforts are underway to fortify foods, but why can't aid agencies simply circumvent the difficulties of fortification and distribute micronutrient supplements to the people who need them? In some cases, that is what they are doing. Supplementation seems to work best for vitamin A, which can be stored in the body for six months. This means that supplements can be given just twice a year.

"Supplementation used to be considered a short-term solution until dietary solutions kick in, but it now seems to be a longer-term prospect," says Schultink. This is because varied diets that include a range of nonstaple foods depend on long-term income increases for the poor. Moreover, recent research has shown that vegetable sources of beta-carotene, which is converted to vitamin A in the body, are not as well absorbed by the body as previously thought.

At certain stages of life, supplementation may be the only way to get people all the nutrients they really need, even people who eat a varied and nutritious diet. This is particularly true during pregnancy, when both the mother and the fetus have an enormous demand for a range of nutrients. "We still need to provide iron supplements during pregnancy," says Stuart Gillespie, research fellow at IFPRI. "It's a fallacy to think we can phase them out. But by targeting supplements to people who need them the most, we can reduce the number of people getting supplements and reduce costs."

Even if you can get the pills to the people who need them, individuals will not always take them. "If you give pregnant women iron and make sure they take it every day, their iron status will be much better," says Mannar. "But in the real world, there are issues of compliance. Communication is a huge part of it."

New Ways of Eating

Nutritionists agree that part of the solution to micronutrient deficiencies is convincing people to make their diets more nutritious. So far, however, most attempts to change people's eating behavior have been unsuccessful. "It's often difficult to make dietary changes using local foods if you're poor. You can't afford a nutritious diet," says Stoltzfus.

One project designed to increase vitamin A consumption among the poor in northeast Thailand showed positive results. The project promoted vitamin A-rich foods as something used by loving and caring mothers, focusing on a locally grown vegetable—ivy gourd—rich in vitamin A that people could cultivate themselves. "It's not that we were interested in promoting only one green vegetable," says Suttilak Smitisiri of the Institute of Nutrition, Mahidol University, Thailand. "We promoted the ivy gourd as representing other green vegetables. And we chose green vegetables not because they are the best sources of vitamin A but because they are the most-available sources for northeast Thailand."

Most projects seeking to change diets, however, end with people returning to their old ways. "Dietary approaches have worked in only limited settings," says Mannar of the Micronutrient Initiative. "They require lots of inputs and education. When they are scaled up, they rarely work, so they tend not to be sustainable."

Putting the Nutrients in Staple Crops

One new strategy for supplying micronutrients to the poor in developing countries involves making the staple foods they eat more nutritious by using conventional plant breeding and biotechnology. This is potentially a low-cost, sustainable strategy: it would not require people to change their eating habits and would not impose the recurring costs that accompany fortification and supplements. The greatest potential for improving nutrition status on a wide scale probably involves rice, which is a staple for billions of people in Asia.

Howarth Bouis, an IFPRI senior research fellow, leads a collaborative initiative among international agricultural research and nutrition centers to breed for nutritionally improved staple food crops. Because different varieties of a crop can have different levels of micronutrients, plant scientists can breed for this trait, he explains. "Iron is in every rice endosperm, with lots of variation in levels. Plant breeders can take a high-iron rice and cross it with a high-yielding plant," says Bouis.

In fact, as part of this initiative the International Rice Research Institute in the Philippines has identified an iron-and zinc-dense rice variety that is also high yielding and disease resistant. One potential obstacle to this approach is that plant sources of iron usually contain compounds that impede iron absorption by humans. "In a pilot feeding trial at a Philippine convent, the iron status of the sisters improved after eating this high-iron rice for four months," according to Glenn Gregorio, IRRI's coordinator of the research. A larger-scale trial with a control group is planned to see if results can be confirmed.

For vitamin A, a conventional plant breeding approach is out of the question, because there is no known rice variety that contains beta-carotene in the endosperm (the milled rice grain). So researchers at the Swiss Federal Institute of Technology used genetic engineering to transfer beta-carotene from another species into rice. In January 2000 they announced that they had created a so-called golden rice, which contains beta-carotene, by inserting two genes from the daffodil and one gene from a bacterium into the genetic material of a rice plant.

"The benefit of having the beta-carotene in the crop is that the delivery system is already there," says Gary Toenniessen of the Rockfeller Foundation, which helped fund the research. "The current generation of improved varieties is being grown in rural areas not being reached by supplements, for instance."

Although golden rice contains only small amounts of beta-carotene, it is an exciting first step in the effort to make staple crops more nutritious. Getting this variety to farmers will still require putting the beta-carotene into rice varieties preferred by farmers and consumers, nutritional and biosafety studies, and field trials. Commercial adoption of golden rice is several years away.

"We hope that our example will encourage other scientists and granting agencies to follow the golden rice case with other traits and other crop plants important for food security in developing countries," says Ingo Potrykus, who led the Swiss research team.

"Nutrient-dense staple crops could play a major role in reducing malnutrition, but up to this point substantial funds have not been invested in the strategy," says Bouis.

No Single Solution

Iron, iodine, and vitamin A are not the only micronutrients that need attention in developing countries—they are just the ones that nutritionists know the most about. But evidence is growing that other micronutrient deficiencies may be as serious. Marie Ruel, a research fellow at IFPRI, says, "We have only recently started to pay attention to zinc deficiency, which has symptoms just as serious as those of iron and vitamin A deficiencies."

No single solution is likely to solve the micronutrients problem. "The consensus among nutritionists now," says Flores, "is that we need to use a combination of approaches: fortification, supplementation, and food-based approaches, including plant breeding. If we wait for a food-based approach alone to work, we will not solve the problem. The magnitude of the problem is so big that we can't wait."

In the end reducing poverty may have the greatest impact on people's nutrition by giving them access to a variety of foods and making it possible for developing countries to afford fortification and supplementation efforts. In the meantime researchers are pursuing new avenues to broaden the options for combating this persistent problem.

Chapter 6

AIDS Mushrooms into a Development Crisis

Reported by Sara E. Wilson

*The gravest long-term impact of the HIV/AIDS
crisis is that on children.*

Each day more than 10,000 people in Sub-Saharan Africa are handed what is almost surely a death sentence, and all of them will likely be dead by 2010. These people are infected with HIV/AIDS. It is now clear that the deaths of so many adults in their most productive years will have a devastating impact not only on individual families, but also on communities and entire countries.

"The realization that we need to focus on AIDS as a development rather than just a health problem has only really come in the last year or two," says Stuart Gillespie, a research fellow at IFPRI. Although health-oriented strategies to combat HIV/AIDS have been under way since the 1980s, attempts to address the socioeconomic repercussions of illness and death on such a massive scale have only just begun.

And the repercussions are enormous. In countries with the highest rates of infection, gains in economic growth, life expectancy, and educational attainment are all being reversed. The sheer number of deaths in Africa is already causing problems for efficiency of businesses and government services. Environmental problems caused by inability to combat agricultural pests and to maintain irrigation systems could occur. The disease is contributing to rapid changes in cultural values, and those changes may alter social bonds. "The epidemic will change these societies, there's no doubt about that," says Tony Barnett, professor of development studies at the University of East Anglia, in the United Kingdom. "But those changes are unpredictable."

Indeed, researchers are still learning what the full range of effects may be. "The research is fragmentary so far," admits Hans Binswanger, the World Bank's sector director for rural development in Africa, "but the signs of what is to come are obvious."

The Scope of the Epidemic

Of the 36 million people worldwide currently infected with HIV/AIDS, 95 percent live in the developing world and 70 percent live in Sub-Saharan Africa, where infection rates in some countries are as high as 35 percent. Sub-Saharan Africa has already lost nearly 14 million to AIDS, and another 23 million will die there by 2020. According to the Worldwatch Institute, life expectancy in Botswana is expected to fall from 66 years to 33 years by 2010.

Infection rates in Asia and Latin America are currently much lower than those in Africa, but many countries there are expected to face rising infection rates and millions of AIDS deaths during the first two decades of the 21st century. It is estimated that India has the highest absolute number of infected citizens. "Even though India is 'only' at a 1 percent infection rate, things can move very fast from there. I believe India, China, and the Philippines, in particular, are at a huge risk," says Binswanger.

Greatest Risk for the Poor

HIV/AIDS takes an especially heavy toll on the poor in the developing world. Poverty and HIV/AIDS can create a vicious circle: conditions imposed by poverty increase the risk of infection, and the effects of the disease in turn exacerbate poverty. The intensification of poverty caused by the disease is not limited to the person dying of AIDS, because survivors are left to live on diminished assets and income.

Poverty increases the risk of infection in a number of ways. The poor in many countries are likely to be uneducated and illiterate, which can make it difficult to reach them with information about preventing infection. People living in poverty sometimes leave their villages to find work in cities. Separated from their spouses and unsupervised by local norms, they may engage in risky sexual behavior. Untreated sexually transmitted diseases are a recognized factor in the transmission of HIV, increasing the risk of HIV infection for women by 300 to 400 percent.

Finally, poverty can make it difficult for people to concern themselves with long-term risks. Gabriel Rugalema, a research fellow in the Group on Technology and Agrarian Development at Wageningen Agricultural University in the Netherlands, says, "Sex workers I've spoken to in Dar es Salaam, for instance, say they have to focus on feeding and educating their children in the here and now."

Cultural stigmas and lack of access to medical care combine to keep most people from being tested. Once they are infected, the disease spreads as people infect their spouses through sexual intercourse and mothers infect their children at birth or through breastfeeding. Because they do not know they are infected, individuals do not prepare themselves and their families for the financial and emotional impact of their impending illness and death.

Even when the poor know they are infected, their time is relatively limited because of the prohibitive cost of life-prolonging drugs. According to nutritionist Vivica Kraak, who led a team of Cornell University researchers in East Africa, "Malnourished people are likely to see a faster progression from HIV infection to full-blown AIDS and to die sooner of AIDS-related complications, especially when they don't have access to prophylactic and antiretroviral drugs."

AIDS Leads to Hunger

Households caring for an AIDS patient turn to a number of different coping strategies, most of which lead to less income and less food security. AIDS decreases income and agricultural production by removing from the labor force not only the sick person, but also other members of the household who must care for the patient. According to a 1999 report from the Joint United Nations Programme on HIV/AIDS (UNAIDS), families in Côte d'Ivoire, Tanzania, and Thailand who were coping with HIV/AIDS experienced a fall in income of 40 to 60 percent. Loss of income and agricultural labor in turn cause a decrease in the household's access to nutritious food. Rural families will often plant root crops because they require less labor, but such crops also offer a lower nutritional value. To raise cash to pay for health care or food, families sell food-producing assets, such as chickens or goats. When cash is lacking, households simply eat less.

The death of a major adult member does not mark the end of a family's food security problems. "In my experience in Cambodia," says Margrethe Juncker, a physician and volunteer with the Catholic organization Maryknoll, "the husband got sick first and the wife had to spend all their money to care for him. Then he dies, the mother is now also infected and has no source of income, and the kids have had to be taken out of school. It's a downward spiral." The survivors may not have the ability or energy to farm the land they retain and may not have the income to hire help, or they may lose land completely because of land tenure practices.

Says Alan Whiteside, director of the Health Economics and HIV/AIDS Research Division at the University of Natal, South Africa, "We need to look at ways to safeguard household assets, both the physical assets like the plow and the cattle, but also the human resources, the knowledge represented by adults. For example, Dad may know not to plant cassava in a particular corner of the field because it always floods there, but his children might not. When Dad is gone, so is that knowledge."

Food insecurity caused by AIDS can extend beyond individual households. When a large enough number of people are ill or dead because of AIDS, food production for an entire region or nation could be compromised. Vivica Kraak found evidence of this during research in East Africa in 1999. "In Uganda farmers in the region around Kampala have traditionally grown matooke [green banana] and supplied it to other regions of the country. Because of the loss of labor caused by AIDS-related illnesses and deaths, the production of matooke has fallen, and this decrease in production has affected not only people growing matooke for their own uses, but also the availability of the crop for people in other parts of the country."

Loss of labor and income can also cause survivors to abandon agricultural practices that raise yields and protect soil fertility, like fallowing and use of fertilizers.

Children Are Hardest Hit

Almost everyone agrees that the gravest long-term impact of the HIV/AIDS crisis is that on children. Even before they face the emotional loss of parents, children may have suffered from the choices their parents have had to make in response to HIV/AIDS. These choices can cause children to suffer from lack of food and parental attention, to be withdrawn from school because fees could not be paid or because their labor was needed, or to be sent away from home to live with relatives.

"The most obvious way children are affected is through orphaning," says Whiteside. "But they're really orphaned before the death of their parents. Orphaning is a series of events, with the death of the parent the culminating one. We are ending up with millions of children who are unloved, unsocialized, and uneducated."

UNAIDS estimates that by 2010 there could be as many as 42 million orphans in Sub-Saharan Africa. "Young children and adolescents are losing more than their parents," says Anita Alban, senior economist in the Policy, Strategy, and Research Department of UNAIDS. "They are losing basic life skills such as caring for one another. The norms of such children might change not only their future but the community they will have to adapt to." Because they are, by definition, years away from adulthood, caring for these children will require the commitment of long-term resources.

Mitigation Efforts Are Changing

Since HIV/AIDS was viewed exclusively as a health issue until recently, most support efforts have focused on providing medical care to the sick and dying. Now attention is being turned to aiding those left behind when AIDS victims die. In general, such mitigation efforts have been carried out by the affected communities themselves. For example, a World Bank study in Tanzania found that 90 percent of assistance to families that had lost a major adult member came from families or communities. These kinds of support strategies include community-based child care; volunteer labor to assist in increasing agricultural output and caring for HIV/AIDS patients; and apprenticeship and training for orphaned adolescents.

Nongovernmental organizations often team with local communities to offer mitigation assistance. Small programs, like the one run by Maryknoll in Cambodia, often start with basic care of AIDS patients and move on to more extensive mitigation efforts. Juncker, for example, started an income-generating activity with patients she cared for in Maryknoll's Seedlings of Hope clinic. Income generated by making patchwork quilts earns people in the program US$62 a month. "After six months, I now have 11 people sewing the quilts and more families working at home to cut donated fabric for the sewers," she says. Juncker hopes to expand the program by opening a creche so that widows with young children will have somewhere to leave their children while sewing. Similar programs throughout the developing world provide opportunities for HIV/AIDS-affected people and families to protect themselves from the worst of the poverty-exacerbating impacts of the disease.

Yet, while these programs are important, they do not reach enough of those who need help. Binswanger of the World Bank refers to them as "tiny boutiques, which do good work but only reach 1 to 2 percent of the population."

Development agencies are more likely to have the financial and organizational capital to reach more of those in need. For instance, the World Bank trains agricultural extension workers to offer advice on what crops to grow when there are fewer adults available to farm the land. The United Nations Children's Fund (UNICEF) works to improve orphan registration efforts and to promote the right of HIV/AIDS children to stay in school. However, according to Daphne Topouzis, a consultant specializing in HIV and agriculture and rural development, international agencies have focused their efforts on research. "It's very hard to generalize," she says, "but it is certain that they have done more on the research side than on practical mitigation efforts."

There are signs that this focus may be changing, among them the fact that in September 2000 the World Bank approved a multicountry HIV/AIDS program for Africa. Funds will go to projects developed by individual countries. According to the World Bank, the program "will support efforts to scale up national prevention, care, support, and treatment programs, and to prepare countries to cope with the unprecedented burdens they will face as the millions living with HIV today develop AIDS over the next decade."

Prevention Is the Ultimate Solution

No matter how widespread mitigation efforts are, the devastating impact of HIV/AIDS will continue unabated until its incidence can be drastically reduced. Since development of a vaccine appears to be at least a decade off, other methods must be found to stem the tide of infection. Some argue that aggressive education campaigns targeting those most at risk can accomplish this goal. That strategy has had significant success in Thailand. In 1990 both Thailand and South Africa had adult infection rates of less than 1 percent. In 1999 South Africa's infection rate was 20 percent; Thailand's was 2 percent.

Despite the case of Thailand, many researchers now argue that prevention strategies will have to aim at the underlying issue of poverty to be truly successful. Rugalema says, "Preventing AIDS through information and messages doesn't really make sense to me. People can't eat information. Where the economy is very weak, sending information is not going to solve the problem. You have to start with re-habilitating the economy so people will have some hope for the future." Gillespie adds, "There has been too much on awareness raising and too little on the specific conditions that have to change before behavior can change."

In a way, then, successful mitigation strategies can themselves be prevention techniques because of the two-way relationship between HIV/AIDS and poverty. Desmond Cohen, former director of the HIV and Development Programme of the United Nations Development Programme, points out, for example, that children who are malnourished, lack education, and have missed out on normal processes of socialization because of the impact of HIV/AIDS on their families and societies are more likely, because of these very conditions, to become "the next cohort of the HIV infected." Improving the conditions under which these children live could pre-vent them from becoming infected and, ultimately, end the epidemic.

Still, even if no new infections were to occur beginning tomorrow, Africa and some areas in Asia and Latin America will be facing severe socioeconomic reper-cussions for decades to come. Vigorous efforts are already under way by donor agencies, NGOs, and communities themselves to understand and act on the ram-ifications of HIV/AIDS. There are some hopeful signs that national governments and the international community are beginning to understand that increased polit-ical will and financial resources must be directed toward this epidemic. Only when that commitment is made will communities, governments, and their partners in the developing world be able to make a real impact on the disaster of HIV/AIDS.

Chapter 7

HIV/AIDS
A Critical Health and Development Issue

Tony Barnett and Gabriel Rugalema

By killing productive adults who are key family providers,
HIV/AIDS shatters the social networks that provide
households with community help and support.

Slightly more than 20 years ago, the first cases of AIDS (acquired immuno-deficiency syndrome) were identified. Since then, scientists not only have identified the human immunodeficiency virus (HIV) that causes AIDS, but also now understand many of the stages in transmission. Naturally, an infection that is transmitted in a predominantly heterosexual manner and that destroys the health and finally the lives of people of prime producing age exerts a considerable socio-economic impact.

Neither a vaccine nor a cheap, assured, and effective treatment for HIV/AIDS exists. The pandemic continues to grow and to affect millions of people worldwide, particularly the poor in the southern hemisphere, where 95 percent of cases are concentrated. With most illness and death occurring in the 15–50 age group, the disease deprives countries, communities, and households of their strongest, most productive people.

Today, approximately 36 million individuals are living with HIV/AIDS. Assuming that each HIV/AIDS case directly influences the lives of four other individuals, a total of more than 150 million people are being affected by the disease. Sub-Saharan Africa is the region most affected by HIV/AIDS, now that area's leading cause of adult morbidity and mortality (see Table 7.1). Most, if not all, of the 25 million people in Sub-Saharan Africa who are living with HIV/AIDS will have

Table 7.1 HIV/AIDS by Region, December 2000

Region	Epidemic Started	Adults and Children Living with HIV/AIDS	Adults and Children Newly Infected with HIV	Adult Prevalence Rate (%)	Percent of HIV-Positive Adults Who Are Women
Sub-Saharan Africa	Late 1970s– early 1980s	25,300,000	3,800,000	8.8	55
North Africa and Middle East	Late 1980s	400,000	80,000	0.2	40
South and South- east Asia	Late 1980s	5,800,000	780,000	0.56	35
East Asia and Pacific	Late 1980s	640,000	130,000	0.07	13
Latin America	Late 1970s– early 1980s	1,400,000	150,000	0.5	25
Caribbean	Late 1970s– early 1980s	390,000	60,000	2.3	35
Eastern Europe and Central Asia	Early 1990s	700,000	250,000	0.35	25
Western Europe	Late 1970s– early 1980s	540,000	30,000	0.24	25
North America	Late 1970s– early 1980s	920,000	45,000	0.6	20
Australia and New Zealand	Late 1970s– early 1980s	15,000	500	0.13	10
Total		36,100,000	5,300,000	1.1	47

Source: www.unaids.org
Note: Adulthood is 15–49 years of age.

died by the year 2020, in addition to the 13.7 million Africans already claimed by the epidemic.

HIV/AIDS also is spreading dramatically in Asia. India leads the world in absolute numbers of HIV infections, estimated at 3 to 5 million. China, too, has a growing HIV/AIDS problem, with approximately 0.5 million AIDS cases and, according to private estimates by Chinese specialists, up to 10 million HIV infections. Asia will overtake Sub-Saharan Africa in absolute numbers before 2010; by 2020 Asia will be the HIV/AIDS epicenter.

HIV/AIDS Morbidity and Mortality and Household Food Security

HIV/AIDS is a huge health problem with profound social and economic implications, including its effect on the ability of households to acquire enough nutritious food for members to lead active, healthy lives. HIV/AIDS has created or contributed to exorbitant health care costs, labor shortages, a declining asset base, breakdown of social bonds, downgraded crops, and loss of livestock. All of these effects contribute to food insecurity.

Households are said to be food-secure when the following four elements are in balance with each other: food availability, equal access to food, stability of food supplies, and quality of food. For rural households, the equitable availability of stable quantities of nutritious food depends on food production (using mainly family labor, land, and other resources); food purchase (using household income); assets that can be quickly turned into food or cash as necessary; and social claims on others through custom and societal structures such as family and community networks.

HIV/AIDS morbidity and mortality affect food security by reducing households' ability to produce and buy food, by depleting assets, and by reducing the insurance value of social networks as the household calls in favors. Morbidity affects agricultural productivity by affecting labor availability, forcing households to reallocate labor from agriculture to patient care. AIDS mortality permanently removes adult labor from the household. This combination of adult morbidity and mortality and the associated reallocation and withdrawal of labor has led to a number of adverse changes.

Downgraded Crops and Loss of Livestock

Households affected by HIV/AIDS often replace valuable and nutritious crops that are labor-intensive with root crops, which are fast-maturing but less profitable. Household members consume this mainly starchy food but cannot easily purchase nutritious food because of lower farm income. Chronic food insecurity and high levels of malnutrition among children, especially orphans, are the likely results of these changing crop patterns. Livestock may be sold to generate cash for patient care or as compensation for a labor shortage, may be taken away from survivors, or may be slaughtered for consumption during funerals—or animals may die because of poor management. When households lose livestock, they also lose fertilizing manure, milk for the family, and "ambulatory" savings.

Loss of Farm Management Resources and Skills

Subsistence agriculture requires the interaction of human, financial, and physical resources, and all adult household members contribute to this interaction in some way. But HIV/AIDS breaks the chain of knowledge transfer and labor sharing between generations. As a result, survivors—notably orphans and the elderly, who cannot manage the family farm due to lack of knowledge, experience, and physical strength—often remain or become malnourished.

Inability to Earn Income

By killing young adults, the key earners of nonfarm income, HIV/AIDS dramatically reduces households' earning power and, therefore, their ability to buy food and related goods and services. Illness and funerals force households to spend most of their cash on care, treatment, and other expenses, with adverse consequences for food availability. Labor shortages force households to forgo cash crops in favor of fast-maturing food crops, curtailing the ability of afflicted households to generate cash. Evidence from eastern and southern Africa shows that households affected by HIV/AIDS not only are eating fewer meals and consuming poorer foods, but also are investing less in the health of surviving members, losing even more labor to frequent morbidity.

Loss of Assets

Food security hinges on household assets, which create a buffer between poor production on the one hand and consumption and exchange needs on the other. In times of need, assets such as livestock, land, trees, and even furniture can be readily converted into cash to buy food. Households accumulate assets as an insurance strategy, but HIV/AIDS forces households to dispose of their assets. They are left not only impoverished, but also vulnerable in the long term.

Disruption of Social Networks

By killing productive adults who are key family providers, HIV/AIDS shatters the social networks that provide households with community help and support. Survivors are left with few relatives upon whom to depend, and strong evidence shows that gender and age are critical determinants of social exclusion in the face of HIV/ AIDS. Widows and their households face critical shortages of food and income, primarily due to disinheritance, lack of sufficient assets, lack of labor supply, and exclusion from wider kinship networks. Orphans, widows, and the elderly find it particularly difficult to depend on other relatives for survival.

Increasing Dependency

Households headed by survivors—notably widows, orphans, and the elderly—are more highly dependent on outside sources of support, further compromising their access to food. Moreover, the centuries-old external support structures that guaranteed the interhousehold transfer of food to cushion the needy are collapsing because of HIV morbidity and mortality.

Policy and Program Implications

Few poverty and distributional policies and programs—particularly in Africa, but also in Asia and Latin America—are unaffected by HIV/AIDS. Households that lose labor are less able to earn cash, with implications for income-generating projects. Less purchasing power reduces the standards of long- and short-term dependent care within those households. Any efforts at mitigating the rural impact of HIV/AIDS, however, must be multisectoral and must take account of local circumstances.

Efforts should be made to identify the most vulnerable farming systems and to ensure the food security of the most vulnerable households. Farming systems and households that remain viable should be supported to prevent individuals from resorting to activities that deplete natural resources (such as bush encroachment).

Research and extension programs should contain an HIV/AIDS education component and should encourage rural people to consider how they would respond to the impact of HIV/AIDS. In some communities, farmers' panels could be established so that those who have coped or are coping with the disease can talk with people from hitherto lightly affected communities.

Development, dissemination, and scaling up of labor-economizing methods of cultivation, food preparation, water supply, and livestock-raising should be encouraged. Agricultural education should be targeted to orphans and out-of-school youth, and land tenure arrangements must safeguard the interests of widowed women and orphaned children.

In general, policies and programs must go beyond HIV prevention and AIDS care to the long-term issues of livelihood maintenance and food security.

Chapter 8

Obesity

An Emerging Health and Nutrition Issue in Developing Countries

Reynaldo Martorell

Obesity is not a problem everywhere in the developing world, but it appears to become a problem as income increases.

O besity is a disease of complex, multiple causes leading to an imbalance between energy intake and output and to the accumulation of large amounts of body fat. It is measured most often as excessive weight for a given height, using the body mass index (BMI)—weight in kilograms (kg) over height squared (m^2). The World Health Organization (WHO) defines overweight as a BMI between 25.0 and 29.9 kg/m^2 and obesity as a BMI of 30.0 kg/m^2 or greater.

A Growing Public Health Problem

The consequences of obesity for adults are well known. Obesity contributes to the development of many diseases, including diabetes, hypertension, stroke, cardiovascular disease, and some cancers. Obesity also increases mortality from all causes, including cardiovascular disease and cancer.

Childhood obesity is a problem because it is an important predictor of adult obesity. About one third of obese preschool children become obese adults, and one-half of obese school-age children become obese adults. Most obese adults, however, were not obese children.

Obesity also affects child health. The risk of hyperlipidemia, hypertension, and abnormal glucose tolerance is somewhat higher among obese children. In the

United States childhood obesity has important psychosocial consequences: obese children frequently are targets of systematic discrimination and, by adolescence, many suffer from low self-esteem.

According to WHO, obesity is increasing worldwide at an alarming rate, in both developed and developing countries. WHO issued this conclusion despite the limited availability of nationally representative data and scarce information about trends. The note of alarm led a U.S. team from Emory University (Reynaldo Martorell and Morgen Hughes) and the Centers for Disease Control and Prevention (CDC) (Laura Kettel Khan and Lawrence Grummer-Strawn) to analyze data from national nutrition surveys in the last 15 years to determine obesity levels and trends in developing countries. Most of these surveys focus only on preschool children and women of reproductive age and therefore provide limited information about obesity patterns.

Obesity in Women

The study compared overweight and obesity rates in women from 38 developing countries with rates in the United States (Figure 8.1). Levels of overweight and obesity were extremely low in South Asia. In poor countries, such as those in Sub-Saharan Africa, obesity levels were low, with the condition concentrated among urban and educated women.

In more developed countries, including those in Latin America and the Central Eastern Europe/Commonwealth of Independent States (CEE/CIS) region, obesity levels were higher and more equally distributed in the general population. Obesity ceased to be a distinguishing feature of high socioeconomic status in Brazil, and in Mexico it is emerging as a marker of poverty, as it is in developed countries.

Obesity in Children

Data regarding obesity in children 12 to 60 months old were available from 50 countries. Obesity was defined as greater than two standard deviations above the mean, using the international reference population recommended by WHO. The prevalence of obesity in the reference population is 2.3 percent. With the exception of Pakistan, where 2.6 percent of children were obese, obesity was rare in South Asia (including India) and in Thailand. The countries examined in Sub-Saharan Africa had low levels of obesity, except Malawi, with 5.2 percent. Seven of 13 countries in Latin America and the Caribbean, 1 of 2 countries in the CEE/CIS region, and all 4 Middle Eastern and North African countries exceeded 2.3 percent. In the United States, 3.1 percent of children were obese.

Figure 8.1 Overweight and Obesity in Women in Developing Countries and the United States

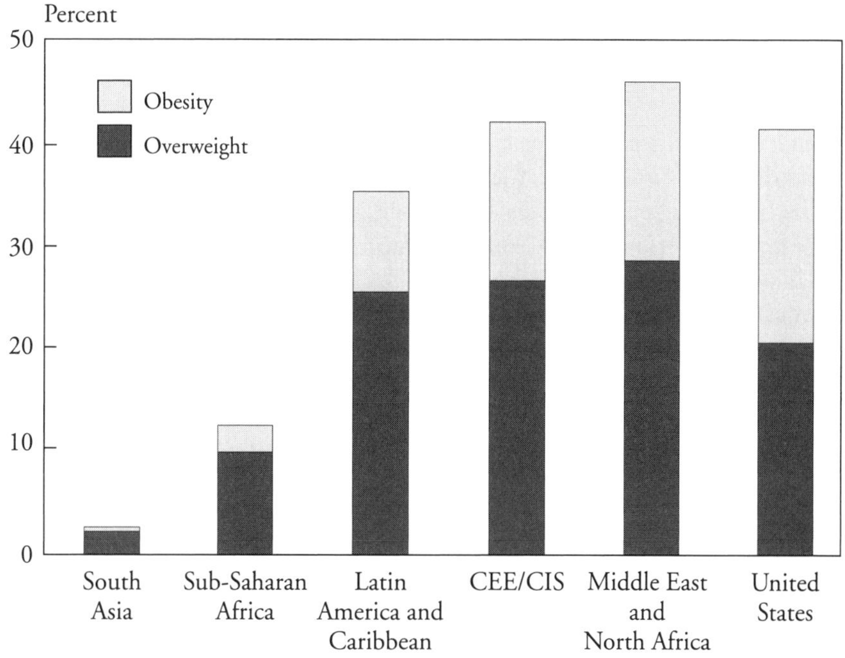

Source: L. Grummer-Strawn, M. Hughes, L. K. Khan, and R. Martorell, "Obesity in Women from Developing Countries," *European Journal of Clinical Nutrition* 54 (2000): 247–252.

Obesity was more common in urban areas and was more prevalent in girls and in children of mothers with higher education. At the country level, child obesity was positively related to gross national product and negatively related to stunting.

Assessing Obesity Trends

In assessing trends in obesity, the research team was severely constrained by lack of data. Only a few countries, mostly in Sub-Saharan Africa and Latin America, had repeat surveys: 6 for women and 17 for children. In the repeat surveys, obesity levels in children in 7 countries in Sub-Saharan Africa did not appear to change over time. By contrast, in Latin America, levels increased in most of the 9 countries with data. In Egypt, obesity levels decreased slightly but remained among the highest in developing countries.

Other sources suggest that obesity, particularly among adults, is increasing in Micronesia, the Middle East, and Latin America as it is in the United States and Europe. Better data are needed, however, to confirm trends in developing countries.

The results of this study of obesity in women and children in developing countries need to be interpreted with caution because of insufficient data as well as methodological concerns. The reference population used to assess obesity in children is derived from measurements of U.S. children, who may have higher than desired levels of fatness. No consensus on how best to measure obesity in children exists, and the interpretation of weight-for-height indexes in populations with significant levels of stunting has been questioned. There is consensus, however, that a BMI over 30 in adults represents a serious clinical concern. Moreover, risk appears at much lower levels of BMI, and just being overweight (BMI of 25 to 29.9) increases health and mortality risks.

Some countries with high levels of obesity also report significant rates of childhood stunting and nutritional deficiencies. Maintaining a dual nutrition agenda—preventing obesity and related chronic diseases while eliminating nutritional deficiencies—presents a difficult challenge to countries with limited resources. In addition, many countries are unprepared to address the changing epidemiology. Because information about the occurrence of obesity and related chronic diseases in the population is limited, these issues are not considered public health problems. Many countries' nutrition policies continue to focus on undernutrition, limiting experience and expertise with chronic diseases.

Preventing Obesity and Related Diseases

Obesity is not a problem everywhere in the developing world, but it appears to become a problem as income increases. Developing countries need to take a number of measures to prevent obesity and related chronic diseases. Information systems should collect data about chronic diseases to support advocacy activities and to help define policies and programs. These efforts must include schoolchildren, elderly women, and men—not just women of reproductive age and young children. Professionals must be trained to design, monitor, and evaluate programs aimed at preventing chronic diseases.

Nutrition and healthy lifestyles should be addressed in the school curriculum, and physical activity should be promoted in schools and in the general population. In Singapore, for example, the "Trim and Fit Scheme"—a comprehensive 10-year program that began in 1992—features teacher education and training, assessment of students, a program to reduce sugar in children's beverages, and more physical activity for children during school hours. A recent evaluation of the Singapore program shows a marked improvement in fitness and some evidence of reduction in obesity.

Urban planners can support increased physical activity by building recreational facilities, such as parks and playgrounds. Public education must be as aggressive and effective as commercial advertisements in promoting healthy diets and lifestyles. Food and agricultural policies can stimulate consumption of healthy diets. Nutrition labeling should be required for all industrially prepared foods to help consumers select food. Industry's role in developing healthier food products and in promoting public health and nutrition should be recognized and encouraged. Agricultural research can help shift the macro- or micro-nutrient composition of the food supply. In the U.S. livestock sector, for example, food processing modifications combined with changes in breeding, feeding, and meat-trimming practices have contributed to lower-fat meat.

In much of the developing world, preventing obesity and related chronic diseases should be a priority of governments, as well as of international, bilateral, and national organizations. At the same time, efforts to eliminate nutritional deficiencies must continue.

PART 3

Demographic Issues: Population Growth and Urbanization

Chapter 9

The Population Boom
What Do the Numbers Mean?

Reported by Ellen Wilson

The high population numbers predicted for the
future should not lead the world to become
complacent about the ability of family
planning programs to have an impact.

Is the earth headed toward massive overpopulation by the year 2020 and beyond? Or is the world's populace destined to decline because of the horrors of disease and war? Whatever the size of the population, will all mouths be fed in the coming years?

The experts seem to agree that by the year 2020, the population will increase from the current 6 billion people to about 7.6 billion people. But after that, the predictions vary wildly. The United Nations provides three possible projections of population after 2020, ranging from 5.6 billion to 17.5 billion people in the year 2100.

Though the far future may be uncertain, there is a current increase in population of 75 million people per year in the developing world. Policymakers must address this reality while paying attention to the realities behind the population growth numbers of the more distant future.

However, according to researchers, policymakers should not just focus on the sheer size of the population, but direct their attention to the implications of the numbers, which will potentially vary more wildly than the numbers themselves. To what geographic regions will the numbers be distributed? Will the regions have the ability—or the "carrying capacity"—to sustain the population in terms of food and income? Will population growth be counter-balanced by new technologies, for example, that increase food production to meet needs? Or will increases in food production lead the population to grow even larger and exhaust the supply of food? What will be the age distribution of the population? Will increased quality of life, social services, and family planning programs help to substantially reduce fertility rates?

Population Movement Versus Population Growth

One of the most important forces behind population growth is the powerful impact of policy incentives in reshuffling people around the globe. According to Steve Vosti, an IFPRI research fellow, "There is an important distinction between population growth and population movement. Policies must be examined to see if they are inducing large numbers of people to migrate to areas where the 'carrying capacity' is lowest—to areas that are least able to sustain the large numbers of people."

"If you have millions of people moving in a five-year period to agriculturally marginal areas," continued Vosti, "you can see that policies that affect population movement might have a more immediate impact on the areas' natural resource base than policies that affect family fertility. Falling mortality rates also lead to population increases that may far surpass policies to slow human fertility rates."

Partially in response to policies that affect population movement, large numbers of people have settled over the past decades in coastal and river regions, according to Thomas Merrick, senior advisor for population at the World Bank. "This causes problems in terms of water resources, for example, in the Eastern Mediterranean. Good governance and good management, planned far in advance, are critical for coping with these pressures. Governments should not distort the incentive system so that the real costs of land and water use are artificially reduced."

But increases in population density don't have to signal an imminent Malthusian crunch. As the population grows, according to Peter Hazell of IFPRI, the carrying capacities of currently productive lands can be increased through environmentally sustainable agricultural technologies. Contrasting with Green Revolution technology where the same improvements could be applied across the board, many sustainable technologies are location-specific and require more complex management schemes. However, such technologies as pest-resistant crops could increase crop yields with little harm to the environment. In fact, some researchers say agricultural technologies, if invested in now, could increase food production enough to feed everyone—no matter which of the projections is realized.

Marginal Areas

But many of the world's poor live in marginal areas, such as hillsides and forest margins, where the prospects for increasing productivity in food are limited. Experts say that more research is needed on how to increase the carrying capacity of this land, but, in the meantime, actions can be taken, including establishing "market linkages."

"In marginal areas, often people are trying to subsist on the food they grow in their own backyard," said Vosti. "But this is extremely demanding on their piece of land, and often not sustainable over the long run. What is needed are 'market linkages'—the ability to grow a cash crop or extract a product from their land and sell it at market for money in order to purchase instead of grow food. Coffee, for example, grows well in some marginal areas where food crops do not. But there has to be a good market for coffee—a mechanism by which coffee can be exchanged for food at reasonable rates throughout the year."

Finally, Vosti notes the importance of considering the proportion of the population that is of working age versus the proportion that is not. "If a large portion of the population is over the age of 60 and under the age of 10, you may have real problems in terms of the ability of working people and governments to keep income and food production up enough to sustain the 'dependent' components of the population."

Quality of Life and Population

Those who are just looking at the population numbers, not the moral issues, may ask: Once people are well fed, whether on marginal or productive lands, won't this increase population growth and exacerbate the world's state of overcrowding and environmental devastation? Just as construction of new highways seems to breed even more cars and traffic jams, will increases in the food supply lead to further increases in population?

Not so, say researchers. "If food is available at affordable prices for poor people—if there is sufficient 'food availability'—this will be a critical factor in increasing the general welfare of the family and, therefore, contributes to decreases in infant and child mortality," said Vosti. "When people are eating better and are better off, they tend to invest more in each child, instead of investing in larger numbers of children, and family fertility rates tend to fall."

Also contributing to increased quality of life and, therefore, reduced fertility rates are investments in social programs, such as in education, particularly for women.

"We have had favorable outcomes in our literacy rates, fertility rates, and infant mortality because of decades of investment in people," said Dr. Rebeca Grynspan Mayufis, past vice president of Costa Rica and a member of the international advisory committee for the 2020 Vision initiative. "Education has been at the center of our concerns since the 19th century and the main factor that explains where we are today. We have obligatory, free education for both girls and boys and have had a recent expansion of secondary school education for both genders. Our literacy rate is now 95 percent, and this makes people more receptive to family planning messages." In the 1960s, the country brought down its population growth rate by more than 33 percent.

Family Planning

Another critical force in controlling and reducing population growth is family planning programs. According to Robert Engelman, director of the population and environment program of Population Action International, the high population numbers predicted for the future should not lead the world to become complacent about the ability of family planning programs to have an impact.

"Population growth is not a mechanistic, easily predictable pattern," said Engelman. "There is a combination of good and bad 'wild cards' that could change the current pattern of population growth tremendously. Birth rates could go down faster than expected or death rates could reverse their historic decline and go up. The numbers provided to us by the demographers are not predictions, but projections based on assumptions, and the low projections are equally as plausible as the high projections."

According to Engelman, one of the main goals of the International Conference on Population and Development in Cairo and population organizations around the world is to put in place policies that encourage worldwide achievement of "replacement" level fertility—2.1 children per family. The average fertility rate is now 4 children per family. He says this reduction could potentially be achieved by meeting all of the world's unmet demand for family planning services, closing the gender gap in education, and improving women's status in the family and workplace.

"The agriculture and population communities have a common cause," said Engelman. "It's in the interest of the agricultural development community to support family planning and social programs because these programs will make their job of feeding the world easier. By the same token, it's in the interest of the population community for people to be well fed, healthy, and able to make choices about their own lives."

However, according to Vosti, "Bringing down fertility rates will be a slow process, and millions of new mouths will have to be fed in the meantime. Yet, these new mouths are most likely to be born in areas least able to feed them, and, therefore, there are three alternatives for preventing hunger: sustainably increasing agricultural productivity, destroying the natural environment, or providing massive food aid. The only reasonable alternative is the first, and the time to begin was yesterday."

Chapter 10

Population Growth and Policy Options in the Developing World

John Bongaarts and Judith Bruce

To be effective, population policies should address all sources of continuing growth, except declining mortality.

The population of the developing world has doubled since 1965 and now stands at 4.8 billion. This growth in human numbers has been a principal cause of a rising demand for food, water, and other life-sustaining resources in the past and will continue to be so for the foreseeable future. The United Nations projects that the developing-country population will reach 6.5 billion by 2020 and 8.2 billion by 2050 (the projected world total is 7.7 billion for 2020 and 9.4 billion for 2050). Although populations throughout the developing world continue to expand rapidly, the rate of growth is declining modestly. The average annual population growth rate was 2.4 percent per year in 1965, is estimated to be 1.7 percent today, and is expected to be 1.2 percent by 2020 (see Table 10.1). The main cause of this decline is a revolution in reproductive behavior that began in the 1960s. Contraceptive use, once rare, is now widespread, and the average number of births per woman has fallen by half—from the traditional six or more in the 1960s to near three today. Fertility declines have been most rapid in Asia and Latin America. Relatively little change has occurred in Sub-Saharan Africa, but significant declines are under way in several countries in the region—Botswana, Kenya, South Africa, and Zimbabwe, for example.

Table 10.1 Population Size and Growth by Region, 1965, 1998, and 2020

Population	Africa	Asia	Latin America	Developing World	World
Size (billions)					
1965	0.32	1.90	0.25	2.38	3.34
1998	0.78	3.59	0.50	4.75	5.93
2020	1.32	4.59	0.66	6.45	7.67
Annual growth rate (percent per year)					
1965	2.6	2.3	2.7	2.4	2.0
1998	2.6	1.4	1.5	1.7	1.4
2020	2.1	0.9	1.0	1.2	1.0
Total fertility rate (births per woman)					
1965	6.7	5.7	5.8	6.0	4.9
1998	5.3	2.7	2.7	3.1	2.8
2020	3.5	2.2	2.2	2.5	2.4

Source: United Nations Secretariat, Department of Economic and Social Affairs, *World Population Prospects: The 1996 Revision* (New York, 1996).

Why Population Growth Continues

Many analysts find it difficult to understand why massive further growth will take place despite declining fertility rates. First, the large decline since the 1960s still leaves fertility about 50 percent above the two-child level needed to stabilize the population. With more than two surviving children per woman, every generation is larger than the preceding one, and population continues to grow. The extent to which high (but falling) fertility rates remain a driving force for population growth varies by region. It is highest in Africa, with a current fertility rate of 5.3 births per woman, and lowest in Asia and Latin America, where fertility has dropped to just below 3 births per woman.

High fertility can, in turn, be attributed to two distinct underlying causes: unwanted childbearing and a desired family size of more than two surviving children. About one in five births is unwanted, and a larger proportion is mistimed. An estimated 25 million abortions are performed each year in developing countries—many of them under unsafe conditions. Many couples have large numbers of children because they fear that some children will die, and they want to be sure that enough children survive to assist them in family enterprises and support them in old age. In most developing countries, the completed family size desired by women still exceeds two children; in Sub-Saharan Africa, for example, desired family size is typically more than five children.

Second, declines in death rates—historically the main cause of population growth—will almost certainly continue. Higher standards of living, better nutrition, greater investments in sanitation and clean water supplies, expanded access to health services, and wider application of public health measures such as immunization will ensure longer and healthier lives in most countries. Only a few countries—mostly in Sub-Saharan Africa, where the AIDS epidemic is most severe—are the exception. Yet, the AIDS epidemic is not expected to eliminate population growth.

The third growth factor is what demographers call "population momentum." This refers to the tendency for a population to keep growing even if fertility were immediately brought to the replacement level of 2.1 births per woman with constant mortality and zero migration. Because the age structure of the population is young, the largest generation of adolescents in history will soon enter the childbearing years. Even if each of these young women has only two children, they will produce more than enough births to maintain population growth over the next few decades.

Of the three factors expected to contribute substantially to continued growth, population momentum is the most important. It will account for 76 percent of the expected increase between 2000 and 2020 in the developing world as a whole and for an even larger portion in Asia and Latin America. Further large increases in the population of the developing world are therefore virtually certain.

Population Policy Options

To be effective, population policies should address all sources of continuing growth, except declining mortality. Among the strategies to be considered are the following.

Expand High-Quality Family Planning and Reproductive Health Services

Unwanted pregnancies occur when women and men who want to avoid pregnancy do not practice effective fertility regulation. Offering individuals and couples appropriate services has been a priority of many governments in the developing world. Despite considerable progress over the last several decades, however, the coverage and quality of family planning services remain less than satisfactory in many countries. In addition, some countries have imposed provider targets on family planning programs, limiting, for example, the number of intrauterine devices to be inserted or the number of sterilizations to be performed, thus actively interfering with trust between clients and providers. To ensure that family planning programs appropriately assist individuals in reaching personal fertility goals, family planning should be strictly voluntary and services should be linked with other reproductive health services. The quality of these programs can be improved by extending services to underserved areas; broadening the choice of methods available (including safe pregnancy termination where it is legal); improving information exchanges between client and provider; promoting empathetic relationships between client and provider; assuring the technical competence of providers; including men in programs; adding service elements to address related health problems, such as diagnosis and treatment of sexually transmitted diseases and treatment following unsafe abortion; and increasing public awareness of the value of and means available for fertility regulation, responsible and safe sex, and the location of services.

Create Favorable Conditions for Small Families

Several social and economic measures have substantial effects on desired family size.

1. *Increase educational attainment, especially among girls.* As economies become less agrarian, the availability of mass education changes the value placed on large families and encourages parents to invest in fewer but "higher-quality" children, capable of entering the emerging labor markets. Higher levels of education are also associated with the spread of nontraditional roles and values, including less gender-restricted behaviors. Educated parents rely less on children for income and old-age support. Educated women want (and have) fewer children with higher survival rates, have higher earnings, and are more able to invest in their children's nutrition and education.

2. *Improve child health and survival.* No developing country has had a sustained fertility decline without first having experienced a substantial decline in child mortality. A high child death rate discourages investments in children's health and education and encourages high fertility because parents believe that excess births are required to ensure that at least the desired number of children will survive to adulthood.

3. *Invest in women and provide them with economic prospects and social identities apart from motherhood.* Improvements in the economic, social, and legal status of girls and women are likely to increase their bargaining power, giving them a stronger voice in family reproductive and productive decisions. As women's autonomy increases, the dominance of husbands and other male household members is reduced, as well as the societal preference for men. As women's status improves, the value of children as insurance against adversity (for example, in old age) and as securers of women's social positions declines.

Delay Marriage and Childbearing by Addressing
the Needs of Young Women

While a young population age structure (the cause of momentum) is not amenable to modification, the age at which childbearing begins and its pace can be altered to offset momentum. Women in general, and young women in particular, are under pervasive pressure to fulfill societal expectations of appropriate feminine behaviors, especially with respect to their sexuality and fertility. This is a disguised form of coercion, as young women often have little choice about whether or not to have sexual relations, when or whom to marry, and whether to defer childbearing. Educating girls to the secondary level; including them in community development efforts, sports, and other publicly visible activities; and encouraging them to generate income begins to lead girls toward autonomy. Social power and economic authority for women are necessary counterpressures to traditional imperatives to marry and have children early.

Conclusion

Well-designed population policies are broad in scope, socially desirable, and ethically sound. They appeal to a variety of constituencies: those seeking to eliminate discrimination against women and improve the lives of children, as well as those seeking to reduce fertility and population growth. Mutually reinforcing investments in family planning, reproductive health, and a range of socioeconomic measures operate beneficially at both the macro and micro levels to slow population growth, increase productivity, and improve individual health and welfare.

Chapter 11

Achieving Urban Food and Nutrition Security in the Developing World

James L. Garrett

*Growth in urban poverty, food insecurity, and malnutrition
and a shift in their concentration from rural to urban
areas will acompany urbanization.*

The trend is inescapable: more and more people in the developing world are living in the cities. By 2020, the number of people living in developing countries will grow from 4.9 billion to 6.8 billion. Ninety percent of this increase will be in rapidly expanding cities and towns. More than half the population of Africa and Asia will live in urban areas by 2020. More than three-quarters of Latin Americans already do.

Growth in urban poverty, food insecurity, and malnutrition and a shift in their concentration from rural to urban areas will acompany urbanization. Although the magnitude and speed of change vary by country, data covering more than half the developing world's population indicate that:

- The proportion and number of poor people living in urban areas grew during the 1980s and 1990s in seven of eight survey countries, including India and China. (Because data are not available, poverty also serves as a reasonable indicator of food insecurity here.) By the early 1990s, the cities of these eight countries alone were home to more than 140 million poor people, up from about 120 million 5 to 10 years earlier.

- From the early to the mid-1990s, the urban share of malnourished children also increased in 11 of 15 countries for which data are available. The total number of malnourished children in urban areas increased in 9 of the 15. Almost 10 million malnourished children in these countries live in urban areas, up from about 7 million in earlier years.

Urban Food Insecurity and Malnutrition: Issues and Policies

A number of factors will affect the future shape of urban food insecurity and malnutrition. Because urban dwellers must buy most of their food, urban food security depends mostly on whether the household can afford to buy food, given prices and incomes. High per-unit costs of food result from inefficient urban food-marketing systems and the fact that the poor usually can buy only small quantities of food at a time rather than in bulk. Macroeconomic policies are also important. Inflation, depreciation in the exchange rate, and the removal of key consumer or producer subsidies can all push prices up. Policies to improve urban food security must therefore seek to improve market efficiency and maintain stable prices.

Logically, income security is also crucial to food security for urban dwellers. Yet with little human or financial capital, the poor are forced to take casual, insecure jobs. These jobs often experience seasonal ups and downs, just as in rural areas. For example, demand for construction workers can decline drastically during the rainy season. Garment workers may be laid off when the holiday rush dies down. With their abundance of labor, but often little else, the poor find competition for jobs is fierce.

To lift the poor from poverty, programs and policies should concentrate on creating jobs and on increasing the capacity of the poor to find and hold more-secure, higher-paying jobs or to expand their own businesses and generate new jobs. Governments, communities, and the private sector should cooperate to provide the elements for private sector success, much of which depends on a capable, if not extensive, government. At the same time, targeted income or food programs and more general social security and unemployment programs will continue to be necessary to provide for those who are left behind or who cannot work, including the elderly and the sick. Programs may also need to address issues of land and housing security, as secure tenure helps ensure that the poor do not lose their investments in tangible assets or in social networks.

However, efforts to improve urban livelihoods must go beyond a focus on urban jobs. Urban and rural lives are intertwined through goods, services, and people. In many cities, a majority of urban dwellers depend indirectly on agriculture for their livelihoods, through employment in food transport, retailing, and processing. Survival strategies may involve maintaining links with a home community in rural areas, through a plot of land or continued connections with family. Policies for improving urban livelihoods, then, must take into account the complexity of urban–rural links and recognize that rural conditions affect urban livelihoods as well.

Urban food security may also have a more direct link with agriculture. Even in large, congested cities, the urban poor may have a home garden or raise small animals as part of a coping strategy. This urban production, often done by women, can complement household incomes and improve the quality of urban diets. Urban planners and local governments should consider how to incorporate environmentally sound urban agriculture in their plans.

Of course, food security is not enough for good nutrition. A healthy household environment and good care and feeding practices are essential as well. The threats to good nutrition for both adults and children in urban areas differ from those in rural areas. The most substantial threats to health of the poor in the cities come from flimsy and overcrowded housing amid filthy conditions—uncollected garbage, unsafe water, overflowing sewers—and from the inability of the poor to get good health care. Even when health facilities are available, the poor often have no access to these services because of an inability to pay. According to UNICEF and the World Health Organization, for example, globally less than 20 percent of the urban poor have access to safe water, compared with 80 percent of the rich. Poverty and inequality are clearly major determinants of health and nutrition outcomes in the city.

Potentially harmful changes in diets also accompany urbanization. Because urban dwellers often face time constraints and have greater exposure to advertising and easier access to supermarkets and fast-food vendors, they often consume more processed and prepared foods. The typical urban diet results in higher levels of some micronutrients and animal proteins than the rural one, but it also means higher intakes of saturated and total fat and sugar and lower intakes of fiber. Combined with a sedentary lifestyle, this diet increases the risk of chronic diseases, including obesity. The public health sector faces a significant challenge in trying to overcome the malnutrition and poor health caused by poverty at the same time it responds to diseases associated with wealth and industrialization.

Challenges to child nutrition come from this unhealthy physical environment and from inadequate caring and feeding practices. Urban women end breastfeeding two to three months earlier than rural women, perhaps depriving their children of needed nutrients and reducing immunity. Women in urban areas also often work outside the home, which may mean they have less time and more difficulty in caring for their children. Policies to promote child nutrition in urban areas should focus not only on increasing incomes, especially women's, but also on encouraging good feeding and caring practices, including provision of easily accessible quality child care for those mothers who work. Good caring practices are possible even for the poor—as they frequently depend more on knowledge rather than income levels—and have been shown to counter the effects of low income on nutritional status.

The greatest difference between solutions to food and nutrition insecurity in rural and urban areas is probably that in rural areas development can often be addressed through broad-brush interventions affecting agriculture, which drives the rural economy. While agricultural growth may also help to reduce urban food insecurity, the income sources in urban areas are more diverse, as are underlying causes and actors in the urban environment. Effective policies and programs will require a holistically conceived response that coordinates actions across actors and levels—from the household (to raise incomes, for example), to the community (to install a water system), to far beyond (to promote labor-intensive growth by the government).

In any case, the most effective, relevant policies will emerge from a system of governance that firmly connects the needs of the poor to a politically responsive local government that has the technical and institutional capacity to act. Programs should work to strengthen the poor's ability to organize, make demands, and affect local authorities and to strengthen the municipality's understanding of its responsibility to respond.

Urban Food Insecurity and Malnutrition: Why Worry Now?

Some argue that concern about urban poverty is misplaced—that rural areas continue to hold most of the poor, food insecure, and malnourished and that they will for many years to come. Many analysts and governments seem complacent because their countries are not industrialized or highly urban. As we look to 2020, is such complacency justified? Clearly not.

First, the experiences of the industrialized world clearly show that developing countries are simply not going to "urbanize" themselves out of poverty. Governments and development agencies must take seriously the shift in poverty, food insecurity, and malnutrition from rural to urban areas. Second, in highly urbanized regions such as Latin America, the geographic center of poverty has *already* shifted: in these countries more poor people *already* live in the cities than in the countryside. Finally, even in countries that are still highly rural and where rural poverty predominates, millions of poor people live in cities. These people deserve not to be forgotten.

The perception that urban poverty exists only in industrialized countries is not matched by reality. In Mozambique, for example, with a poverty rate of 69 percent, 2 million poor people live in urban areas, more than the number of urban poor in highly urbanized Colombia and more than half the number of urban poor in much more populous Indonesia.

Even in highly rural countries, then, urban poverty, food insecurity, and malnutrition are problems of today, not tomorrow. For the sake of the millions of hungry and undernourished people living in cities today, as well as for the sake of those millions who may be forced to live there tomorrow, governments, development agencies, and communities must act now. They must work forcefully, confidently, and reasonably to promote policies, including those that promote rural development, to confront the rising specter of urban poverty, hunger, and malnutrition and so achieve the 2020 vision of sustainable food and nutrition security for all.

Chapter 12

Urbanization and Agriculture to the Year 2020

Reported by Ellen Wilson

*Though malnutrition in the cities is often not
as severe as in rural areas, there are pockets
of urban malnutrition that can rival the
poorest areas of the countryside.*

At present, the global population is half rural and half urban, but the world's cities are swelling. By 2025, two-thirds of the world's people will live in urban areas, and 80 percent of these urban residents will live in developing countries. As urbanization increases, policymakers in developing countries will be challenged to design ways to feed their cities ideally by relying mostly on their countries' own agriculture sectors. They must also work to prevent undernutrition, cope with changing diets among urban residents, and seek to quell the trend toward obesity.

"The developing world is now experiencing urbanization in the way developed countries did in the past, with urban populations doubling and tripling in one or two decades," says Wally N'Dow, secretary-general of Habitat II. "The difference is that urban dwellers in the developing world earn as little as $200 per person in annual income, compared with more than $20,000 in the United States. That means that cities must manage their money aggressively because there is less to invest in services and infrastructure."

"Urbanization means good news and bad news," said Jorge Wilheim, deputy secretary-general of Habitat II. "Urbanization contributes to national economic and social development. However, when the speed of urbanization is great, it is almost impossible for governments to follow the growth with water, energy, and other basic services."

The result is often poverty, unemployment, inadequate shelter, poor or non-existent sanitation, contaminated or depleted water supplies, air pollution, and other forms of environmental degradation. Substandard housing, unsafe water, and poor sanitation in densely populated cities are responsible for 10 million deaths worldwide every year, according to the United Nations. The UN reports that 600 million urban dwellers now live in life- and health-threatening housing situations in Africa, Asia, and Latin America.

Reducing Pressure on the Cities

Much of the current and future urbanization in developing countries, particularly in Africa and Asia, is occurring as a result of rural-urban migration and the transformation of rural areas to urban centers. According to IFPRI, one way to reduce the pressure on cities is for developing-country governments to invest in the rural areas, particularly in the agriculture sector—the base of the economy in most developing countries. This would make people less inclined to leave their agrarian lifestyles in search of better jobs in the cities. An investment in agriculture reverberates across the whole economy, generating more income and employment. According to IFPRI, each additional dollar of agricultural production spurs more than two dollars in spending in other sectors of the economy.

"If you increase agricultural productivity, then farmers make more money and have more to spend on other goods and services such as food, clothing, housing, education, and health care," said James Garrett, a researcher with IFPRI. "If the rural areas are not supported and the well-being of rural people improved, the cities will implode. People will continue to move to the cities, but the cities won't be able to support them in terms of either jobs or services."

Generally, urban areas offer people more jobs and health and social services than are available in the rural areas. As people move to cities, birth rates also tend to go down, mainly because fertility tends to fall as women's level of education rises, and cities offer greater educational opportunities. "Urban areas offer a higher life expectancy and lower absolute poverty and can provide essential services more cheaply and on a larger scale than rural areas," says Mathias Hundsalz, coordinator of the *Global Report on Human Settlements* by the United Nations Centre for Human Settlements (Habitat).

But experts agree that policies should not favor cities over the countryside. "People vote with their feet," said Richard Stren, director of the Center for Urban and Community Studies at the University of Toronto. "They perceive that their lives will be better off in the cities, and this is often the case. But, even though people are able to live better in urban areas, development should not favor urban areas over rural areas or vice versa. We don't want to discourage development in one sector at the cost of development in the other. We must invest in the whole economy so that people will have the freedom to live where they want and so that there continues to be a dynamic interaction between the rural and urban areas."

The Rural-Urban Connection

But urban policies are greatly needed to help manage urbanization. "The trend has been for urbanization to be concentrated in one city, and hence we've seen the growth of the megacities of the South such as São Paulo, Mexico City, and Cairo," said Wilheim of Habitat II. "We are encouraging countries to set up urban policies to stimulate a network of medium-sized cities. This would help provide people in the rural areas with employment and other benefits."

According to Stren from Toronto, this trend is already taking place. "The megacities have stopped growing rapidly in the South with the exception of cities in China. Since the 1980s, small and middle-sized cities have begun to grow more rapidly. This has implications for agricultural production because these cities are more connected to the agricultural hinterlands and, with good communication systems, can interact with the rural agricultural sector."

Better channels of communication between farmers and the cities, and new methods for transporting food cheaply from rural areas to cities will be crucial for stimulating economic growth in the rural sectors and low food prices throughout a country. "There must be ways for farmers to obtain information on what types of food products the urban areas are going to demand so that they can respond accordingly," said Garrett. "Communications and transportation systems should be improved so that farmers know what prices to charge and can get their goods to market."

In many countries, the current costs of "food marketing"—the process by which crops leave farmers fields and are transported to food processing plants or to urban markets to be sold—are extremely high. Of these food marketing costs, high transportation costs, caused by factors such as poor roads, high gas prices, and high automotive maintenance bills, can be major inflators of food prices for urban and rural residents. These factors can spur malnutrition by preventing the poor from being able to buy the food they need. Countries need to improve food marketing systems so that these costs remain low.

However, for farmers to take advantage of markets in urban areas, they must have education and other assistance. "You can have great roads, but if you are a poor, small farmer with no access to credit or the right seeds or you are not healthy enough to farm your land, these things don't matter," said Garrett. "Governments need to invest in rural people so that they can gain access to agricultural markets."

Meeting the Demands of Urban Appetites

As people move to the cities, they have less time and are exposed to a wider range of food items than in the rural areas they came from. These factors and others spur significant changes in diets in urban areas. Urban populations tend to eat more meat and processed foods and less rice and other grain and root dishes. This trend has already taken place in the rapidly urbanizing areas of Asia, such as Japan, Taiwan, and the Republic of Korea, and in Latin America. Some of the demand for meat will be fulfilled by rural areas outside of cities. Imports will also help take care of the increased demand for meat. According to IFPRI, developing-country imports of meat are expected to increase 20-fold from 2000 to 2020.

But no matter how developing countries' increasing appetite for meat is satisfied, urbanization and the accompanying more sedentary lifestyle, as well as diets that include more animal fat, sugar, and processed food, will lead to more obesity. Obesity is closely associated with chronic diseases, such as heart problems, diabetes, and hypertension. Significant increases in obesity have occurred in all regions of the developing world since 1957.

"As they eat more fat than they need or too many processed foods with comparatively low nutritional value, the urban poor begin to experience the worst of both the developed and developing worlds—both obesity and undernutrition sometimes in the same household," said Garrett. "Processed foods are often inexpensive, but can rob families of essential vitamins and minerals that can be found in more expensive fresh fruits, vegetables, and grains. While families may be increasing their calorie intake, they are not getting other nutrients they need."

Malnutrition in the Cities

Though malnutrition in the cities is often not as severe as in rural areas, there are pockets of urban malnutrition that can rival the poorest areas of the countryside. "For kids in the rural areas, milk comes from a cow," said Wilheim from Habitat II. "For kids in the cities, milk comes from the refrigerator. The milk must be purchased. Food and nutrition in the urban sector are almost totally dependent on the income of the family."

But sometimes money for food is in short supply, for example, if the family loses a job or if the husband does not give spending money to the wife for food. One way to help ward off hunger among low-income households of the future may be through "urban agriculture"—the farming of small plots of land available in urban environments or on the perimeter of the city. Urban agriculture might be able to supplement the family's diet, according to Dan Maxwell, a Rockefeller fellow at IFPRI.

However, urban agriculture must be managed carefully to address important food safety and environmental concerns. Urban residents must not irrigate edible crops with raw sewage or farm intensively with fertilizers and pesticides in highly populated areas. "Urban agriculture can have a beneficial impact on food security for low-income urban residents, but there are also potential risks, particularly where water is scarce and municipal governments are weak or ill informed," said Maxwell.

As urbanization increases, policymakers have multiple challenges with which to contend. Habitat II will seek to deal with many of these policy issues. However, it will also seek to improve overall human solidarity as more and more people in the world live closer together in the smaller quarters of urban cities.

"There is an urban war in the cities now with divisions between races and ethnic groups," said Wilheim. "We want to reconquer human solidarity. People must learn to be convivial, to live together. We want to prevent cities from becoming Sarajevos. Human diversity is as important as biodiversity."

PART 4

Diet Trends: Increasing Demand for Livestock and Fish

Are We Ready for a Meat Revolution?

Reported by Heidi Fritschel and Uday Mohan

*"Most people in India, including government officials, don't
believe a huge increase in meat consumption will happen,
but I think they're in for a big surprise."*
—Peter Hazell

I t happens in developing countries the world over—when poor families in Africa, Asia, and Latin America get access to a little more money, they spend a sizable share of it on meat to supplement their meager diet of staple grains. On a worldwide scale, this tendency produces dramatic results. For all developing countries combined, per capita consumption of beef, mutton, goat, pork, poultry, eggs, and milk rose by an average of about 50 percent per person between 1973 and 1996.

"As populations and urbanization increase and economic reforms lead to higher gross domestic product levels, the demand for livestock products will only grow stronger," says Simeon Ehui, coordinator of the Livestock Policy Analysis Project in the Ethiopia office of the International Livestock Research Institute (ILRI). "We are in the midst of an animal food product revolution," says Christopher Delgado, an IFPRI research fellow and coauthor of a 2020 Vision discussion paper on trends in livestock supply and demand.

Work conducted at IFPRI shows that in 2020, each person in the developing world is likely to demand about 29 kilograms of meat and 63 kilograms of milk a year, up from 21 kilograms and 41 kilograms, respectively, in 1993. Can the world produce the livestock necessary to meet this future demand? Even if it can, what will be the consequences for health and the environment and for small-scale farmers?

Income Is Not the Only Factor

"The poor consume cereals first to keep from going hungry, because cereals are cheap," says Howarth Bouis, an IFPRI research fellow. "The very poor don't have any money left over. But as people's income goes up, that's what they buy: meat and dairy products." In China and other countries of East Asia, which have seen large jumps in income since the early 1980s, meat consumption has grown by more than 5 percent a year.

Another important contributor to rising demand for meat products is urbanization. As people move to cities, studies show they start to eat more meat, milk, and other livestock products. "We're not sure of the cause," says Bouis. "It may be reduced activity patterns and, thus, lower cereal consumption—farming is more strenuous than most urban occupations. It may be that in cities people have more choices about what to eat and are exposed to new foods and recipes."

This trend will probably mean large increases in meat consumption in coming decades. In the future, the rural population in developing countries is expected to remain about constant while the urban population will increase rapidly.

Urbanization is already changing diets in India, according to Vijay Vyas, professor emeritus of the Institute of Development Studies in Jaipur, India, but not necessarily leading to much higher consumption of meat. "The importance of cereals in the food basket is declining, even among the poorest of the poor," says Vyas. "But the increase in meat consumption is not happening at the same speed in India as in China and other Southeast Asian countries. We are seeing a large increase in consumption of milk and eggs, as well as other noncereal foods like vegetables and fruits." Vyas attributes the shift partly to urbanization and partly to increased availability of these products and the religious sanctions against eating beef. "India has surpassed the United States to become the world's largest producer of milk," says Vyas.

But Peter Hazell, an IFPRI researcher and coauthor of a study on food balances in India, believes India is poised for an explosion in demand for meat, as well as more milk and eggs. "Most people in India, including government officials, don't believe a huge increase in meat consumption will happen, but I think they're in for a big surprise. Our study showed that in the last 10 years prices for livestock products went up and income growth for rural people in India was slow. So you wouldn't think that consumption of meat products would rise much. In fact, however, consumption shot up. Imagine what will happen if real incomes do grow more rapidly as a result of India's ongoing policy reforms."

The reasons, says Hazell, are many. Television is everywhere. Restaurants and street foods are more prevalent. Transportation is better, so rural people travel to town more often. The middle class is growing larger, and others see how they live. And advertising works.

The Meat Factor

By developed-country standards, people in the developing world still eat very small amounts of meat and livestock products. In the early 1990s, on average, each person in the developed world ate nearly four times as much meat and consumed nearly five times as much milk as each person in the developing world. And many poor people in developing countries still do not get enough calories or protein.

There are sound nutritional reasons for poor and malnourished people to wish to add more meat to their diet. Food staples like rice and maize offer calories but are not dense in micronutrients or protein. Christopher Delgado says, "You can get complete protein from vegetables, but you need to eat a wide variety of them. Eating meat is an easy way to get usable protein into your diet."

Meat can also aid in the absorption of other nutrients. "Meat contains iron, but it also helps the body absorb iron from other foods. This trait is known as the meat factor," says Catherine Geissler of the Department of Nutrition and Dietetics at King's College London. "Only small amounts of meat are required to do this. Vegetarians can get an adequate diet, but a mixed omnivore diet is an easier way to get all your nutrients."

In Bangladesh, says Bouis, people get only about 2 to 3 percent of their calories from meat, and their diet contains insufficient amounts of bioavailable iron. "More than half of adult women and 40 to 45 percent of preschool children are anemic," Bouis explains. "This iron deficiency retards mental development, particularly for infants, and reduces work capacity for adults. More meat, fish, and dairy consumption would be the best thing for nutrition in Bangladesh."

"Our research shows that a fivefold increase in meat, fish, and dairy consumption would lower the prevalence of anemia by 50 percent," says Bouis. "But with their income level, such an increase is totally infeasible, so finding ways to reduce prices of animal products is really important."

The Nutrition Transition

While some developing countries are struggling with how to add more meat to their diets, others are already facing the problem of too much meat consumption. "A nutrition transition is occurring in some developing countries," says Geissler. "The diseases of affluence are beginning to take over from the diseases of poverty. China is seeing a shift from undernutrition to such problems as heart disease partly caused by a rich, high-fat diet."

"China is trying to increase the consumption of traditional protein-rich products like soy through education, but it's not working too well. The general demand is for meat and other animal products," says Geissler. "Now that trade in food is freer, the government has less control. Farmers are freer to produce what they want."

To complicate matters, countries like China have a mixture of poor and better-off communities, containing both undernourished and "overnourished" people. "So targeted policies are needed," says Geissler.

"Meating" Demand

Increases in demand have been met largely by substantial growth in livestock production in developing countries. Meat production grew 5.4 percent annually between the early 1980s and early 1990s, a rate almost five times the developed-country average of 1.1 percent. Although per capita meat production in developing countries is still only a little more than a fourth of the developed-country average, the developing world supplies almost half the world's meat. Asia is the fastest growing supplier, accounting for more than 80 percent of the net increase in meat output of developing countries.

"Globally, livestock will become the most important economic subsector within agriculture," predicts Henning Steinfeld, senior officer in the Animal Production and Health Division of the Food and Agriculture Organization of the United Nations.

Increases in the supply of livestock products in developing countries—with pork and poultry production growing particularly fast, at 6.1 and 7.8 percent per year, respectively—are coming predominantly from industrial production. Steinfeld says there are several reasons why the traditional, small-scale producer cannot respond to the surge in demand: "Traditional livestock production uses feed resources, such as grazing, that simply cannot expand at a fast enough rate. There is also the difficulty that livestock products are easily perishable, and rural producers often don't have adequate market access. Economies of scale in production and processing favor large-scale livestock production, which is now found in the vicinity of virtually every large developing-country city. And policies do tend to favor the large producers with capital subsidies."

Nonetheless, Steinfeld sees livestock offering "a great development opportunity that could be missed." He worries that donors and development agencies have turned away from livestock mainly because of environmental and social concerns. "But these problems have little to do with livestock activities themselves," says Steinfeld, "and much more to do with the broader policy framework that has not dealt effectively with health, environment, and poverty issues as they relate to livestock."

How Will the Smallholder Fare?

The rewards of a dynamic livestock sector could especially benefit the poor, many of whom derive a larger share of their income from livestock than do the well-off.

About half a billion pastoralists depend on livestock for their livelihood, and at least 200 million smallholder farm families in the developing world derive most of their income from livestock. In some African countries, livestock contributes roughly 80 percent of cash income in crop-livestock farming systems. "As livestock production increases," says Ehui, "smallholders will increasingly walk away from poverty."

Joyce Turk, senior livestock adviser at the U.S. Agency for International Development, enumerates the ways livestock can help the poor: "In addition to improved human nutrition, of course, livestock generates economic growth through cash stability in the form of collateral and savings that aren't easily dissolved by inflation, reduces the need to purchase inorganic soil amendments, and provides products that can be sold at market." Delgado agrees but warns, "If research and policy do not find market-oriented ways for the smallholder to compete with large-scale commercial farming, the smallholder may well be shut out from an unprecedented growth opportunity."

Some analysts fear that booming livestock production could divert cereals away from food and toward feed markets, pushing prices for staple cereals out of the reach of the poor. But such concerns are misplaced, says Delgado. "World cereal prices are experiencing a long-term trend downward, because a substantial reserve capacity for production exists. IFPRI's projections to 2020 show that increasing livestock consumption will prevent inflation-adjusted cereal prices from falling below their already low levels, or raise them marginally, but nowhere near the high levels of the 1980s."

Dairy production has been one means the poor have used to improve their lives through the livestock sector. "Women especially tend smaller livestock, and this gives them increased control over products and the income from their sale, all of which promotes gender equity," says Jim De Vries, head of international programs at Heifer Project International, a U.S.-based nongovernmental organization (NGO) that supplies poor families with livestock to help them become self-reliant. "We have seen that one of the primary benefits of our work with goat husbandry, for example, is that the increased income particularly benefits the nutrition and education of girls," adds De Vries.

Market-oriented dairy production is also an avenue for smallholder women farmers to increase income and food security. In some cases, however, women do not gain as much as men despite providing as much or more livestock labor. "Only in areas where women traditionally dominate in agriculture do they control most of the income from dairying," explains Steve Staal, an economist at ILRI. "And even where men and women control income fairly equally, women's participation in dairying can be constrained because of lack of access to adequate investment resources," he adds.

Effects of Production on Health and the Environment

In addition to its benefits, livestock production presents enormous environmental challenges. Cees de Haan, livestock adviser at the World Bank, says, "The large increase in demand for livestock products expected in the developing world over the next decades will put tremendous pressure on natural resources. Livestock production can help the rural poor to escape the poverty trap, but policymakers and researchers will have to meet the challenge of putting in place the policies and technologies to make livestock production more sustainable."

About 37 percent of the world's meat supply comes from industrialized livestock production. In recent years, industrial production, which concentrates large numbers of animals in confinement, has grown twice as fast as production in farming systems that mix crops and livestock, and six times as fast as production in grazing systems. Increased industrial production has brought its own environmental problems as well as animal diseases. "In East Asia," says Steinfeld, "increased animal density near urban centers now results in unparalleled waste loads, with the capacity of plants to use nutrients from manure sometimes exceeded by 1,000 kilograms of nitrogen per hectare, which poses risks to flora and fauna and ultimately to humans." Manure also produces greenhouse gases—16 percent of annual methane emissions and 7 percent of the more aggressive nitrous oxide—that cause global climate change.

The Natural Resources Defense Council (NRDC), an NGO based in the United States, reports that "factory" farming in 29 U.S. states is poisoning drinking water supplies and contributing to hazardous air pollution. Robbin Marks, senior resource specialist at NRDC, points to the large corporate farms that dominate livestock production as "the culprits that create pollution problems when their enormous manure storage sites contaminate bodies of water and release toxic fumes into the air." Tightening regulations, involving communities in decisions about setting up factory farms, and banning manure runoff and open-air cesspools are some of the solutions Marks proposes. The U.S. Department of Agriculture and the Environmental Protection Agency are now drafting a strategy to limit these problems.

Livestock can improve environmental quality when used in traditional farming systems. De Vries says that "ownership of livestock is a great motivation for farmers to plant forage bearing trees and shrubs, grass contours, and pasture, all of which help to control erosion and conserve water."

But without proper training and incentives for smallholders, livestock can damage the environment, especially through overgrazing on open rangeland. "There are too many people raising too many animals in the low-rainfall areas in West Asia and North Africa," says Hazell. "The encroachment of cropping further erodes the soil in these lands, some of which are already drought-prone." He believes livestock production should rely less on grazing systems and more on intensive production in higher-potential areas. Hazell agrees, however, that problems arise with this method as well, including waste disposal and transfer of disease from animals to humans: "In Hong Kong the lethal flu virus that jumped from poultry to humans didn't learn to spread from human to human, otherwise we could have seen millions of people die in a worldwide epidemic. We were lucky that time."

Another problem is the conversion of forest to ranches in the Amazon, Central America, and elsewhere. "The truth is," Hazell says, "cattle are more profitable than forest." He sees deforestation and degradation increasing if the world's demand for livestock products goes up substantially and if countries fail to intensify and industrialize their production in a sustainable way.

Milking the Benefits of Livestock Production

With rising incomes and freer markets in developing countries, it will be difficult, if not impossible, for governments to control their people's demand for meat products. The key for policy, therefore, is to ensure that meat, milk, and eggs are available to the poor, who are likely to derive the greatest health benefits, and that livestock production is organized to bring the greatest benefits to the poor and to minimize damage to the environment. "The worst thing that well-motivated agencies can do is prevent investments in small-scale, sustainable, market-oriented livestock production," says Delgado. "Such investments won't stop the animal food product revolution, but they will help ensure that it contributes as much as possible to poverty alleviation and environmental sustainability."

Chapter 14

Livestock to 2020

The Next Food Revolution

Christopher Delgado, Mark Rosegrant, Henning Steinfeld,
Simeon Ehui, and Claude Courbois

*Lack of policy action will not stop the Livestock Revolution,
but it will ensure that the form it takes is less favorable
for growth, poverty alleviation, and sustainability
in developing countries.*

A revolution is taking place in global agriculture that has profound implications for human health, livelihoods, and the environment. Population growth, urbanization, and income growth in developing countries are fueling a massive increase in demand for food of animal origin. These changes in the diets of billions of people could significantly improve the well-being of many rural poor. Governments and industry must prepare for this continuing revolution with long-run policies and investments that will satisfy consumer demand, improve nutrition, direct income growth opportunities to those who need them most, and alleviate environmental and public health stress.

Transformation of Consumption and Production

Unlike the supply-led Green Revolution, the "Livestock Revolution" is driven by demand. From the early 1970s to the mid-1990s, the volume of meat consumed in developing countries grew almost three times as much as it did in the developed countries. Developing-world consumption grew at an even faster rate in the second half of this period, with Asia in the lead (Table 14.1).

Beginning from a small base, developing countries have begun to catch up with developed-world consumption levels, but they have a fairly long way to go, prima-

Table 14.1 Actual and Projected Meat Consumption by Region

Region	Annual growth of total meat consumption (percent)		Total meat consumption (million metric tons)		
	1982–94	1993–2020	1983	1993	2020
China	8.6	3.0	16	38	85
Other East Asia	5.8	2.4	1	3	8
India	3.6	2.9	3	4	8
Other South Asia	4.8	3.2	1	2	5
Southeast Asia	5.6	3.0	4	7	16
Latin America	3.3	2.3	15	21	39
West Asia/North Africa	2.4	2.8	5	6	15
Sub-Saharan Africa	2.2	3.5	4	5	12
Developing world	5.4	2.8	50	88	188
Developed world	1.0	0.6	88	97	115
World	2.9	1.8	139	184	303

Source: FAO annual data. Total meat consumption for 1983 and 1993 are three-year moving averages. 2020 projections come from IFPRI's global model, IMPACT.
Notes: Meat includes beef, pork, mutton, goat, and poultry. Suspected overestimation of meat production in China in the early 1990s suggests that actual 1993 consumption was 30 million metric tons (a 6.3 percent annual growth rate since 1983). If so, the level of world meat consumption for 1993 is overestimated here by at most 4.3 percent and by even less than that for 2020 because IMPACT incorporates pessimistic assumptions that are compatible with the conservative view for 1993.

rily because of low income levels. People in developed countries obtain an average of 27 percent of their calories and 56 percent of their protein from animal food products. The averages for developing countries are 11 and 26 percent, respectively. The difference in consumption levels gives an indication of the dramatic changes in store for global food production as the Livestock Revolution unfolds.

Production of animal food products grew most rapidly where consumption did. Total meat production in developing countries grew by 5.4 percent per year between the early 1980s and mid-1990s, more than five times the developed-world rate. Per capita production kept up with population in most developing regions, except in Sub-Saharan Africa (for meat) and West Asia/North Africa (for milk).

Whether these consumption trends will continue in the future is a question explored through IFPRI's global food model, which includes data for 37 countries and country groups and 18 commodities. Known as IMPACT (International Model for Policy Analysis of Agricultural Consumption), the model's baseline scenario projects that consumption of meat and milk in developing countries will grow 2.8 and 3.3 percent per year between the early 1990s and 2020. The corresponding developed-world growth rates are 0.6 and 0.2 percent per year. By 2020 developing countries will consume 100 million metric tons more meat and 223 million metric tons more milk than they did in 1993, dwarfing developed-country increases of 18 million metric tons for both meat and milk.

Growth rates for meat production through 2020 again follow those for meat consumption quite closely in most regions. Meat production will grow about four times as fast in developing countries as it will in developed countries. By 2020 developing countries will produce 60 percent of the world's meat and 52 percent of the world's milk. China will lead meat production and India milk production.

Implications for World Food Prices

The increase in livestock production will require annual feed consumption of cereals to rise by 292 million metric tons between 1993 and 2020. While some are concerned that such large increases will raise cereal prices substantially over time, the inflation-adjusted prices of livestock and feed commodities in fact are expected to fall by 2020, though not as rapidly as they have in the past 20 years. In a "worst-case" scenario, which by common accord is much too pessimistic, feedgrain requirements per unit of meat are assumed to rise 1 percent per year through 2020 due to increased industrialization of production and lack of a countervailing increase in livestock feeding efficiency. Even so, IMPACT shows that real maize prices in 2020 would be at most one-fifth above their present levels and remain substantially below their levels in the early 1980s.

Even with increases in livestock productivity far below historical trends, enough meat, milk, and feed will be available in 2020 without prices rising above 1992–94 levels. The key issue, then, is not availability, but what direct effect rapidly escalating livestock production and consumption will have on the poor, the environment, and human health.

Livestock and the Poor

Far from being a drain on the food available to the poor, increased consumption of animal products can help increase the food purchasing power of the poor. Considerable evidence exists that the rural poor and landless, especially women, get a higher share of their income from livestock than better-off rural people (with the main exceptions found in areas with large-scale ranching, such as parts of Latin America). Furthermore, livestock provide the poor with fertilizer and draft power, along with the opportunity to exploit common grazing areas, build collateral and savings, and diversify income. The Livestock Revolution could well become a key means of alleviating poverty in the next 20 years. But rapid industrialization of production abetted by widespread current subsidies for large-scale credit and land use could harm this major mechanism of income and asset generation for the poor.

Policymakers need to make sure that policy distortions do not drive the poor out of the one growing market in which they are presently competitive.

Livestock products also benefit the poor by alleviating the protein and micronutrient deficiencies prevalent in developing countries. Increased consumption of even small additional amounts of meat and milk can provide the same level of nutrients, protein, and calories to the poor that a large and diverse amount of vegetables and cereals could provide.

Environmental Sustainability and Public Health

At the low levels of calories consumed by the poor, lack of access to animal products, not overconsumption, should be the concern of policymakers. The greater health risks from livestock products in developing countries come from animal-borne diseases, such as avian flu and salmonella, microbial contamination from unsafe handling of foods, and a build-up of pesticides and antibiotics in the food chain through production practices.

The effects of the Livestock Revolution on the environment are also potentially worrisome. Livestock typically contribute to environmental sustainability in mixed farming systems that strike a proper balance between crop and livestock intensification. In these systems livestock provide the manure and draft power to sustain intensive crop production. But the larger concentrations of animals in periurban areas needed to meet growing urban meat and milk demand have led to the degradation of grazing areas and pollution problems. Policies have also encouraged overstocking or deforestation by shielding producers and consumers from the true costs of environmental degradation. In high-intensity systems, the large quantities of greenhouse gases and excess levels of nutrients produced by livestock pose dangers to the environment. This pollution needs to be, but rarely is, reflected in financial costs to the producer and consumer.

Conclusions for Policy

Some want to halt the Livestock Revolution. But the ongoing nutritional transformation in developing countries driven by income, population, and urban growth leaves little room for policy to alter the widespread increase in demand for animal food products. Policy can, however, help make the form of the revolution as beneficial as possible to the overall well-being of the poor. To do this, policymakers will have to focus on four key issues:

Small-scale producers have to be linked vertically with processors and marketers of perishable products. The poor find it difficult to gain access to productive assets such as credit and refrigeration facilities and to information such as knowledge about microbial infection prevention. The integration of small-scale livestock producers and larger-scale processors would combine the environmental and poverty-alleviation benefits of small-scale livestock production with the economies of scale and human health benefits that can be had from larger-scale processing.

Policy can help facilitate the incorporation of smallholders into commercial production by remedying distortions that promote artificial economies of scale, such as subsidies to large-scale credit and grazing. Success in this effort will require political commitment as well as public and private partnership to develop the technologies and practices necessary to minimize risks from animal disease that are inevitable when animals from large numbers of small-scale producers are mixed in a single finishing or processing facility. Much greater attention should be given to livestock productivity and health issues, including in postharvest processing and marketing.

Regulatory mechanisms for dealing with the health and environmental problems arising from livestock production need to be developed. Technologies that address environmental and public health dangers will not work unless regulatory enforcement backs them up. Such institutional developments will likely occur when the political demands for better regulation become strong.

Above all, small-scale producers need to be included in the response to this dynamic opportunity. Lack of policy action will not stop the Livestock Revolution, but it will ensure that the form it takes is less favorable for growth, poverty alleviation, and sustainability in developing countries.

Chapter 15

Overfished Oceans, Booming Fisheries
What Does This Mean for World Food Security?

Reported by Ellen Wilson

*"We've reached the point where we have
the technology to catch the last fish."*
—Gerry Leape

The adage "Give a man a fish, and feed him for a day; teach a man to fish, and he can feed himself for a lifetime" no longer holds true in today's world. Families that rely on fishing for their sustenance and livelihood are facing poverty and food insecurity as bounty from the oceans is depleted the world over.

Aquatic resources, including fish caught from the oceans and fish grown on saltwater and freshwater farms, were valued at US$70 billion in 1991. The fishing industry—in everything from dug-out canoes to giant trawlers using the advanced technology of the 1990s—is struggling to meet the world's appetite for fish. The result has been overexploitation of natural fish stocks and severe degradation of marine and coastal environments—resources once thought to be unlimited gifts of nature.

"The fishing industry's aggressive and expanding search for fish from the sea reached a turning point in 1990," said Meryl Williams, director general of the Philippines-based International Center for Living Aquatic Resources Management (ICLARM). "After many years of increasing production, the global marine and inland catch from natural stocks declined from the 1989 peak of about 89 million tons to 85 million tons in 1993. Despite a rebound to 91 million tons in 1994 and

1995, all indications are that the global catch will not resume the fairly steady production increase that marked the period from the 1940s to the 1980s."

The depletion of the world's natural fish stocks will have no small effect on the world food supply now and in the coming years. About 1 billion people—a fifth of the global population—rely on fish as their primary source of protein. Fish are also an important source of income, particularly for artisanal fisherfolk—people who live along coastal areas of developing countries. These people are at risk not only because their waters are overfished, but also because competition for access to coastal resources is increasing, mainly as a result of the recent phenomenal growth in shrimp and lobster exports to developed countries. This fisheries boom has marginalized many artisanal fisherfolk. With the global population growing fast, the world will need to further expand aquaculture to make up for the lost food and income supply for the poor.

Overfishing

Natural fish stocks are depleted worldwide because of unbridled access and super-advanced fish harvesting technology. Better enforcement of international agreements is needed to sustainably manage natural fish stocks and allow the oceans to recover. "We've reached the point where we have the technology to catch the last fish," said Gerry Leape, legislative director for ocean issues at Greenpeace. "We can no longer continue to develop our fishing fleets. But the world still subsidizes commercial fleets to the tune of a billion dollars a week. To put that in perspective, the world spends US$124 billion to catch US$70 billion worth of fish."

Industry is pumping so much money into increasingly more sophisticated equipment, such as trawlers with drift nets that span 40 kilometers, computerized searching mechanisms, and larger fishing vessels and fleets, because the fish are getting harder to find. In 1950, no marine fish stocks were known to be overfished. In 1994, the United Nations Food and Agriculture Organization (FAO) estimated that almost 70 percent of those stocks of marine fish for which assessments were available were fully exploited, overfished, or otherwise in urgent need of management.

"All of the oldest fishing grounds of the Northern Hemisphere are overfished," said Chris Delgado, research fellow at the International Food Policy Research Institute (IFPRI). "Europe and North America's traditional high-quality halibut, sole, and flounder fisheries are under severe pressure; previously abundant stocks from the North Sea between Denmark and Britain are at their lowest point ever; and, more recently, there has been the collapse of and subsequent ban on the fishing of Canada's cod. It remains to be seen how long it will take for these stocks to regenerate."

Overfishing is also taking place in Asia, in some African countries, in parts of Latin America, and in many small island countries, according to a report by the Denmark-based Institute for Fisheries Management and Coastal Community Development. Overfishing by local fishers in these areas is often aggravated by fishing fleets from industrialized countries.

Restrictions on Fishing

As fish have become increasingly scarce, countries have established 200-mile fishing limits off their coasts, which, to some degree, restrict access to fish on the continental shelf in much of the world. They have also created licensing and quota restrictions, such as "effort quotas," "individual transferable quotas" (ITQs), and limited entry into fisheries. Developed countries back up these limits with military force. However, few developing countries have been able to implement comprehensive and effective management measures for their waters.

"There is an international agreement and many laws," said Max Agüero, general director of the Chile-based research organization the Inter-American Centre for Sustainable Ecosystems Development (ICSED). "But industrial fleets do not fully respect the regulations, and developing countries do not have the resources to enforce them, such as through good fleets to monitor the waters within their own boundaries. We need more means to police the oceans if we want to implement the regulations, and, as an international community, we must find ways to self-regulate."

Some areas are still in dispute, such as those between China and the Philippines, the United States and Canada, and Canada and Spain. And these limits do not take into account fish that migrate from one country's jurisdiction to another, such as tuna and salmon.

Another major problem is the high rate of discarded fish, estimated by FAO's report The State of the World Fisheries and Aquaculture 1996 to be in the neighborhood of 27 million tons per year, or about 32 percent of the total reported annual production of marine capture fisheries. Trawling and other technologies sweep the ocean floor, but most of the catch is thrown out and wasted.

Policy groups call for increased enforcement of treaties to restrict fishing around the world, and some strides have been made in recent years. "For many years, the law of the sea under the United Nations was a pious wish that wasn't being implemented," said Delgado. "Now, after years of foot-dragging, it is being better implemented under the Agreement on Straddling Stocks and Highly Migratory Fish Stocks, and this has signified a major change in the way the world does business."

The Fisheries Boom

As the industrialized world's fish stocks have been depleted, the fish trade has increasingly turned to developing countries for fish. The United States, for example, has gone from the world's second largest exporter of fish to a net importer in a 10-year period, according to an IFPRI report. Among developing countries, fish exports have become the major foreign exchange success story of the last decade. From 1985 to 1994, foreign exchange earnings from fish exports from developing countries, mainly from Asia, have gone up from US$9 billion in 1983 to US$17 billion in 1993 after adjusting for inflation. This is an 87 percent increase in real terms over 10 years. Increased trade in fish has driven up fish prices. This has been good news for many debtor nations. Increased earnings from fish have come at a time when receipts from traditional exports of tropical agricultural products from developing countries were declining as a result of sharp price decreases for those items on the world market.

"The numbers are astounding," said Delgado. "The traditional money earners in many developing-country economies—sugar, coffee, tea, and cocoa—are together earning less now on a global scale than large-scale fisheries exports, which tend to be concentrated in countries like Indonesia, India, Mexico, and Thailand."

But there is a dark side to the new fish boom in developing countries. Most of the new fish on the market are coming from industrial fisheries in developing countries. These are often capital-intensive enterprises, mainly financed by and earning profits for large investors, favored by national governments because of their contributions to markets, exports, and the national economy. Although they provide employment, industrial fisheries are not producing food for the poor. They produce high-value fish for industrialized countries and low-value fish for fish meal that is fed to livestock. Yet they are overtaking the waters of small-scale, artisanal fisherfolk, particularly in Asia, where there are many poor, coastal communities.

"Generating income is one thing," said Agüero. "Who gets the income is another, and it is not the small-scale fishers. With new trends toward a global economy and more foreign investment, outsiders take advantage of the income fish resources can generate. Increasingly, resources from these enterprises are going into very few hands, and the community at large is not benefiting.

"There needs to be an emphasis on producing more low-cost fish like tilapias and carps on fish farms, rather than emphasizing the high-value fish that generally appeal to high-income population," continued Agüero. "While the production of high-value fish has increased the income and foreign exchange of many developing countries, it does not address the food problem."

Artisanal Fisherfolk

The significance of small-scale artisanal fisherfolk cannot be overemphasized, as they account for the major part of the fish landed for direct human consumption in developing countries, according to an IFPRI report. "The contribution of small-scale fisheries to income and employment, often in areas where there is no alternative employment, is also considerable, with at least 100 million people wholly or partly economically dependent on it."

According to the 1996 FAO report on fish, "it is important to ensure that traditional fisherfolk also benefit directly from higher fish values and are fully involved in decisions affecting their livelihoods."

One way for artisanal fisherfolk to participate in the fisheries boom is through fish cooperatives or comanagement of fisheries, whereby authority for fisheries management can be shared between various levels of government and the local fishing community. According to a report by ICLARM, some countries such as Malawi and Viet Nam have adopted comanagement as an official policy. In others, such as in Bangladesh and the Philippines, it is being pursued selectively as an interim measure through local and community initiatives or with the assistance of nongovernmental organizations.

Nonetheless, in the years ahead, there will be a shortfall in inexpensive protein for people who once relied on fish. According to Williams from ICLARM, better research is needed on the freshwater farming of affordable food fish in developing countries. Increasing the supply of substitute products through improved aquaculture can help solve the conflicting problems of overfishing and the world's increased demand for fish. This technical solution must be complemented by social and policy measures to help make aquaculture environmentally sustainable and to improve fisheries management.

"Fish is unlikely to ever return to being the poor man's protein," she said. "However, we must maximize use of aquatic resources. Efficiency improvements, such as reducing postharvest losses, hold great potential."

Williams also raised the issue of using aquatic resources as livestock and aquaculture feed, crop fertilizer, and food and nonfood additives. The critical question to ask of lower-priced uses is whether a greater contribution could be made by using the resources more directly for human food.

Looking to the future, economists project that under optimistic conditions, overfishing—and the resulting loss of fish for human consumption—could be offset by the adoption of wise fish management strategies and the increased use of low-value fish to the year 2010.

"Over the next 25 years, the challenge will be to maintain present or near-present levels of natural harvests while sustainably increasing aquaculture production," said Williams.

"The next few transition decades pose a host of uncertainties for users of fisheries, consumers, and management institutions. It is also a time of opportunities, when even small actions could have important effects."

PART 5

Food Production and the Environment

Chapter 16

The Earth's Environmental Woes

Is Agriculture Part of the Problem
Or Part of the Solution?

Reported by Ellen Wilson

*One of the major causes of the environmental stress in
the developing world is poverty, and one of the major
causes of poverty is environmental stress.*

Every year, nearly 17 million hectares of tropical rain forests are destroyed, thousands of irreplaceable plant varieties are lost, and millions of hectares of land turn into deserts.

Will increased agricultural production, with its associated use of fertilizers, pesticides, irrigation, and farm machinery only exacerbate these severe global environmental problems? In short, does the goal of meeting the world's future food needs conflict with the goal of protecting the environment?

According to researchers, one of the major causes of the environmental stress in the developing world is poverty, and one of the major causes of poverty is environmental stress.

"The relationship between poverty and environmental degradation is close and complicated," said Per Pinstrup-Andersen, director general of IFPRI. "The rural poor depend on agriculture, and hence on natural resources, for 40 to 85 percent of their income. Environmental degradation sets in when the poor lose the capacity to sustainably support themselves from their natural resource base. Population pressures and a lack of adequate agricultural technologies, among other factors, are major forces driving the poor to make desperate choices."

The negative relationship among poverty, population, and environmental degradation can end only, according to researchers, with the help of more productive agriculture in the areas that have already been cultivated by the poor. This will slow encroachment on rain forests, hillsides, and desert margins.

Yet at the same time, changes need to be made where agriculture is more advanced, such as on former Green Revolution lands. More environmentally sound management of fertilizers, pesticides, and irrigation is needed to reduce the negative environmental impact of agricultural intensification.

Increasing agricultural productivity in both the fragile and the more productive areas of the developing world is essential for meeting future global food needs. According to researchers, this is one of the most important ways of better managing the world's natural resources.

Putting Nutrients Back into Soils

According to the 1994 UNICEF *State of the World's Children* report, "Land cleared by burning forests loses stability and fertility within a very few years; steep hillsides quickly become eroded without investments in soil conservation; marginal agricultural lands gradually become infertile when those who farm them can afford neither fertilizer nor fallow periods. . . ."

It used to be that farmers could allow land in fragile areas to recover between crop rotations, but this practice is fast becoming a luxury as a result of population pressures. Much of the population pressure is coming from migrations of people from wars, social strife, natural disasters, and environmental degradation. According to an IFPRI report, 500 million people live on severely degraded hillsides, 200 million live in tropical rain forests, and 850 million live in dry areas threatened by desertification.

As the population density increases, farmers must produce even more food than before. To do this, there is no other way except to put nutrients back into soils. The methods for doing this, however, are still being debated by agriculturalists and environmentalists. There are inorganic and organic methods—use of synthetic fertilizers and use of organic materials such as compost and nitrogen-fixing legumes that add nutrients to the soils.

According to Carlos Baanante, director of the Research and Development Division at the International Fertilizer Development Center, "Organic fertilizers, such as composted livestock manure and plant residues, help to maintain the soil's organic matter and supply nutrients. But the nutrients supplied may not be sufficient. The best management is the use of both organic and inorganic sources of nutrients."

But some members of the environmental community disagree. "The assumption that we should keep adding nitrogen fertilizer to soils indefinitely is weak," said

Jonathon Landeck, director of international programs at the Rodale Institute. "The ideal agriculture is that which does not incorporate any synthetic chemicals. For those who say that organic fertilizers are not viable in the long run, I have to point out that synthetic fertilizer use will likewise reach yield plateaus. Additionally, use of organics could mean fewer energy inputs, making them cheaper than synthetic chemicals. But we don't know this because we have not been investing equally in research on agriculture that is clean of synthetic chemicals."

According to researchers, other needs in fragile areas are diverse cropping systems instead of intensive monocultures of annual crops; better integration of livestock and green manures into farming systems; and generation of nonfarm sources of income. Other needed reforms include changes in land tenure rights. "In many instances," said Pinstrup-Andersen, "poor people do not own the land they farm. They, therefore, have few or no incentives to conserve soils, harbor groundwater, or preserve trees."

People versus Trees

Fragile areas not only supply food, fuel, water, and income to the poor, they are also home to some of the world's most important caches of biodiversity. The Nature Conservancy, through its assistance to developing-world organizations to purchase and preserve ecologically valued land, often wrestles with the dilemma of "people versus trees."

According to Alan Randall, director of major program development at the Conservancy, "Our philosophy is to make these reserves an instrument of economic development and employment for the people who live around them rather than an instrument for taking land away. The bottom line is that a forest reserve or park cannot exist if it is surrounded by poverty."

The Conservancy is working with the Bertoni Foundation, a conservation group, to protect the Mbaracayu Forest Nature Reserve—146,000 acres in Paraguay. The land was purchased in advance of a company that planned to raze the trees and convert the land to industrial-scale soybean and cotton farming. Instead of opposing the poor farmers who sought land claims on the reserve, the Bertoni Foundation is assisting community members to file land claims in the buffer areas outside the reserve, and to adopt sustainable agricultural practices.

The Foundation and the Conservancy are also helping the community to develop alternative sources of income that do not degrade the land, such as poultry production and beekeeping. They are also encouraging sustainable harvesting of nontimber forest products, such as tea leaves, from the reserve. Indirect byproducts of the reserve have been government-sponsored improvements to the rural roads and electrification of the local village.

Agricultural Ills

Some perceive agriculture as an environmental enemy. In some of the highly productive Green Revolution areas, dramatic increases in food production have been associated with environmental degradation: waterlogging and salinization of soils from irrigation; contamination of surface and groundwater; loss of beneficial insects; buildup of chemical resistances in insects and weeds; poisoning of farm workers from pesticides; and loss of traditional plant varieties from the planting of monocultures. According to researchers, these ills do not necessarily have to come hand in hand with agricultural development.

"Agricultural 'inputs'—irrigation, fertilizers, and pesticides—have been heavily subsidized by governments, making them far too cheap, and leading many to overuse them," said Peter Hazell of IFPRI. "Between 10 and 24 percent of all irrigated land, for example, suffers from salinization caused by overirrigation. In India, about 7 million hectares of land have been abandoned because of salts."

What is needed, according to Hazell, is better design and management of irrigation systems, fewer subsidies on fertilizers and pesticides, development of economic incentives to reduce excessive use of water and chemical inputs, regionally diversified crop breeding programs, and farmer education on safe application, storage, and disposal of pesticides.

"Irrigation and chemical inputs, if applied properly, at the right time, and sparingly, do not have to degrade the environment," said Hazell. "And using chemicals that are specifically designed for the problems at hand will decrease the negative environmental consequences as well."

Studies have found that pesticides are only needed in very small amounts, and work is progressing on ways to replace them completely. Says Hazell, "There is a shift toward biological control—using natural predators to control pests instead of pesticides. We are also breeding into plants natural resistances to pests and diseases.

"Agriculturalists and environmentalists are becoming better informed," continued Hazell. "Few agriculturalists think that Green Revolution technology should be applied to fragile areas. On the other hand, in highly productive areas, more environmentalists agree that we have to continue to use modern inputs, but do so in a more environmentally responsible way. As we look to the future, biotechnology will provide more and more substitutes for chemicals. Who knows, maybe one day we can breed a nitrogen-fixing gene into wheat and rice."

But according to Natural Resources Defense Council senior attorney Jacob Scherr, policymakers should also look beyond technology to political and social issues affecting environmental protection, poverty, and the food supply. "For example, take Africa," said Scherr. "If you consider its natural resource base, the continent should be able to meet its own food needs. However, Africa is experiencing a food shortfall, which is expected to become worse. The solution will not come from a Green Revolution 'magic bullet.' The issue of adequate food supply in Africa is extraordinarily complex. It involves markets, distribution, governmental policies—all of which are vulnerable to disruption by political unrest. It is going to take much more than improved seeds to avoid chronic hunger and food shortages."

Chapter 17

Agricultural Growth Is the Key to Poverty Alleviation in Low-Income Developing Countries

Per Pinstrup-Andersen and Rajul Pandya-Lorch

*Very few countries have experienced rapid
economic growth without agricultural growth
either preceding or accompanying it.*

The extent and depth of poverty in the developing world is a disgrace. Over 1.1 billion people—30 percent of the population—live in absolute poverty, with only a dollar a day or less per person to meet food, shelter, and other needs. Not surprisingly, hunger, malnutrition, and associated diseases are widespread: more than 700 million people do not have access to sufficient food to lead healthy, productive lives; millions more live on the edge of hunger; and more than 180 million preschool children are significantly underweight. Every second person in South Asia and Sub-Saharan Africa is absolutely poor. Unless concerted action is taken now, poverty is not expected to diminish much in the near future. South Asia will continue to be home to half the developing world's poor, and Sub-Saharan Africa, where the number of poor is projected to increase 40 percent between 1990 and 2000, will emerge as an increasingly important locus of poverty.

Poverty is a rural phenomenon in most of the developing world, especially the low-income developing countries. The rural poor make up more than 75 percent of the poor in many Sub-Saharan African and Asian countries. Latin America's high urbanization rates have led to a higher prevalence of urban poverty, but even in that region the majority of the poor are rural.

Agriculture Is Key to Poverty Alleviation

Most of the world's poor are rural-based and, even when they are not engaged in their own agricultural activities, they rely on nonfarm employment and income that depend in one way or another on agriculture. Moreover, agricultural growth is a catalyst for broad-based economic growth and development in most low-income countries: agriculture's linkages to the nonfarm economy generate considerable employment, income, and growth in the rest of the economy. Very few countries have experienced rapid economic growth without agricultural growth either preceding or accompanying it. Economic growth is strongly linked to poverty reduction. Diversification out of agriculture will occur in the long term, but in the short term many countries lack alternatives.

Agricultural growth and development must be vigorously pursued in low-income developing countries for at least four reasons: (1) to alleviate poverty through employment creation and income generation in rural areas; (2) to meet growing food needs driven by rapid population growth and urbanization; (3) to stimulate overall economic growth, given that agriculture is the most viable lead sector for growth and development in many low-income developing countries; and (4) to conserve natural resources. Poverty is the most serious threat to the environment in developing countries: lacking means to appropriately intensify agriculture, the poor are often forced to overuse or misuse the natural resource base to meet basic needs.

National and international investments in agriculture have declined since the mid-1980s. In many countries, agriculture has been taxed explicitly and implicitly. The downward trend in support for developing-country agriculture must be reversed, not only to assure future food supplies and to protect natural resources, but also to promote general economic growth and poverty alleviation.

Accelerated public investments are needed to facilitate agricultural and rural growth through

- Yield-increasing crop varieties, including improved crop varieties and hybrids that are more drought-tolerant and pest-resistant, and improved livestock;

- Yield-increasing and environmentally-friendly production technology such as small-scale irrigation and irrigation management systems and techniques such as integrated pest management;

- Reliable, timely, and reasonably priced access to appropriate inputs such as tools, fertilizer, and, when needed, pesticides, and the credit often needed to purchase them;

- Strong extension services and technical assistance to communicate timely information and developments in technology and sustainable resource management to farmers and to relay farmer concerns to researchers;

- Improved rural infrastructure and effective markets; and

- Primary education, health care, and good nutrition for all.

These investments need to be supported by an enabling policy environment. This includes trade, macro, and sectoral policies that do not discriminate against agriculture, and policies that provide appropriate incentives for the sustainable management of natural resources.

Investments in Research and Technology Are Crucial

Agricultural research and technological improvements are crucial to increase agricultural productivity and returns to farmers and farm labor, thereby reducing poverty and meeting future food needs at reasonable prices without irreversible degradation of the natural resource base. Accelerated investment in agricultural research is particularly urgent for low-income developing countries, partly because these countries will not achieve reasonable economic growth and poverty alleviation without productivity increases in agriculture, and partly because comparatively little research is currently undertaken in these countries. Many poor countries, which depend the most on productivity increases in agriculture, grossly underinvest in agricultural research (Figure 17.1). Per capita agricultural research expenditures in low-income countries are one-tenth those in high-income countries, even though agriculture accounts for much larger shares of average incomes. Expenditures in public-sector agricultural research in low-income countries are still less than 0.5 percent of the agricultural gross domestic product, compared with about 2.0 percent in high-income countries, a share that has doubled since the early 1960s.

Sub-Saharan Africa, which desperately needs productivity increases in agriculture, has only 42 agricultural researchers per million economically active persons in agriculture compared with 2,458 in industrialized countries. Figure 17.2 shows that the annual growth of African agricultural research expenditures has declined since the 1960s. Sub-Saharan Africa is also missing out on biotechnological research, which is concentrated in industrial countries and a few large developing countries such as Brazil. By failing to capitalize on the new opportunities biotechnology offers, Sub-Saharan Africa may lose export markets to competitors and synthetic substitutes.

Figure 17.1 Agricultural Research Expenditures, 1981–85

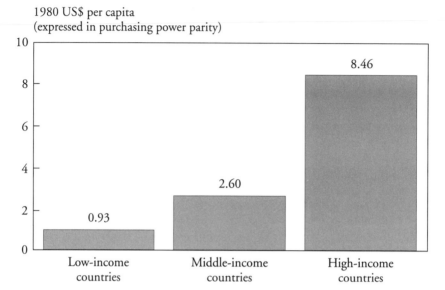

Source: P. Pardey, J. Roseboom, and J. R. Anderson, eds., *Agricultural Research Policy: International quantitative perspectives* (Cambridge: Cambridge University Press, 1991).

A large share of the poor reside in areas with high risks of environmental degradation. The low priority given to research to develop appropriate technology for these areas in the past is a major reason for the current rapid degradation of natural resources and high levels of poverty. In addition to assuring sufficient research investment in the high-potential areas, much more research must be directed to the development of appropriate technology for marginal areas. Outmigration is not a feasible solution for these areas in the foreseeable future simply because of the large numbers of poor people who reside there and the lack of opportunities elsewhere.

While the private sector is expected to play an increasing role in research and technology development for developing-country agriculture, much of the research needed to reduce poverty is of a public goods nature—the benefits are not easily captured by individual farmers or firms but extend to society as a whole—and will not be undertaken by the private sector. Fortunately, extremely high social rates of returns of past and current agricultural research justify public investment. The major share of such investments should occur in the developing countries' own research institutions. However, to be fully effective, those institutions must be supported by international research. The centers under the auspices of the Consultative

Figure 17.2 Annual Growth Rate of Expenditures in African national Agricultural Research Systems

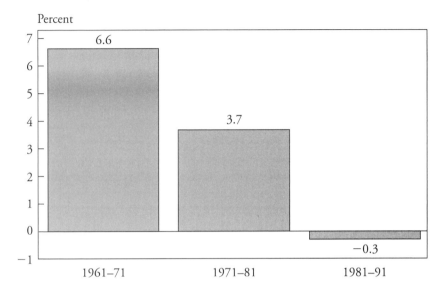

Source: P. Pardey, J. Roseboom, and N. Beintema, *Agricultural Research in Africa: Three Decades of Development.* Briefing Paper No. 19 (The Hague, Netherlands: International Service for National Agriculture Research, 1995).

Group on International Agricultural Research (CGIAR) play an essential role in undertaking research of a public goods nature with large international benefits. Such research is of critical importance to developing countries and must be accelerated if poverty is to be significantly reduced.

Research and technology alone will not drive agricultural growth. The interaction between technology and policy is critical. The full and beneficial effects of agricultural research and technological change will materialize only if government policies are appropriate. Distortions in input and output markets, asset ownership, and other institutional and market distortions adverse to the poor must be minimized or removed. Access by the poor to productive resources such as land and capital needs to be enhanced. Human resources must be improved through expanded investments in education, health care, nutrition, and sanitary environments. Rural infrastructure and institutions must be strengthened. The policy environment must be conducive to and supportive of poverty alleviation and sustainable management of natural resources.

Agriculture must be in the forefront of the national and international agenda to eradicate poverty in low-income developing countries. Failure to significantly expand agricultural research in and for developing countries and failure to invest in agricultural development will make poverty eradication an elusive goal. Lack of foresight today comes with a high price tag for the future. As usual, the weak and powerless will pay the largest share of the price. We must all share the blame for inaction or inappropriate action.

Chapter 18

Reducing Poverty and Protecting the Environment

The Overlooked Potential of Less-Favored Lands

John Pender, Peter Hazell, and James L. Garrett

Strategies to get agriculture moving in less-favored
areas will typically have to be different from
the Green Revolution model.

Poverty, low agricultural productivity, and natural resource degradation are severe interrelated problems in less-favored areas of the tropics. Less-favored areas include lands that have low agricultural potential because of limited and uncertain rainfall, poor soils, steep slopes, or other biophysical constraints, as well as areas that may have high agricultural potential but have limited access to infrastructure and markets, low population density, or other socioeconomic constraints. In other words, less-favored lands may be less favored either by nature or by man.

According to a recent study by the Technical Advisory Committee of the Consultative Group on International Agricultural Research, nearly two-thirds of the rural population of developing countries—almost 1.8 billion people—lives in less-favored areas, including marginal agricultural areas, forest and woodland areas, and arid areas. These areas include most of the semiarid and arid tropics of Africa and South Asia, mountain areas in South America and Asia, much of the highlands of East and Central Africa, hillside areas in Central America and Southeast Asia, and large portions of the humid tropics of Africa and Latin America. The available evidence suggests that most of the rural poor in developing countries live in these less-favored areas. Low agricultural productivity and land degradation are severe in these areas. Cereal yields of less than one metric ton per hectare are common, and deforestation, overgrazing, soil erosion, and soil nutrient depletion are widespread.

The conventional wisdom in policy circles has said that strategies for development in developing countries should emphasize public investments in favored areas. Many experts have believed that returns to investment would be greatest in favored areas and that increased food production and rapid economic growth in these areas would ensure food security and allow people to migrate out of less-favored areas, reducing poverty and pressure on the resources in such areas.

In the past, many governments and donors have adopted this strategy and provided high-potential areas with better roads, communications, schools, health facilities, and agricultural technologies. Credit programs as well as pricing policies for production and for agricultural services and inputs have also tended to favor these areas, or at least the crops produced there. Yet, despite considerable outmigration, population and agricultural production in less-favored areas continue to grow, often in association with worsening poverty and resource degradation. At the same time, after years of intensive use of irrigation and chemical inputs, erosion and salinization are affecting many high-potential areas, and growth in yields has stagnated, leading to diminishing returns to new investment. In some instances, as capital-intensive technologies displace workers, the development of high-potential areas has actually encouraged migration to less-favored areas. Thus, the sustainability of this strategy is even now in doubt. Success is especially uncertain for predominantly agrarian countries, like many in Africa, with only limited high-potential land and nonfarm opportunities.

Although less-favored areas often have an absolute disadvantage in producing many types of crops compared with favored areas (that is, productivity is lower than in favored areas), they invariably have a comparative advantage in some type of agricultural production or in nonfarm activities (that is, production is profitable given alternative uses of the land and labor of people in these areas). The diversity of situations in less-favored areas can allow them to exploit their different comparative advantages, provided that necessary investments in infrastructure and institutions are made. Increasing evidence suggests that investments in less-favored areas can yield relatively high rates of economic return and significantly reduce poverty in some countries. Anecdotal evidence also suggests the possibility of reducing resource and environmental degradation alongside economic growth and poverty reduction. However, the evidence on such strategies is still very limited.

Government and donor agencies could, of course, try to increase incomes in less-favored areas by promoting nonagricultural or postharvest activities, instead of agriculture. But in most rural areas, the generation of significant nonfarm income depends critically on having a dynamic agriculture sector. If regional agriculture stagnates, the local economy has no engine to drive nonfarm activities.

In Africa, for example, less-favored areas are often isolated from the rest of the economy. Low incomes limit demand. With investment, agriculture starts to grow; incomes and expenditures of local people increase. Opportunities to diversify production of agricultural and nonagricultural goods and services, including microenterprises and agroprocessing, open up.

Although there are large gaps in knowledge about the underlying causes of the problems facing less-favored areas and the appropriate strategies to address them, several key lessons emerge from recent assessments:

- Less-favored areas offer opportunities for socially profitable investments. Recent research shows high returns to various kinds of public investment in lower-potential areas of China and India (in many instances higher than returns to investments in favored areas), in terms of both economic growth and poverty reduction. Investments in agricultural research and development, education, roads, and irrigation had greater incremental impact in less-favored areas in these countries, in part because the opportunities for investment in these areas had been neglected.

- The success of alternative investments in less-favored areas depends upon differences in comparative advantage across these diverse areas. Given the variety of situations in less-favored areas, no one-size-fits-all strategy is likely to succeed everywhere. Three factors are particularly important for determining comparative advantage: agricultural potential, access to markets and infrastructure, and population density. In less-favored areas having high agricultural potential but poor market access—as in much of humid West Africa, parts of the East African highlands, and the Southeast Asian uplands—high-value nonperishable perennial crops such as coffee, cocoa, or oil palm often have a comparative advantage. Areas with low crop production potential are likely to have comparative advantage in extensive livestock production, particularly if they are far from markets and not densely populated, as in much of semiarid West Africa and the Altiplano of the southern Andes. In remote areas where population densities are greater, mixed-crop livestock production is more important, even where crop production potential is low, as in parts of the East African highlands. Areas with low crop production potential but good access to markets—as in periurban areas of semiarid India and other low-potential areas—are likely to have a greater comparative advantage in forestry, intensive livestock production, or nonfarm activities. Development strategies will be more successful if they recognize and build upon such comparative advantages.

- Strategies for developing and disseminating technologies must take into account the special characteristics and demands of less-favored areas. A high degree of diversity in biophysical and socioeconomic conditions is one of the main challenges. Other challenges may include susceptibility to droughts, pests, diseases, temperature extremes, and other risks; the fragility of land and other resources; remoteness from markets and services; and the subsistence orientation of farmers in these areas. A technological strategy should there-fore be participatory and demand driven, stimulating and building upon farmer innovation and adapting to local circumstances. Technologies that help reduce risks (by increasing tolerance to drought, pests, or frost, for example) and conserve and improve resources may be more effective than those that simply promote high yields in response to high levels of inputs.

- Sustainable and profitable technologies are needed to conserve and efficiently use scarce water, control erosion, restore soil fertility, and increase the supply of useful biomass. Such technologies are often labor or land intensive (such as terrace building) and may be unattractive to farmers where labor costs are high or where land is scarce. Labor- or land-saving technologies such as improved fallows during a short rainy season or agroforestry on farm boundaries may have more potential. In areas with limited rainfall, scarcity of biomass and high demands for alternative uses of biomass (for fodder and fuel, for example) limit the potential of many organic approaches to land management. In such circumstances, technologies and policies for conserving water and profitably increasing the production of useful biomass (such as promotion of woodlots) should have high priority.

- Strategies for less-favored areas will be most effective if they are linked to the development pathways that have comparative advantage in particular circumstances. Small-scale irrigation development is likely to yield the highest returns in areas with good market access and otherwise suitable soil conditions, since this can enable high-value crop production as well as intensified food crop production. Road development is likely to have the highest returns in densely populated areas with good agricultural potential but limited market access, by enabling marketing of high-value commodities and inputs for these. Improved management institutions for common property resources such as community grazing lands or woodlots are critical in many less-favored areas, particularly low-potential areas with limited opportunity to increase crop productivity. Investments in education and training are also important, particularly in low-potential areas with limited market access, where emigration is likely to be an important element of people's livelihood strategies for the foreseeable future.

- Secure property rights and effective institutions must be ensured. When farmers do not have assured long-term access to land, do not bear the full cost of resource degradation, or are not sure they will receive the benefits of their investments, they are more likely to pursue unsustainable farming practices and fail to invest in improving and conserving resources. Governments should ensure that farmers have secure property rights, and should remove restrictions that inhibit the most efficient and environmentally sustainable use of private, public, and common property. Many community-based land tenure systems provide farmers with adequate security. When appropriate, governments should strengthen these indigenous systems and facilitate their adaptation to changing circumstances, instead of replacing them. This is particularly true of local organizations that manage common properties such as rangelands, woodlands, and wetlands. When adequately empowered, they are often best able to take account of resource interdependencies and establish regulations that recognize the rights of many users over the same land. Such regulations are especially important in watersheds or drought-prone areas that require the ability to move animals over wide areas as an integral part of risk management.

- Effective risk management is needed. Risks of crop disaster due to bad weather or pests can discourage investments by farmers in land improvements and their adoption of higher-yielding technologies. Agricultural research can help reduce risk, for example, by improving drought resistance in crops or developing better ways to conserve soil moisture. Additionally, governments may need to assist farmers in coping with catastrophes and work to provide effective safety net programs and credit and insurance markets. However, care should be taken in designing such interventions, for they can easily backfire. Subsidized drought insurance, for example, increases the profitability of more risky farming practices, some of which may be environmentally unsuitable for drought-prone areas. Subsidized fodder programs in drought years for rangeland users can also encourage overstocking, which over time degrades the range.

- Policymakers must provide the right policy environment. Market reforms, including price and trade liberalization, are also necessary to ensure that prices provide the right production signals to farmers and that production and input markets are competitive and work well. Governments should make sure that farmers have access to good roads, telecommunications, and a strong credit and savings system. Without them, farmers cannot be sure that they will be able to sell their crops or get the inputs, like credit and fertilizer, that they need.

Governments and donors should look more closely at the benefits of investing in the agriculture of less-favored areas. Even without including social and environmental benefits, the line can already be redrawn on what is economically justified. This line may well shift even further in favor of less-favored lands as agricultural research opens up new development possibilities. These investments become even more compelling when the social benefits from reducing poverty, food insecurity, and environmental degradation are considered.

Addressing the complex challenges of less-favored areas will not be easy or inexpensive. It will typically require significant policy and institutional changes, investments in agricultural research, rural infrastructure, human capital, and the active involvement of local communities. Success will depend on the development of stronger linkages between agricultural researchers, local governments, farmers, community leaders, nongovernmental organizations, national policymakers, and donors. On their own, none of these agents of change are likely to succeed. But by working together, they can take advantage of significant opportunities now and in the future to reduce poverty and protect the environment in the areas that until now have been less favored.

Chapter 19

The Potential of Agroecology to Combat Hunger in the Developing World

Miguel A. Altieri, Peter Rosset, and Lori Ann Thrupp

With increasing evidence and awareness of the advantages of agroecology, why hasn't it spread more rapidly and how can it be multiplied and adopted more widely?

Proponents of a second Green Revolution generally argue that developing countries should opt for an agroindustrial model that relies on standardized technologies and ever-increasing fertilizer and pesticide use to provide additional food supplies for growing populations and economies. In contrast, a growing number of farmers, nongovernmental organizations (NGOs), and analysts propose that instead of this capital- and input-intensive approach, developing countries should favor an agroecological model, which emphasizes biodiversity, recycling of nutrients, synergy among crops, animals, soils, and other biological components, and regeneration and conservation of resources.

It is argued here that agroecology—a science that provides ecological principles for the design and management of sustainable and resource-conserving agricultural systems—offers several advantages over the conventional agronomic or agroindustrial approach. First, agroecology relies on indigenous farming knowledge and selected modern technologies to manage diversity, incorporate biological principles and resources into farming systems, and intensify agricultural production. Second, it offers the only practical way to restore agricultural lands that have been degraded by conventional agronomic practices. Third, it provides for an environmentally sound and affordable way for smallholders to intensify production in marginal areas. Finally, it has the potential to reverse the anti-peasant bias of strategies that emphasize purchased inputs as opposed to the assets that small farmers already possess, such as their low opportunity costs of labor.

Case Studies

Thousands of examples exist of rural producers, in partnership with NGOs and other organizations, promoting resource-conserving yet highly productive farming systems. Critics of such alternative production systems point to lower crop yields than in high-input conventional systems. But all too often it is precisely the emphasis on yield of a single crop that blinds analysts to broader measures of sustainability and the greater productivity per unit area obtained in integrated agroecological systems that feature many crop varieties together with animals and trees. Below are some examples of the agroecological approach from Latin America.

Stabilizing the Hillsides of Central America

Perhaps the major agricultural challenge in Latin America has been to design cropping systems for hillside areas that are productive and reduce erosion. World Neighbors took on this challenge in Honduras in the mid-1980s. The program introduced soil conservation practices, such as drainage and contour ditches, grass barriers, and rock walls, and organic fertilization methods, such as the use of chicken manure and intercropping with legumes. Grain yields tripled, and in some cases quadrupled, from 400 kilograms per hectare to 1,200–1,600 kilograms. The yield increase has ensured that the 1,200 families participating in the program have ample grain supplies.

In the same region, a local NGO helped some 300 farmers experiment with terracing, covering crops to smother weeds, and other new conservation techniques. More than half of the farmers tripled their corn and bean yields. Many have gone beyond staple production to grow vegetables for local markets.

Several NGOs in Central America have promoted the use of legumes as green manure, an inexpensive source of organic fertilizer. Farmers in northern Honduras are using velvet beans with excellent results. Corn yields are more than double the national average, erosion and weeds are under control, and land preparation costs are lower. Taking advantage of well-established farmer-to-farmer networks in Nicaragua, more than 1,000 peasants recovered degraded land in the San Juan watershed in just one year using this simple technology. These farmers have decreased use of chemical fertilizers from 1,900 to 400 kilograms per hectare while increasing yields from 700 to 2,000 kilograms per hectare. Their production costs are about 22 percent lower than those for farmers using chemical fertilizers and monocultures.

Agroecology in the Andean Region

NGOs in Peru have studied pre-Columbian technologies in search of solutions to contemporary problems of high-altitude farming. A fascinating example is the revival of an ingenious system of raised fields surrounded by ditches filled with water that evolved in the Peruvian Andes about 3,000 years ago. These *waru-warus* were able to produce bumper crops despite floods, droughts, and the killing frosts common at altitudes of nearly 4,000 meters.

In 1984 several NGOs and state agencies assisted local farmers in Puno to reconstruct the ancient systems. The combination of raised beds and canals moderates soil temperature, thereby extending the growing season and leading to higher productivity on the *waru-warus* than on chemically fertilized normal pampa soils. In the district of Huatta, the *waru-warus* have produced annual potato yields of 8–14 metric tons per hectare, contrasting favorably with the average regional potato yields of 1–4 metric tons per hectare.

Beginning in 1983 an NGO and some peasant communities in Cajamarca planted more than 550,000 trees and reconstructed about 850 hectares of terraces and 173 hectares of drainage and infiltration canals over the course of 10 years. About half the population in the area—1,247 families—now has land under conservation measures. For these people, potato yields have increased from 5 to 8 tons per hectare and oca (wood sorrel) yields have jumped from 3 to 8 tons per hectare. Enhanced crop production, fattening of cattle, and raising of alpaca for wool have increased family income from an average US$108 per year in 1983 to more than US$500 today.

Various NGOs and government agencies in the Colca valley of southern Peru have sponsored terrace reconstruction by offering peasants low-interest loans or seeds and other inputs to restore abandoned terraces. First-year yields of potatoes, maize, and barley showed a 43–65 percent increase compared with yields from sloping fields. A native legume was used as a rotational or associated crop on the terraces to fix nitrogen, minimizing fertilizer needs and increasing production. Studies in Bolivia, where native legumes have been used as rotational crops, show that though yields are greater in chemically fertilized and machinery-prepared potato fields, energy costs are higher and net economic benefits lower than with the agroecological system (see Table 19.1). Surveys indicate that farmers prefer this alternative system because it optimizes the use of scarce resources, labor, and available capital and is accessible to even poor producers.

Integrated Production Systems

A number of NGOs have promoted diversified farms in which each component of the farming system biologically reinforces the other components—wastes from one component, for instance, become inputs to another. Since 1980 an NGO has

Table 19.1   Performance of Traditional, Modern, and Agroecological Potato-
based Production Systems in Bolivia

Performance indicator	Traditional low-input	Modern high-input	Agroecological system
Potato yields (metric tons/hectare)	9.2	17.6	11.4
Chemical fertilizer (nitrogen + P_2O_5, kilograms/hectare)	0.0	80 + 120	0.0
Lupine biomass (metric tons/hectare)	0.0	0.0	1.5
Energy efficiency (output/input)	15.7	4.8	30.5
Net income per invested Boliviano	6.2	9.4	9.9

Source: S. Rist, "Ecología, economía y tecnologías campesinas," *Ruralter* 10 (1992): 205–227.

helped peasants in south-central Chile reach year-round food self-sufficiency
while rebuilding the productive capacity of the land. Small, model farm systems,
consisting of polycultures and rotating sequences of forage and food crops, forest and fruit trees, and animals, have been set up. Components are chosen according to their nutritional contributions to subsequent rotations, their adaptability
to local agroclimatic conditions, the local peasant consumption patterns, and market opportunities.

Soil fertility on these farms has improved, and no serious pest or disease problems have appeared. Fruit trees and forage crops achieve higher than average yields,
and milk and egg production far exceeds that on conventional high-input farms. A
nutritional analysis of the system shows that for a typical family it produces a 250
percent surplus of protein, 80 and 550 percent surpluses of vitamin A and C,
respectively, and a 330 percent surplus of calcium. If all of the farm output were
sold at wholesale prices, the family could generate a monthly net income 1.5 times
greater than the monthly legal minimum wage in Chile, while dedicating only a few
hours per week to the farm. The time freed up is used by farmers for other on- or
off-farm income-generating activities.

Recently a Cuban NGO helped establish a number of integrated farming systems in cooperatives in the province of Havana. Several polycultures, such as cas-
sava-beans-maize, cassava-tomato-maize, and sweet potato-maize were tested in
the cooperatives. The productivity of these polycultures were 1.45 to 2.82 times
greater than the productivity of the monocultures. The use of green manure
ensured a production of squash equivalent to that obtainable by applying 175 kilograms of urea per hectare. In addition, such legumes improved the physical and
chemical characteristics of the soil and effectively broke the cycle of insect-pest
infestations.

Conclusions

The examples summarized above are a small sample of the thousands of successful experiences of sustainable agriculture implemented at the local level. Data show that over time agroecological systems exhibit more stable levels of total production per unit area than high-input systems; produce economically favorable rates of return; provide a return to labor and other inputs sufficient for a livelihood acceptable to small farmers and their families; and ensure soil protection and conservation and enhance agrobiodiversity.

With increasing evidence and awareness of the advantages of agroecology, why hasn't it spread more rapidly and how can it be multiplied and adopted more widely? Clearly, technological or ecological intentions are not enough. Major changes must be made in policies, institutions, and research and development to make sure that agroecological alternatives are adopted, made equitably and broadly accessible, and multiplied so that their full benefit for sustainable food security can be realized. Existing subsidies and policy incentives for conventional chemical approaches must be dismantled, and institutional structures, partnerships, and educational processes must change to enable the agroecological approach to blossom. In addition, participatory, farmer-friendly methods of technology development must be incorporated. The challenge is to increase investment and research in agroecology and scale up projects that have already proven successful, thereby generating a meaningful impact on the income, food security, and environmental well-being of the world's population, especially millions of poor farmers yet untouched by modern agricultural technology.

Chapter 20

Sustainable Farming

A Political Geography

Robert L. Paarlberg

*The sustainable farming debate will remain
deadlocked until it is recast in a region-specific and
politically aware form that emphasizes the vastly
different circumstances of farmers in different
parts of Asia, Africa, and Latin America.*

F arming is a threat to the natural environment in rich as well as poor countries, but the human stakes are now much higher in the developing world, where food needs are acute and growing rapidly. Roughly 700 million people in developing countries do not have access to sufficient food supplies to meet their needs for a healthy and productive life. Already because of population growth, the developing world is being asked to feed 88 million additional people every year, the equivalent of feeding a new Mexico every year. How can this production task be met if environmentally destructive farming practices continue?

In much of Africa, where crop yields will have to increase, the "mining" of soil nutrients is now helping to push average crop yields into decline. In much of South Asia, old irrigated lands are becoming saline and waterlogged and are going out of use almost as fast as new irrigated lands are coming into production. From Honduras to Java, soils are washing away on newly cleared sloping lands. In East Asia, South Asia, and Central America, the natural biological controls for crop pests are being poisoned with farm chemicals, even while the pests themselves are becoming more poison resistant.

Worsening this crisis today is a paralyzing technical debate between agriculturalists and environmentalists over what environmentally sustainable farming would actually look like. Production-oriented agriculturalists argue that environmental protection—especially protection of forests and topsoil—can be advanced through modern, input-intensive farming. Environmental advocates, by contrast, associate high-input farming with chemical pollution, a faster exhaustion of water supplies, and a dangerous loss of biodiversity. They feel it is better to hold onto traditional farming techniques suited to local ecologies and to the circumstances of ordinary resource-poor farmers.

These divergent technical preferences between agriculturalists and environmentalists have helped paralyze the international policy community. Bilateral and multilateral assistance organizations, not wishing to antagonize powerful environmental lobby groups, have become increasingly wary of sponsoring input-intensive, science-based farm modernization projects. This is one reason international assistance to farming and to farm research has recently faltered. Yet the number of people needing food in the developing world grows larger every year, while the quality of their farm resource base continues to degrade.

How can this paralyzing policy deadlock be broken? Paying more attention to geography and to politics is one way to start. In some regions of the developing world the agriculturalists are right to argue for more use of purchased inputs, while in other regions less input use is needed, so the environmentalists are right. In some regions neither group will be entirely correct, since appropriate technical changes will not take place without more fundamental political and social change.

The Geography of Resource Abuse

In Africa, agriculturalists tend to be right: use of purchased inputs will have to increase if food production is ever to increase at an acceptable cost to the rural environment. Fertilizer use in Africa today, at 12 kilograms per hectare, is only 1/4 the level of India and only 1/36 the level of Japan. Irrigation covers only 4 percent of cultivated area in Sub-Saharan Africa, compared with 26 percent in India and 44 percent in China. Africa's rural environment is at risk because too many farmers are trying to produce more simply by extending traditional low-input practices—such as shifting cultivation—into forest land, or onto drier and more fragile lands, or by shortening fallow times.

In Africa, and also in much of nonirrigated dry or upland Asia, the only way to boost production in pace with local food needs, without having to cut more trees or plow up more land, will be to move toward higher purchased input use and higher-yield farming. The experience of India is telling. By switching to highly responsive seeds, more fertilizer use, and expanded irrigation, India was able to double its total wheat production between 1964/65 and 1970/71. This not only helped India avoid a famine, it also helped protect the rural environment. If India had attempted to use traditional low-yield farming techniques to secure the same wheat production gain, it would have had to plow up an additional 36 million hectares of cropland, resulting in further deforestation, substantial habitat destruction, and soil erosion. Environmentalists who criticize India's Green Revolution should acknowledge the need to boost total production and weigh the environmental damage that would have taken place if this had been attempted without a switch to input-intensive farming.

On the other hand, the environmentalists' preference for reduced input use is fully justified in some of the more advanced Asian countries now undergoing rapid industrial development, such as Taiwan and Korea. An earlier switch to high-yield farming in these countries helped ease a first generation of rural environmental problems—soil erosion, tree cutting, and habitat destruction—but it has now become associated with a dangerous "second generation" of problems, including excess water and fertilizer use, inadequate nutrient and animal waste containment, loss of biodiversity, and excessive reliance on pesticides.

Agriculturalists argue that most of these are technical problems that need not permanently accompany a switch to high-yield farming. If given proper policy signals (tighter pollution regulations, more liberal trade policies, and input or credit subsidy reductions), input supply industries will innovate cleaner and safer products, and farmers will learn to profit by using inputs in smaller quantities and with greater precision. Just as these farmers originally learned to substitute larger quantities of purchased inputs for land, soon they will learn to replace input quantity with better quality and with improved management (for example, by switching from exclusive reliance on pesticides to integrated pest management).

This optimistic vision has merit, but too often it discounts political realities. Environmentally damaging input mismanagement has persisted in the rapidly industrializing countries of East Asia in part because farmers there (similar to well-organized farm lobbies in all mature industrial countries) tend to gain disproportionate political influence and then to use that influence to demand subsidies and trade protection. The predictable result is a policy set (artificially high commodity prices, combined with artificially cheap inputs) that induces damaging input use habits. Similar to politically powerful farmers in Europe or North America, farmers in these rapidly industrializing countries also use their organized influence to escape accountability for the adverse effects (mostly off-farm) that result from their careless and excessive water and chemical use.

The Politics of Resource Abuse

At a deeper level, resource abuse in farming often reflects power abuse. In East Asia, where farmers tend to be politically stronger within their sector than nonfarmers, much of the environmental damage they do reflects the subsidies they are able to command, and most of the suffering from that damage is felt by politically weaker nonfarmers (as when animal wastes pollute congested urban areas or when excessive irrigation and chemical use depletes or pollutes off-farm surface and ground water supplies). In Africa, by contrast, where farmers tend to be politically weaker than urban dwellers and vulnerable to the whims of centralized government ministries, the environmental damage they do grows out of this weakness. They use too few inputs rather than too many because their production tends to be overtaxed rather than subsidized. Lacking secure local control over the resource base, they tend to exploit and overuse good resources when given the chance, while skimping on investments in long-term protection. The environmental damage they do mostly takes place on the farm (overgrazing, loss of trees, soil nutrient depletion), so it harms farmers more than nonfarmers in yet another manifestation of the underlying power relationship at work.

These links between political power and environmental resource protection can be seen in a slightly more complex pattern in Latin America. This is a region where a politically weak rural majority, often without secure access to good land, farms alongside a politically privileged minority of commercial farmers. The result is a dualistic pattern of environmental resource abuse. Privileged commercial farmers on high-potential lands use government subsidies to overmechanize, overirrigate, and overspray, even while nearby peasant farmers, with insecure access even to low-potential lands, are mining soils, invading forest margins, and plowing hillsides in an environmentally damaging "hit-and-run" fashion.

Where first-generation and second-generation forms of environmental damage are taking place side by side, due to persistent rural social inequities and insecurities, technical solutions alone (either agriculturalist or environmentalist) will miss the point. The solution must include more fundamental rural social and political reform.

Conclusions

The sustainable farming debate will remain deadlocked until it is recast in a region-specific and politically aware form that emphasizes the vastly different circumstances of farmers in different parts of Asia, Africa, and Latin America. If regional precision is maintained, paralyzing technical arguments between powerful agriculturalists and environmentalists can be minimized, and important reform imperatives that go beyond technical choice can be highlighted as well.

Chapter 21

Land Degradation in the Developing World

Issues and Policy Options for 2020

Sara J. Scherr and Satya Yadav

*Although some types of degradation are
irreversible, most can be prevented or reversed.*

By the year 2020, land degradation may pose a serious threat to food production and rural livelihoods, particularly in poor and densely populated areas of the developing world. Appropriate policies are required to encourage land-improving investments and better land management if developing countries are to sustainably meet the food needs of their populations.

Land degradation takes a number of forms, including depletion of soil nutrients, salinization, agrochemical pollution, soil erosion, vegetative degradation as a result of overgrazing, and the cutting of forests for farmland. All of these types of degradation cause a decline in the productive capacity of the land, reducing potential yields. Farmers may need to use more inputs such as fertilizer or manure in order to maintain yields, or they may temporarily or permanently abandon some plots. Degradation may also induce farmers to convert land to lower-value uses. For example, farmers may plant cassava, which demands few nutrients, instead of maize, or may convert cropland to grazing land.

Farmland degradation can also have important negative effects off the farm, including deposition of eroded soil in streams or behind dams, contamination of drinking water by agrochemicals, and loss of habitat.

Existing estimates of the current global extent and severity of the problem should be considered indicative at best. The Global Land Assessment of Degradation

Figure 21.1 Regional Land Degradation by Type of Land Use, 1945–90

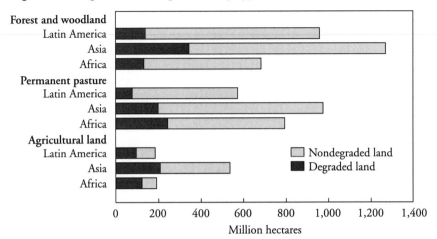

Source: L. R. Oldeman, *Global Extent of Soil Degradation* (Wageningen, the Netherlands: International Soil Reference and Information Centre, 1992); L. R. Oldeman, R. T. A. Hakkeling, and W. G. Sombroek, *World Map of the Status of Human-Induced Soil Degradation: An Explanatory Note,* rev. ed. (Wageningen, the Netherlands: International Soil Reference and Information Centre, and Nairobi: United Nations Environment Programme, 1990).
Note: Degraded land includes slightly, moderately, strongly, and extremely degraded areas.

(GLASOD), based only on the impressions of experts, estimates that nearly 2 billion hectares worldwide (22 percent of all cropland, pasture, forest, and woodland) have been degraded since mid-century. Some 3.5 percent of the 2 billion total is estimated to have been degraded so severely that the degradation is reversible only through costly engineering measures, if at all. Just over 10 percent has been moderately degraded, and this degradation is reversible only through major on-farm investments. Of the nearly 1.5 billion hectares in cropland worldwide, about 38 percent is degraded to some degree. Africa and Latin America appear to have the highest proportion of degraded agricultural land, and Asia has the highest proportion of degraded forestland (Figure 21.1).

Various sources suggest that 5 to 10 million hectares are being lost annually to severe degradation. If this trend continues, 1.4 to 2.8 percent of total cropland, pasture, and forestland will have been lost by 2020. Declining yields (or increasing input requirements to maintain yields) could be expected over a much larger area. These data are, however, likely to overestimate the problem, as they do not account for the effects of land improvements, which also appear to be widespread.

The Impact on Global Agricultural Production

Globally, there are few studies of the impact of degradation on agricultural production. Pierre Crosson, in a 1994 study, analyzed GLASOD results and other data and concluded that there has been a 17 percent cumulative productivity loss over 45 years (1945–90) as a result of degradation. During that same period, growth in global food production and long-term declines in grain prices were unprecedented; clearly other factors offset the effects of degradation on aggregate performance.

A 1995 study by Rattan Lal of the impact of degradation in Africa based on field data estimated that yield reductions due to past erosion may range from 2 percent to 40 percent, with a mean of 8.2 percent for the continent and 6.2 percent for Sub-Saharan Africa. If accelerated erosion continues unabated, yield reductions by the year 2020 may be 16.5 percent for the continent and 14.5 percent for Sub-Saharan Africa. Evidence from four Southeast Asian and three Middle Eastern countries indicates a degradation-induced decline in productivity greater than 20 percent.

Although the economic importance of this observed degradation has long been a matter of debate, an extensive literature has developed only recently. A review of this literature, even with its limitations, suggests that economic effects may be of much greater importance than previously thought.

The cumulative productivity loss for cropland from soil degradation over the past 50 years is estimated to be about 13 percent, and for pasture lands 4 percent. Crop yield losses in Africa from 1970 to 1990 due to water erosion alone are estimated to be 8 percent. Subregional studies have documented large aggregate declines in crop yields due to degradation in many parts of Africa, China, South Asia, and Central America. A global agricultural model suggests a slight increase in degradation relative to baseline trends could result in 17–30 percent higher world prices for key food commodities in 2020, and increased child malnutrition.

Besides affecting aggregate food supply, soil degradation also diminishes agricultural income and economic growth. In South and Southeast Asia, estimates for total annual economic loss from degradation range from under 1 to 7 percent of agricultural gross domestic product (AGDP). Given that more than half of all land in this region is not affected by degradation, the economic effects in the degrading areas would appear to be quite serious. Estimates for eight African countries show annual economic losses ranging from under 1 percent of AGDP in Madagascar to 9 percent in Zimbabwe. Country models simulating the effects of soil degradation in Ghana and Nicaragua find annual economic growth to be reduced by nearly a percentage point. The effects of soil degradation on the environment and longer-term national wealth in soil resources have not been studied adequately, but are likely to add considerably to the economic impact.

Because the poor are particularly dependent on agriculture—on annual crops (which generally degrade soils more than perennial crops) and on common property lands (which generally suffer greater degradation than privately managed land), and because they often lack the capacity to make land-improving investments—the poor tend to suffer more than the nonpoor from soil degradation. In West Africa, for example, the proportion of children who died before the age of five was highest (more than 30 percent) in areas with high soil degradation. The link between poverty and soil quality, however, has not been studied widely.

Hot Spots

Declining food supplies from specific regions due to degradation are likely to have only a modest effect on global food supplies, because of the potential for substitution from other producing areas. However, land degradation could have dramatic effects in specific countries and subregions.

Nutrient depletion is predicted by the experts to cause serious problems in the mid-altitude hills of Nepal; in poor soil quality areas of northeastern India and Myanmar, now undergoing transition to permanent agriculture; and in areas in northeastern Thailand, where farmers consistently extract more nutrients from the soil than they put in. It is also expected to cause major problems in large areas of Africa under transition to short fallow or permanent cropping, in areas of reduced silt deposits in the Nile delta, in the subhumid Mesoamerican hillsides, and in the semi-arid Andean valleys, northeastern Brazil, and the Caribbean Basin lowlands, where agriculture is undergoing intensification.

Salinization will be a major threat in the irrigation systems of the Indus, Tigris, and Euphrates River basins, in northeastern Thailand and China, in the Nile delta, in northern Mexico, and in the Andean highlands.

Agrochemical pollution is expected to be critical in cotton-producing areas in Turkey, in high-density and coastal areas in East and Southeast Asia, on banana plantations in Central America, in areas of intensive agriculture in Bolivia, and in peri-urban agriculture in Southeast Asia and Mexico City.

Soil erosion will create serious production problems in southeast Nigeria, in Haiti, and on the sloping lands of the Himalayan foothills, southern China, Southeast Asia, and Central America. Major wind erosion problems will develop in West Asia as rangelands are converted to grain production, in the Sahel, in West Africa owing to poor mechanization techniques, in the dry Andean Valley, and in the Brazilian cerrados.

Vegetative degradation of rangelands will accelerate by 2020, as a result of overgrazing and overexploitation of vegetation for fuel, in the trans-Himalayas and in Southern and North Africa. The spread of Imperata grassland areas in Southeast Asia will also contribute to degradation.

Agriculture-induced deforestation by 2020 will threaten critical habitats in parts of Southeast Asia, Madagascar, the humid Amazon, the hillsides and Atlantic lowlands of Central America, the Pacific rain forest of Colombia and Ecuador, and the Chaco region of Latin America.

Strategies to Reduce Land Degradation

Historical and socioeconomic evidence suggests that farmers often respond actively to degradation by modifying their farming systems or practices and through land-improving investments. Unfortunately, no global or even national data are yet available estimating the scale and effects of land improvements (for example, area under terracing or other soil conservation practices), although data collection efforts are beginning.

Although some types of degradation are irreversible, most can be prevented or reversed by, for example, adding nutrients to nutrient-depleted soil, rebuilding topsoil through soil amendments, reestablishing vegetation, or buffering soil acidity. The practicality of rehabilitating degraded landscapes depends on the costs relative to the value of the output or environmental benefits expected.

Despite the lack of quantitative data, it is clear that land-improving investments are creating a number of "bright spots" in the developing world. Agroforestry, community forestry, and afforestation are beginning to have large-scale positive impacts in numerous countries. Conservation farming is spreading widely in countries including Morocco, the Philippines, and Thailand and regionally in East Africa, parts of West Africa, Mesoamerica, and parts of South America. Water management is improving through water-saving irrigation, water harvesting, aquaculture, small-scale irrigation, and salinization control.

Diversification into higher-value perennial crops is protecting soils in Africa, Asia, and Latin America. Dryland range rehabilitation schemes are showing positive results in Syria and Jordan, Southern Africa, Mexico, and northern Argentina. Farmer incentives for land investment are improving through range cooperatives in Jordan; more favorable property rights in Cambodia, Ethiopia, Laos, and Viet Nam; and community-based natural resource management in many areas.

Policy Recommendations

An effective response to land degradation calls for improving the incentives for farmers to care for their land and improving their access to the knowledge and inputs required for proper care. Based on lessons learned from past successes and failures in managing land degradation, the following policy actions should be considered:

- Increase research and technology development for land management, and improve the spread of information, through widely linked, user-friendly information systems for farmers.

- Promote land-improving investments (for example, building up soil organic matter, planting trees, and installing small-scale irrigation) through technical assistance and new financing arrangements suitable for low-income farmers.

- Encourage long-term land improvements by securing property rights and rights of access to natural resources, particularly for the poor.

- Develop planning systems for sustainable land use that involve key resource user groups.

- Improve the economic environment for farmers by developing market infrastructure, correcting distorted price incentives, and encouraging rural income growth and diversification.

- For marginal regions, encourage more public investment in infrastructure, social services, and agricultural support services.

Chapter 22

The Role of Agriculture in Saving the Rain Forest

Stephen Vosti

When a farm household in the humid tropical forest margin slashes and burns as the initial step in an agricultural cycle, it starts a clock ticking.

Is Conversion of Forest to Agriculture the Problem?

Tropical forests are disappearing rapidly—with potentially high social costs in biodiversity loss and carbon emissions. But what does agriculture have to do with this? Consider the role of small farmers: they account for about two-thirds of rain forest destruction, by converting land to agriculture (Figure 22.1). Most of them are poor. They moved to forest margins to escape from poverty elsewhere, and they deforest in order to survive. Deforestation is not likely to slow until these people can earn a living and meet their food needs. And their numbers are growing, even where in-migration has slowed or stopped, as families reconstituted at the forest margin move through the life cycle. Agriculture to meet these food needs may lie behind much forest clearing—true. Still, only improvements in agriculture's performance as part of an opening up of alternatives for meeting basic welfare requirements can save the rain forest.

Why Do Small Farmers Deforest?

Like rural households throughout the developing world, farm households in the forest margins strive to put enough food on the table for the next day, week, or month. In their struggle, farmers do not view natural resources as the most important asset,

Figure 22.1 Tropical Forest Depletion by Proximate Cause

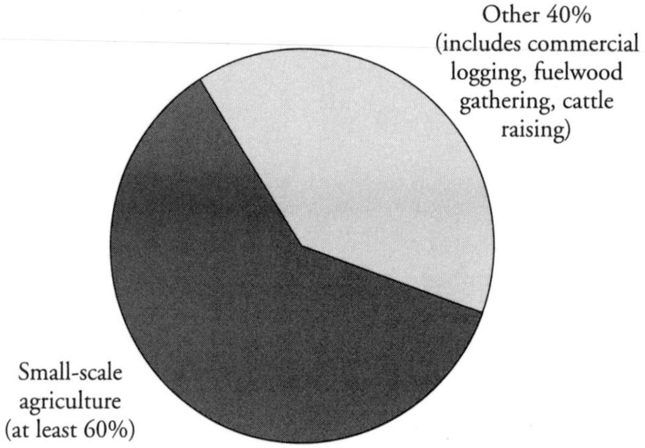

Other 40%
(includes commercial
logging, fuelwood
gathering, cattle
raising)

Small-scale
agriculture
(at least 60%)

Source: N. Sharma, ed. *Managing the World's Forests* (Washington D.C.: World Bank, 1992).

to be conserved at all costs, especially human costs. Although degradation is viewed as undesirable by the farmer and society as a whole, economic necessity predictably leads to land degradation.

In fact, when a farm household in the humid tropical forest margins slashes and burns as the initial step in an agricultural cycle, it starts a clock ticking. During the first tick of the clock, annual crops are the crops of choice. Fertilized by forest residue, the nutrient-poor soils can support such crops, and recently arrived families, needing food (and without the resources to purchase food), plant them. Annual crop production, however, depletes soil, narrowing the crop choice of farm households at the next tick of the clock. At this point, they favor perennials, which in turn deplete the land (though at much slower rates). Finally, pasture and fallow—lower than the original forest in biomass and lowest in per hectare productivity for the farmer—become the only viable options. While farm households in other agroclimatic zones may see some narrowing of land-use options over time, in the humid tropical forest margins, it is the speed and certainty of this sequence (over several agricultural cycles) that is striking.

This does not mean that successful agricultural intensification is out of reach in these areas: with technical innovations, the range of agricultural choices open to the farmer could widen from current patterns, but few such innovations are currently available to resource-strapped farm households, and policies for promoting them are often lacking.

Well-known off-farm externalities, such as smoke and carbon dioxide emissions, which dissipate into the air above the farm, have no direct production consequences for the farmer; therefore, they do not play a major role in farm household decisionmaking. These environmental effects are important on a global basis, but from the farmer's perspective, private costs and benefits—the farmer's—matter most.

What Has Gone Wrong in the Past?

Because the poverty-stricken small farmer has a short time horizon for planning, incorporation of pro-environment choices can be difficult. This short-term perspective is not myopic, but rational: natural resource mining may be the only way, not the short-sighted way, to meet short-term goals. Policies that ignore this constraint generally fail.

For example, farmers must diversify income sources to survive, and improved infrastructure is key to such diversification. However, national and regional governments, often under pressure from the international community looking toward long-term environmental protection, make limited investments in all-weather transportation infrastructure. The problem for the small farmer is that even the investment in infrastructure needed to link existing communities is limited, which can make farmers more reliant on their natural resource base for survival.

The emphasis often placed on extracting forest products as an alternative livelihood activity is also illustrative, in that little is known as yet about the interdependence of different components of ecosystems; the impact of different techniques for extraction on these systems; the potential for marketing extracted products; and the consequences of, and scope for, expanding extractive activities.

Farmers often have insufficient knowledge to successfully implement sustainable agriculture. Populations transplanted from different agroecological environments do not carry with them the stock of knowledge about local conditions helpful in designing an environmentally compatible farming system. Where indigenous knowledge about sustainable livelihood practices does exist, it often cannot support the higher population density that migration has brought.

Labor conditions must also be right: coffee production, desirable from an environmental and income viewpoint, requires high labor input and might be ruled out where labor is scarce. Cattle raising requires much less labor and might be chosen regardless of environmental consequences.

The bottom line: forest conversion will continue so long as it makes sense to rural households, given the incentives and constraints they face, regardless of the costs to society.

What Can Be Done?

If output generated from deforested plots and the value of natural products extracted from forests cannot be increased and sustained, the pressure on standing forests will remain. The "tools of the trade" for development planning—policies, technologies, and institutional arrangements—play a role in lifting constraints to implementation of environmentally sound practices. And they help encourage agricultural practices that use natural resources to boost livelihood security without using them up.

Policies need to change to take into account needs of current resident farmers, on land already deforested. This means helping them intensify their agriculture through improved technology and access to well-integrated, reliable markets; credit; and roads that remain open in all seasons.

The generation and use of new, more sustainable agricultural technologies is absolutely critical. This requires focusing sights not on agricultural technologies that just meet growth goals or those that meet only sustainability goals, but on those that meet both growth and sustainability goals. The approach is controversial: there are fears that successes in agricultural intensification could attract new waves of migrants, and that introduction of nontraditional crops might disrupt the ecosystem in unforeseen ways. But clear definition and enforcement of property rights can help allay these concerns.

The third "tool" of development planning, the set of institutional arrangements (formal and informal, public and private) charged with generating, distributing, and implementing information and policies to achieve sustainability, growth, and poverty alleviation goals, has expanded dramatically over the past 15 years and now includes a vast array of governmental, nongovernmental, and hybrid forms. The forest margins have seen a dramatic proliferation of organizations—local, state, and international—but little is known about their relative sustainability or effectiveness, particularly cost-effectiveness, in meeting development goals.

Interregional Linkages

Forest margin areas generally do not enjoy a comparative advantage in the production of food staples: poor soils, severe pest problems, and intense, seasonal rainfall all keep yields low. These areas do, however, have a comparative advantage in agroforestry products, some types of livestock, and products extracted from primary or secondary forests. But poor infrastructure leading to inefficient or even missing markets can *lower* and destabilize prices for nonfood items produced in the forest margins and *raise* and destabilize prices of the foods rural households purchase. These economic signals induce rural households to allocate time, money, and land to producing their own food, even though they do so inefficiently. To improve natural resource management in the forest margins, therefore, it is necessary to improve infrastructure and thereby promote the flow of nonfood and food products across regions.

Importance of Agriculture to Long-Term Solutions

Looking toward 2020, three scenarios are possible. First, if all goes well, improvements in social and physical infrastructure will integrate forest margin areas into the economy. The combined agricultural productivity growth of the breadbasket and forest margin areas will be adequate to feed the larger population, lessening the pressure to convert forests to agricultural uses. In the second scenario, regional integration will only partially be successful. Productivity growth will be swift in the breadbasket areas, but it will languish in the forest margins, and deforestation will continue. Under the disastrous third scenario, regional integration will largely fail, agricultural growth will stagnate everywhere, and deforestation will accelerate. Which of these scenarios will prevail largely depends on agricultural intensification.

While agriculture is critical to the long-term solution of sustainable livelihood and food security in the humid tropics, it is only part of the story. To take pressure off land, nonagricultural sectors of rural economies must be strengthened in addition to improving agricultural productivity. In short, what is called for is a portfolio of agricultural, extractive, and nonagricultural activities that involve technological innovation designed for higher productivity of land and labor. These activities must translate into higher profitability for the farmer at lower cost to the environment and must be compatible with the constrained resource position of the small farmer.

Chapter 23

Dealing with Water Scarcity in the 21st Century

Mark W. Rosegrant

*Most of the world does not treat water
as the scarce resource that it is.*

Reform of water policy is urgently needed to avert severe national, regional, and local water scarcities that will depress agricultural production and worsen water-related health problems. Water is abundant globally but scarce locally. Of the earth's 1,360 million cubic kilometers of water, 97 percent is in the oceans. Three-quarters of the freshwater is in glaciers and icebergs, another fifth is groundwater, and less than 1 percent is in lakes and rivers. Almost two-thirds of the renewable freshwater provided by annual rainfall over land evaporates. Much of the rainfall transformed into runoff is lost to floods.

Given current global water use of 4,000 cubic kilometers, the remaining 14,000 cubic kilometers of effective runoff would be adequate to meet demand for the foreseeable future if supplies were distributed equally across the world's population. But freshwater is distributed extremely unevenly across countries, across regions within countries, and across seasons.

When does water scarcity become a serious problem? Water analysts use the following rule of thumb: countries with freshwater resources of 1,000 to 1,600 cubic meters per capita per year face water stress, with major problems occurring in drought years. Countries are considered water scarce when annual internal renewable water resources are less than 1,000 cubic meters per capita per year. Below this threshold, water availability is considered a severe constraint on socioeconomic development and environmental quality. Currently, some 30 countries are considered water stressed, of which 20 are absolutely water scarce. By 2020, the number of water scarce countries will likely approach 35. Equally worrisome, virtually all developing countries, even those with adequate water in the aggregate, suffer from debilitating seasonal and regional shortages that urgently need to be addressed.

Challenges for the Future

Low Water Use Efficiency

The foremost challenge related to water scarcity in developing countries is the need to increase generally inefficient water use in agriculture, urban areas, and industry. Irrigated area accounts for over two-thirds of world rice and wheat production, so growth in irrigated output per unit of land and water is essential. Improved efficiency in agricultural water use is required both to maintain productivity growth and to allow reallocation of water from agriculture to urban and industrial uses.

Expensive New Water

New sources of water are increasingly expensive to exploit. Water to meet growing household and industrial demand may thus need to come increasingly from water savings from irrigated agriculture, which generally accounts for 80 percent of water diverted for use in developing countries. To truly contribute to reducing water scarcity, improved efficiency in agricultural use should be accompanied by improved efficiency in urban and industrial use.

Resource Degradation

The quality of land and water must be sustained in the face of mounting pressure to degrade these resources through waterlogging, salinization, groundwater mining, and water pollution.

Water and Health

Pollution of water from industrial effluents, poorly treated sewage, and runoff of agricultural chemicals is a growing problem. Unsafe water, combined with poor household and community sanitary conditions, is a major contributor to disease and malnutrition, particularly among children. One billion people are without clean drinking water, and 1.7 billion have inadequate sanitation facilities. As many as 1 billion episodes of diarrhea occur annually in developing countries. The World Bank has estimated that access to safe water and adequate sanitation could result in 2 million fewer deaths from diarrhea among young children.

Massive Subsidies and Distorted Incentives

Most of the world does not treat water as the scarce resource that it is. Both urban and rural water users receive massive subsidies on water use; irrigation water is essentially unpriced; in urban areas the price of water does not cover the cost of delivery; capital investment decisions in all sectors are divorced from management of the resource. In Mexico, subsidies to operate and maintain water systems (that is, not including capital costs) total 0.5 percent of gross domestic product, far more than is spent on agricultural research. In Jordan, despite severe water scarcity, subsidies encourage overuse of irrigation water. Strict rationing is then required to allocate the resulting scarcities. In most countries, water subsidies go disproportionately to the better-off: irrigated farmers and urban water users connected to the public system. The inequity is exacerbated because subsidies are often financed from regressive taxes.

Development of New Water

The development of new water has slowed considerably since the late 1970s owing to escalating construction costs for dams and related infrastructure, relatively low prices of staple cereals, and concerns over the environmental effects and dislocation of persons caused by dam and reservoir construction. Although the construction boom of the 1970s will not return, a portion of new demand for water must be met by carefully selected, economically efficient development of new water, both from impoundment of surface water and sustainable exploitation of groundwater resources. In some river basins, efficiency gains from existing systems may be limited, because whole-basin reuse and recycling of drainage water already occur, even though individual water users are inefficient. Under these circumstances, new water development could be necessary.

As scarcity increases, the rising economic value of water should improve the cost-effectiveness of some new water development projects, particularly multipurpose dams that both supply new water and generate revenue from hydropower. The environmental costs and benefits must be carefully weighed in evaluating new water sources. In Laos, for example, new water and hydropower development on the Mekong could offer an alternative energy source to fuelwood, reducing deforestation. This benefit, however, must be weighed against the potentially harmful consequences of construction, including displacement of indigenous people and inundation of reservoir sites.

Sustainable development of groundwater resources also offers significant opportunities for some countries. The extent of groundwater storage and recharge is poorly understood in much of the developing world. Investment in a "groundwater revolution" in Bangladesh beginning in the 1980s was a key stimulant to rapid agricultural growth in the 1980s and early 1990s. Nearly 1.5 million hectares of land was newly irrigated after 1980, in significant part from private installation of shallow tubewells spurred by deregulation of tubewell imports. Although localized problems of groundwater mining have occurred, in most areas in Bangladesh further expansion of groundwater use within the bounds of natural recharge is possible. If dry season water scarcity worsens, investments to divert wet season river flows for artificial recharge of aquifers may become feasible, and could also reduce wet season flooding.

Comprehensive Water Policy Reform

A large share of water to meet new demands must come by saving water from existing uses through comprehensive reform of water policy. Such reform will not be easy, because both long-standing practice and cultural and religious beliefs have treated water as a free good, and because entrenched interests benefit from existing arrangements.

The precise nature of water policy reform will vary from country to country, depending on underlying conditions such as level of economic development and institutional capability, relative water scarcity, and level of agricultural intensification. Additional research is required to design specific policies within any given country. However, key elements of comprehensive reform include the following:

Secure Water Rights

Reform must provide secure water rights vested in individual water users or groups of water users. In some countries and regions, these rights should be tradable, which further increases the incentives for efficient water use. Such a reform can empower water users, provide investment incentives, improve water use efficiency, reduce incentives to degrade the environment, and increase flexibility in resource allocation.

User Management of Irrigation Systems

In many developing countries, devolving irrigation infrastructure and management to water user associations will be beneficial. In the past, such steps often failed because they were not accompanied by secure access to water. Well-defined water rights provide the incentive for user groups to economize on water use, to bargain effectively with the water conveyance bureaucracy for timely and efficient service, and to undertake operations and management.

Reformed Price Incentives

Privatization and regulation of urban water services, together with reduced subsidies for urban water consumption, can also improve efficiency. When incremental water can be obtained at low cost owing to subsidies there is little incentive to improve either physical efficiency (such as through investment in pipes or metering) or economic efficiency. Secure water rights held by the urban companies and an active market have encouraged the construction and operation of improved treatment plants that sell water for agricultural or urban use. Removing subsidies on urban water use can have dramatic effects. An increase in the water tariff in Bogor, Indonesia, from US$0.15 to US$0.42 per cubic meter resulted in a 30 percent decrease in household demand for water. In the industrial sector, increased water prices will lead to investment in water recycling and conservation technology. Increased water tariffs induced a 50 percent reduction in water use over a five-year period by a fertilizer factory in Goa, India. In São Paulo, three industries reduced water consumption by 40 to 60 percent in response to effluent charges.

The reforms described would free up substantial resources for both productive investment and targeted subsidies to the poor and groups who might be left out of the reform process. For example, in Chile the removal of general water subsidies has allowed the government to increase the level of subsidies targeted directly to the rates paid for urban water by the poor. Subsidies also go to small farmers to allow them to acquire water rights from new infrastructure.

Appropriate Technology

Availability of appropriate technology will be essential as incentives are introduced for water conservation. Small-scale water harvesting techniques can have high pay-offs in certain agro-climatic environments. As the value of water increases, sprinklers, computerized control systems, and drip irrigation using low-cost plastic pipes, all of which are common in developed countries, could have promising results for developing countries. In Malaysia's Muda irrigation system, real-time management of water releases from the dam, keyed to telemetric monitoring of weather and streamflow conditions, has significantly improved water use efficiency.

Environmental Protection

Greater protection must be afforded to water and soil quality. The appropriate approach to environmental protection is likely to include both regulatory and market elements. In Mexico, the new water law establishing tradable water rights is the first to establish strong explicit protection of the environment. The law stipulates a regulatory, rather than a market or tax/subsidy approach. The government must specify the quality of discharge for nonagricultural uses when it grants a water right, and it can restrict water use in the event of damage to ecosystems, overexploitation of aquifers, and other environmental effects.

Increased water prices or establishment of tradable water rights can cause farmers to take account of the costs their water use imposes on other farmers, reducing the pressure to degrade resources. A simple example is the farmer at the head of a canal who overuses water, thereby waterlogging other farmers' land through excess return flows, seepage, and percolation. If he could trade the excess water instead, he would conserve resources. Although any society can design effective environmental protection policies, how much environmental protection will be provided will be a matter of political choice and commitment.

International Cooperation

Water policy reform must transcend national boundaries. In many regions, long-term solutions will require international cooperation between countries sharing scarce water resources. Intergovernmental activities to settle conflicts over shared bodies of water have had mixed success. A 1977 agreement between India and Bangladesh allocated 63 percent of the dry season flow of the Ganges at the India/Bangladesh border to Bangladesh. However, the agreement has not been in effect since 1988, and water disputes remain a serious source of conflict.

More significant headway has been made on talks between Jordan and Israel over the Jordan and Yarmuk Rivers and on shared groundwater resources. However, the lack of participation of Lebanon and Syria in these talks has made it difficult to reach comprehensive settlement on the use of water from the Jordan and Yarmuk Rivers.

Cooperation between countries sharing the same water basin will become increasingly important as water becomes scarcer. Reconciliation is cheaper than armed conflict. A key to defusing potential international conflicts over water is national water policy reform to ensure the most efficient use of available water supplies. Countries must therefore begin the painful process of reforming national water policies and treating water as a scarce resource.

Chapter 24

Global Warming Changes the Forecast for Agriculture

Reported by Sara E. Wilson

*"In the most fundamental way, climate change
will bring change to agriculture wherever
it is practiced around the globe."*
—Cynthia Rosenzweig

In January 2001, representatives of 99 countries gathered in Shanghai to consider evidence on global warming as part of the United Nations' Intergovernmental Panel on Climate Change (IPCC). Their conclusions, while not new to scientists, set off alarm bells among laypeople and policymakers around the world. The scientific evidence on global warming is now stronger than ever and points to a rise in temperatures of 1.4 to 5.8 degrees Celsius over the next century, higher than earlier predictions. Higher temperatures will be accompanied by rising sea levels and more frequent occurrence of extreme weather events, such as droughts, floods, and violent storms.

The IPCC has studied not only the projected changes in climate, but also how those changes will affect many human activities, including agriculture. "In the most fundamental way, climate change will bring change to agriculture wherever it is practiced around the globe," says Cynthia Rosenzweig, senior research scientist at the National Aeronautics and Space Administration (NASA) and Columbia University.

Agriculture Will Feel the Heat

Although scientists are uncertain about exactly how the world's climate will change and how that change will bear on agriculture, they are in increasing agreement on some likely effects. On the bright side, global warming could increase water availability in some currently water-scarce areas, increase global timber supply, and raise crop yields in temperate and some subtropical zones, according to a February 2001 report issued by the IPCC.

Higher crop yields and increased timber supplies could result from "the carbon dioxide fertilizer effect." Richard Adams, professor of agricultural and resource economics at Oregon State University, explains, "As the amount of carbon dioxide in the atmosphere increases, some plants will grow faster and produce more yield."

Experiments show the potential benefit of elevated levels of carbon dioxide, but Adams cautions, "The experiments that have studied this effect have controlled for all other conditions. That will not be the case in farmers' fields. Water or nitrogen, for example, may not be sufficient under field conditions to fully utilize the increased carbon dioxide, and therefore the carbon dioxide fertilizer effect may not be as great as it seems in the experiments."

The benefits of the carbon dioxide fertilizer effect may not be on hand for long either, because increased carbon dioxide appears to boost crop yields only if average annual temperatures increase by less than a few degrees. If average temperatures rise beyond that, temperate zones will lose the carbon dioxide fertilizer effect and their crop yields will fall. Other regions do not even have the hope of many potential benefits from climate change. "Very little positive effect is projected in the tropics, even in the short term," says Rosenzweig. The IPCC predicts reduced crop yields in most tropical and subtropical regions, increased risk of flooding, and decreased water supply, especially in the subtropics.

In addition to the direct effects of rising temperatures, changes in levels of precipitation, and more common extreme weather events, agriculture will also suffer from the indirect effects of climate change: pests and pathogens may increase, soil is expected to erode and degrade because of more intense rainfall patterns, and rising levels of ozone may increase air pollution damage to crops. "These indirect effects may potentially be more important than the direct effects that have received most of the attention in existing studies," says Adams.

Crops will not be the only food source affected by climate change. For example, says Meryl Williams, director general of ICLARM—the World Fish Center, "More and more severe climate and weather events will further stress fish production systems, natural and artificial, and increase greatly the challenges for people whose food and livelihoods depend on them." Livestock will also suffer from rising and more extreme temperatures and may also have less forage and feed available to them. As a result, individual animals may produce less food for human consumption and overall herd numbers may decrease.

Current projections indicate that global food security will not be threatened by the end of the 21st century. However, climate change is expected to be more pronounced in developing nations, which already experience lower agricultural yields and suffer more from extreme weather events. Even if global food security is not imperiled, climate change is likely to cause hunger and displacement in many parts of the developing world.

Climate change will not only affect different geographic regions disproportionately, but will also vary over time. "People don't seem to recognize that climate isn't necessarily going to change in a smooth manner," says Paul Faeth, program director of the Economics and Population Program at the World Resources Institute. Severe weather events, for example, could devastate agriculture in some years and have little impact in other years.

Agriculture Is a Culprit

Agriculture itself produces about 20 percent of greenhouse gases that are responsible for global warming. Farming activities release substantial amounts of the gases methane and nitrous oxide. Methane is produced by the decomposition of organic matter, particularly in the soil of flooded rice fields and by the digestive process of ruminant livestock like cattle. Converting land to agricultural use emits nitrous oxide, as does the use of nitrogen fertilizer. Agriculture is responsible for about 50 percent of human-related methane emissions and 70 percent of nitrous oxide emissions.

Agriculture plays a relatively small role in by far the biggest contributor to rising concentrations of greenhouse gases: carbon dioxide from the burning of fossil fuels as well as from deforestation and tilling practices. "When you convert from forest or grassland to agricultural usage, you lose a lot of carbon," says Stanley Wood, an IFPRI senior scientist. "After conversion, much less carbon is usually stored in the soil and in crops and pasture, and carbon is released when crops are harvested and processed." Limiting the loss of carbon due to agricultural practices is one way that farmers can begin to help mitigate the problem of climate change.

Putting the Brakes on Climate Change

"Because agricultural ecosystems are responsible for 18–24 percent of green-house gas emissions, there have to be some significant things agriculture can do to mitigate the problem," says Sara Scherr, adjunct professor in the Agricultural and Resource Economics Department at the University of Maryland and a fellow at

Forest Trends. "Reduction in emissions from the burning of fossil fuels has to be the highest priority, but it would be foolish to overlook what agriculture can contribute."

By cutting overuse of nitrogen fertilizer, for example, farmers can help lower nitrous oxide emissions. They can reduce methane emissions from livestock by using improved feed.

Strategies to store more carbon in soil, trees, and other plants will also help reduce global warming through a process called carbon sequestration, the increased retention of carbon in soils and vegetation. Examples of this strategy include limiting deforestation through better agricultural techniques (higher yields means less land needed for agriculture) and reducing the amount of carbon lost during conventional tilling of agricultural lands.

Carbon sequestration can also occur by intentionally creating carbon "sinks" to increase the amount of carbon stored on the planet. Regrowing forests is the most obvious example of this policy, but another promising solution can be found in agroforestry, the use of trees on agricultural lands. This practice is finding increasing support, according to Pedro Sanchez, director general of the International Centre for Research in Agroforestry, because it not only helps store carbon, but can also improve yields on agricultural lands by enhancing soil fertility, preventing soil erosion, and helping to control weeds. By planting trees on their lands, poor farmers can increase their own food security while also helping to reduce the amount of carbon dioxide in the atmosphere. "What's important in these efforts," says Sanchez, "is to bring together the human element of people who are hungry and poor and, at the same time, get a global environmental benefit for all of us."

Agroforestry is an example of what is often called a "win-win" strategy among climate change experts: it not only slows climate change, but also provides an immediate and direct benefit to farmers. "It's true of all long-term problems: you have to look for immediate rewards to convince people to make changes that will have a longer-term benefit," says Faeth. "There are lots of things that help productivity and also have a climate benefit. The synergies are pretty amazing."

Robin Reid, systems ecologist at the International Livestock Research Institute, agrees that win-win strategies might have an important role to play but offers a caveat. After describing a strategy whereby the use of better feed in livestock improves meat and milk production while also reducing methane emissions, she says, "But you need to be skeptical of win-wins because they don't always spell out the full carbon accounting of the situation. For example, to produce better quality feed for livestock, you might have to use more fertilizer to grow it. Ultimately, the emissions from the increased fertilizer might overcompensate for the reduction in emissions from the livestock."

Adjusting to a Global Greenhouse

The effects of climate change are already being felt. According to the IPCC, it is likely that the 1990s was the hottest decade in the Northern Hemisphere in the past one thousand years. International efforts to mandate reductions in greenhouse gas emissions have been underway since the 1980s. Even if emissions are drastically cut, however, farmers will have to adapt to the changes in climate that are preordained by the levels of greenhouse gases already in the earth's atmosphere.

"Our current research continues to support the idea that farmer adaptations will be the main mechanisms for keeping world agricultural production from falling very much even if mean global temperature increases by 5 degrees Celsius," says Roy Darwin, an agricultural economist at the Economic Research Service of the United States Department of Agriculture.

Agricultural adaptations include increasing irrigation where water is available, growing different crop varieties, changing planting and harvesting dates, expanding access to markets, and shifting agricultural production from one area to another. Some of these coping efforts can be undertaken by individual farmers, while others will require the joint action of farmers and outside organizations, including development agencies, private industry, and national governments.

"Farmers will adapt. There's no doubt about that," says Rosenzweig. "But it's important to note that we're not even completely adapted to our climate today. Agriculture already has to respond to many dynamic factors, such as changing markets, regulations, and demands. Climate change puts another stress on agricultural systems."

The capacity to adapt to the kinds of changes predicted, the IPCC points out, will require access to information, infrastructure, and technology—resources that poor people in developing countries already lack. Because many of these people live in the tropical and subtropical countries most likely to experience the negative effects of climate change, they are in a position of double jeopardy.

Unfortunately, developing countries are doing little to plan for either mitigation or adaptation. "One reason is the learning curve on the science of climate change. It's just an incredibly complex issue that takes a long time to get a handle on," says Scherr. "Even in developed countries, where a lot of sophisticated research has taken place for many years, policymakers are only beginning to be aware of the urgency of climate change and willing to do something about it."

The Standoff over Global Climate Change

"The real problem," according to Brian Fisher, executive director of the Australian Bureau of Agricultural and Resource Economics, "is getting people to face up to problems that may not greatly affect us for one hundred years or more. This is especially true in developed countries in temperate zones, which won't feel much impact even if some of the worst climate projections come true." Efforts led by the United Nations Framework Convention on Climate Change (UNFCC) to complete negotiations on the Kyoto Protocol, a proposed international agreement on restrictions of greenhouse gas emissions, stalled in late 2000 but are scheduled to resume in summer 2001. A major stumbling block is the fundamental disagreement between developed and developing countries about the fairest way to cut greenhouse gas emissions.

Developing countries, which are responsible for a relatively small amount of the greenhouse gases currently in the atmosphere, believe those who caused the problem should carry the lion's share of the burden of solving it. On the other hand developed countries fear that restricting greenhouse gas emissions, particularly those caused by the burning of fossil fuels, will slow their economies, and they want more flexible methods to meet proposed reduction requirements. Whether any agreement at all can be reached under the Kyoto Protocol was recently thrown into doubt by the announcement of the United States that it plans to withdraw from the talks scheduled for this summer.

While efforts to set international emissions restrictions are progressing slowly, some promising initiatives are already underway, especially in the area of carbon trading. Trading carbon allows those who emit greenhouse gases to earn counteracting credits by investing in carbon sinks. Pedro Sanchez of ICRAF gives an example: "A European airline that flies to Nairobi several times a week is exploring ways to compensate farmers in Kenya for the carbon they sequester in agroforestry systems to counterbalance the greenhouse gases the airplanes emit in the stratosphere."

In the end, no one will remain unaffected by climate change. To cut emissions and encourage adaptations in agriculture, many other cooperative efforts will be needed. Governments and development organizations will need to help farmers, especially in resource-poor areas, cope with the temperature increases, reduced water supply, extreme weather events, and reduced soil moisture that are likely to exacerbate food insecurity in those regions of the globe that are already worst-off. Current projections do not extend beyond the 21st century, but if mitigating and adaptive steps are not taken soon, climate change and the agricultural problems associated with it will only increase, putting the food security of future generations further at risk.

PART 6

The Hot Spots: Sub-Saharan Africa and South Asia

Chapter 25

Nutrient Depletion in the Agricultural Soils of Africa

Julio Henao and Carlos Baanante

Depletion of nutrients from soils has
caused crop production to stagnate or
decline in many African countries.

About two-thirds of Africans depend on agriculture for their livelihoods. The fate of agricultural production, therefore, directly affects economic growth, social improvement, and trade in Africa. As the region's population continues to grow rapidly, outpacing the growth rate in other regions of the world, its agricultural land is becoming increasingly degraded. Farmers are intensifying land use to meet food needs without proper management practices and external inputs. The resulting depletion of nutrients from soils has caused crop production to stagnate or decline in many African countries. In some cases, notably in the East African highlands, the rate of depletion is so high that even drastic measures, such as doubling the application of fertilizer or manure or halving erosion losses, would not be enough to offset nutrient deficits. Unless African governments, supported by the international community, take the lead in confronting the problems of nutrient depletion, deteriorating agricultural productivity will seriously undermine the foundations of sustainable economic growth in Africa.

The Extent of Nutrient Depletion

All African countries, except Mauritius, Reunion, and Libya, show negative nutrient balances every year (see Figure 25.1). In the semiarid, arid, and Sudano-Sahelian

Figure 25.1 Average Annual Nutrient Depletion (NPK) in Africa, 1993–95

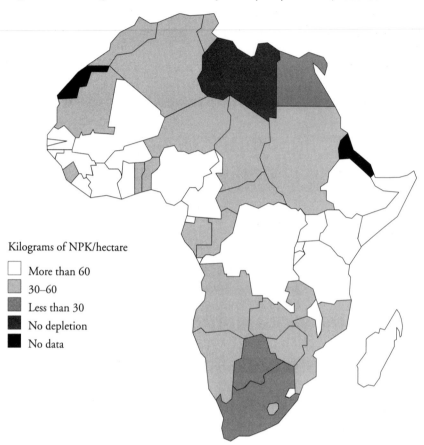

Kilograms of NPK/hectare

☐ More than 60

▨ 30–60

▨ Less than 30

▨ No depletion

■ No data

areas that are more densely populated, soils lose 60–100 kilograms of nitrogen, phosphorus, and potassium (NPK) per hectare each year. The soils of these areas are shallow, highly weathered, and subject to intensive cultivation but with low levels of fertilizer application. Limited water availability and intensified land use due to increasing population size have restricted crop diversification and the adoption of proper management practices. Short growing seasons contribute to additional pressure on the land.

In other important agricultural areas, such as those located in the subhumid and humid regions and in the savannas and forest areas, nutrient losses vary greatly. Rates of nutrient depletion range from moderate (30 to 60 kilograms of NPK per hectare per year) in the humid forests and wetlands in southern Central Africa, to high (above 60 kilograms) in the East African highlands.

In 1993–95 the difference between nutrient inputs and nutrient losses in the continent ranged from –14 kilograms of NPK per hectare per year in South Africa to –136 kilograms in Rwanda. Burundi and Malawi also experienced rates of nutrient depletion above 100 kilograms of NPK per hectare per year. About 86 percent of African countries show annual nutrient deficits greater than 30 kilograms of NPK per hectare per year. More countries fall into the high depletion range than the medium range. Nutrient imbalances are highest where fertilizer use is particularly low and nutrient loss, mainly from soil erosion, is high. The low gains in nutrients, inherently low mineral stocks in these soils, and the harsh climate of the interior plains and plateaus aggravate the consequences of nutrient depletion.

The estimated net annual losses of nutrients vary considerably by subregion: 384,800 metric tons for North Africa, 110,900 metric tons for South Africa, and 7,629,900 metric tons for Sub-Saharan Africa. This represents a total loss of US$1.5 billion per year in terms of the cost of nutrients as fertilizers. Forfeited yields cause additional financial losses. Most crop yields in Africa did not change substantially between 1981 and 1995, remaining close to the average obtained by smallholders with rainfed land and moderate to low soil fertility.

More nitrogen and potassium than phosphorus get depleted from African soils. Nitrogen and potassium losses primarily arise from leaching and soil erosion. These soil problems result mainly from continuous cropping of cereals without rotation with legumes, inappropriate soil conservation practices, and inadequate amounts of fertilizer use. Guinea Bissau and Nigeria experience the highest annual losses of nitrogen and potassium in West Africa. Nitrogen loss in East Africa is highest in Burundi, Ethiopia, Malawi, Rwanda, and Uganda, and phosphorus loss is highest in Burundi, Malawi, and Rwanda.

Losses of potassium are associated with severe erosion. The highest rates of potassium depletion occur in Guinea Bissau and Nigeria in West Africa, and Burundi, Kenya, Malawi, Rwanda, Swaziland, and Uganda in East and Southern Africa.

Nutrient Requirements and Soil Management Practices

Nutrient gains in African soils come about mainly through mineral fertilizer application, nutrient deposition, and nitrogen fixation. The negative nutrient balances clearly indicate that not enough nutrients are being applied in most areas. The current annual use of nutrients in Africa averages about 12 kilograms of NPK per hectare. Fertilizer use ranges from nearly 234 kilograms per hectare in Egypt to 46 kilograms in Kenya to less than 10 kilograms in most countries in Sub-Saharan Africa. North Africa, with about 20 percent of the continent's land area, accounts for 41 percent of the fertilizer consumption.

Figure 25.2 Annual Requirements for Maintaining Current Yields without Depleting Nutrients, 1993–95

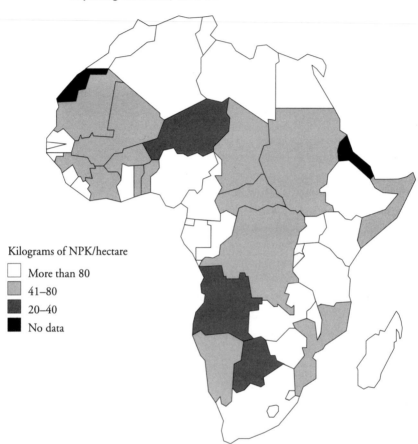

Kilograms of NPK/hectare

☐ More than 80
▨ 41–80
▨ 20–40
■ No data

Fertilizer tends to be used mostly on cash and plantation crops because of the high profitability of fertilizers in the production of export crops. Food crops get less fertilizer because of unfavorable crop/fertilizer price ratios and financial constraints faced by farmers.

To maintain current average levels of crop production without depleting soil nutrients, Africa will require approximately 11.7 million metric tons of NPK each year, roughly three times more than it currently uses (3.6 million metric tons) (see Figure 25.2). Sub-Saharan Africa will need by far the largest proportion of this amount, 76 percent, because its current average level of fertilizer use is so low. Total nutrient requirements per hectare per year in this subregion range from Botswana's 24.5 NPK (a figure 350 percent above current usage) to Reunion's 437.3 NPK (about 20 NPK per hectare less than the country consumes). Burkina Faso would have to increase its NPK consumption more than 11 times to maintain crop production levels without depleting nutrients, and Swaziland would have to double its consumption. Estimated average use for Africa as a whole would have to increase about 4 times to meet nutrient needs at the current level of production. Generally more nitrogen is required than potassium, and more potassium than phosphorus.

Although increasing the use of mineral fertilizer may be the centerpiece of the strategy to balance nutrient depletion and improve soil productivity in Africa, it should not be taken to mean that fertilizer levels should be increased beyond basic requirements. Indeed, surpassing recommended levels for less-responsive varieties and in poorly managed cropping systems can lead to high nutrient losses and low yields. Moreover, to achieve intended goals, fertilizer use must be combined with a broad spectrum of complementary practices, such as soil conservation, recycling of crop residues, livestock management, and use of organic fertilizers. Such practices could reduce the mineral fertilizer required to maintain current average yields by as much as 44 percent.

Implications for Policy

If nutrient depletion and land degradation continue at current rates, one has to wonder how farmers in African countries will be able to grow enough food for ever-larger populations in the next century. To avoid possible crises, national governments and donors should address the threat of nutrient depletion and land degradation through policies and programs that promote increased productivity of land resources and conservation of the resource base. Significant policy changes will be required to establish an environment that makes agricultural inputs easily available, that encourages farmers to use these inputs more efficiently, and that helps improve local extension services and farmer support. Structural adjustments, market development, trade and price policies, credit systems, infrastructure improvement, and institutional support services should be reevaluated and assessed for their impact on the resource base and the sustainable expansion of agricultural production and productivity.

Many countries and regions need to integrate natural resource management with economic and sector policies. More economic and environmental impact analyses at the country level are needed to help set priorities for agricultural land issues, to assess the costs and benefits of policy decisions, and to expedite identification of the type of investments that will be required to prevent land degradation and increase production. Prevention of nutrient mining through sound economic policies, research, information dissemination, and human resource development should be actively promoted in Africa.

Chapter 26

Applying Science to Sub-Saharan Africa's Food Needs

Reported by Ellen Wilson

*In the drive to develop the best technology to solve
Sub-Saharan Africa's mounting food needs,
indigenous knowledge should not be forgotten.*

With biotechnology and other new agricultural technology on the horizon, millions of Sub-Saharan Africans have reason to wonder whether there will be a magic bullet that will save their countries from massive food shortages. The answer, as given by African leaders and researchers and other global agriculture experts, seems to be "no, there will not be a magic bullet." But biotechnology should be in the mix of solutions to food insecurity in Sub-Saharan Africa. And equally, if not more important, are food policy changes and new technology that focus on a range of issues from increasing cassava crop yields to more-effective ways to capture and store water during the rainy season.

"Africans cannot afford to be left behind in the area of biotechnology," said Professor Francis Idachaba, vice-chancellor of the University of Agriculture in Makurdi, Nigeria. "African farmers must be prepared for advances in biotechnology so that they can replace their seeds with genetically engineered seeds. However, there are many other policy problems that need to be addressed first. Food insecurity is not due to the fact that we have little or no biotechnology."

Unlike many parts of Asia where famine was averted through Green Revolution technologies that could be applied consistently across millions of hectares of land, Sub-Saharan Africa has special challenges—poor soils, unsuitable conditions for irrigation, and overall wide variations in growing conditions. Millions of people subsist in fragile areas—on hillsides, forest margins, and in drylands—areas where growing any kind of crop is a challenge.

"We're behind in the development of new technologies that can be applied to the diverse growing conditions of Sub-Saharan Africa," said Per Pinstrup-Andersen, director general of IFPRI. "Much of the agricultural research that has been done in the past was focused on high-potential areas of Asia and is not well-suited to Sub-Saharan Africa. We need more research to help these farmers increase production per unit of land without damaging the environment. We need more drought tolerance in crops grown in these regions, such as cassava, maize, sorghum, and millet, and we need varieties that are more high-yielding and resistant to pests and diseases."

Traditional Plant Breeding Delivers the Goods

Some say that biotechnology is not likely to assist in the process of improving these crops. "In the area of increasing yields, traditional plant breeding has been delivering the goods, not biotechnology," said Margaret Mellon, director of the agriculture and biotechnology project at the Union of Concerned Scientists. "Biotechnology cannot deal with complex traits and multiple gene transfers needed in African crops. All the hype surrounding biotechnology, with the implication that traditional plant breeding should be swept aside, needs to be deflated. Biotechnology has a role, but a minor one."

Agricultural researchers agree that biotechnology is not yet capable of dealing with complex traits. "Many of the concerns in Sub-Saharan Africa, like most of the tropics, are environmental stresses—drought, flooding, and soil stresses," said Roger Beachy, co-director of the International Laboratory for Tropical Agriculture and Biotechnology at the Scripps Research Institute in La Jolla, California. "It has thus far not been demonstrated that genetic engineering can confer resistances to these complex biological traits. But we can certainly expect that in the next 5 or 10 years, genetic engineering will help to arm plants against some of these problems."

However, according to Indra Vasil, plant biologist at the University of Florida and chair of the United Nations Educational, Scientific, and Cultural Organization's (Unesco's) Biotechnology Action Council, biotechnology can be put to great use in traditional plant breeding in Africa right now. "Biotechnology helps to identify new genes, through gene mapping, which makes it easier for plant breeders to select for the right gene combinations." In the case of insects such as aphids, white flies, and caterpillars, biotechnology will also likely be the primary method of control, replacing chemicals and pesticides, according to Beachy. There has been noteworthy progress in the transfer of genes from the bacterium, *Bacillus thuringiensis* or "Bt," into cotton and corn to combat caterpillars.

But understanding local ecology could potentially be the only environmentally safe way to control the primary culprits that limit production of crops in Sub-Saharan Africa—locusts, grasshoppers, and mealybugs, according to Beachy. He notes that in the past, these voracious insects have been controlled through massive chemical spraying. Recently, the Nigerian-based International Institute of Tropical Agriculture and other organizations have had great success in keeping insects in check through biological control by identifying and using natural predators or using natural fungi or bacteria in sprays.

National Research Programs

The ability to upgrade agriculture in Africa also hinges on the existence of strong national agricultural research programs. "There has been no Green Revolution in Africa," said Vernon Ruttan, regents professor in the Department of Agricultural and Applied Economics at the University of Minnesota. "And the reason is that agricultural technologies that lead to large increases per hectare of land are typically very location-specific. But they can only be adapted to particular locations to the extent that there are strong research programs in those locations."

Furthermore, the national agricultural research programs offer improvements in crop technology to farmers free of charge. "Innovation in Africa will not be accomplished through the private sector," said Klaus Leisinger, executive director of the Ciba-Geigy Foundation for Cooperation with Developing Countries. "It must be accomplished through the public sector, such as through the work of the Consultative Group on International Agricultural Research (CGIAR), combined with national programs and other academic institutions. The reason is that the commercial market in Africa is too small to be developed by the private sector and because, once you create improved crop varieties, they must be within the purchasing power of the small farmer in Africa."

But agricultural research capabilities have deteriorated in Sub-Saharan Africa. "Less is being invested in these programs by African governments than was invested before," said Pinstrup-Andersen. "And overall investment in agricultural research by donors has also declined."

According to Ruttan, the way to build national research programs is by having them develop new technology. "It's a process of learning by doing. You have to have experiment stations and trained scientists, they have to be supported by international funding and by national governments, and they have to be in Africa."

But there is also reason to hope for more productive relationships between the private sector and the developing world agriculture sector. According to Leisinger,

"I would hope that there can be closer collaboration between the private sector and the CGIAR System so that knowledge and patents could be made available in the developing world either on commercial terms through licenses or through 'soft conditions'—lower than market prices or for free."

Dissemination to Farmers

But new technology is only as good as the mechanism of its dissemination to farmers. And, according to African leaders, this link has been quite weak. "In my country, a lot of agricultural research has been undertaken in the last 60 years," said Speciosa Wandera Kazibwe, the vice president of Uganda. "But the bulk of these findings are allowed to gather dust in our archives and research institutions. The challenge is to communicate the findings to the people who need this information—the farmers."

Extension services are also needed to spread the word about better agronomic practices that could help increase crop yields. Fungal and viral plant diseases are particularly devastating in Sub-Saharan Africa, according to Beachy, because of the presence of weeds and the lack of freezing temperatures that help to control them. Weeds are a major reservoir for viruses and diseases. But extension services have not delivered this information to many rural and nomadic farmers, who traditionally plant crops such as cassava on the edge of the forest instead of in plots that are tilled and kept clear of weeds.

Most of Africa's agriculture is rainfed, instead of irrigated, and vulnerable to drought. African leaders cite a need for new, small-scale technologies to irrigate Africa's lands during the dry spells. "We must move to agriculture that relies on water collected during the rainy season," said Vice President Kazibwe. "We must tap underground water and the water in our fresh water lakes and rivers. But we must adopt technologies for storing and using water that are appropriate for our small farms."

Technology Part of a Larger Mosaic

There are many sociopolitical issues that mire new technology once it has been developed. "The developmental impact of recombinant genetics and biotechnology is only as good as the sociopolitical soil in which they are planted," said Leisinger. "Technological innovation is just one stone in a large and complex mosaic."

According to Idachaba, unsound food policies and governmental instability in large part hinder the ability of technology to help the small farmer. Some of the poor policies have included government taxation of agriculture to finance nonagricultural products; lack of government support of agricultural extension services; poor rural infrastructure, including roads, water supplies, and physical markets in which to buy, sell, and store crops; and unfriendly macroeconomic policy environments, including poor exchange rates that hinder African agricultural exports.

Throughout the 1980s and continuing into this decade some of the poor food policies were reversed, according to Idachaba. "Policy changes are being made that define the proper role of the government in agriculture," he said. "But still, from government to government and from country to country, policy failures persist because their political cost has been too low. We must raise the cost of governmental neglect of African agriculture. Rural people must put political pressure on governments to support improvements in agricultural technologies. In African countries, there are no 'farm lobbies,' but they are urgently needed."

In the drive to develop the best technology to solve Sub-Saharan Africa's mounting food needs, indigenous knowledge should not be forgotten, according to Kazibwe. It was not long ago that Africa was self-sufficient in its own food production. Certainly, some of the lessons of the past can be applied to the future. "Our people who have been engaged in agriculture since the beginning of time have accumulated a lot of knowledge about crops, soils, insects, the weather, and so on," she said. "This body of knowledge should be tapped and related to modern science. If this knowledge sustained our ancestors in the past, it cannot be totally useless today."

Chapter 27

Pushing Back Poverty in India

Reported by Heidi Fritschel and Uday Mohan

*Reaching India's millions of rural poor will require
jump starting growth in the rural areas.*

In August 1999, India's population reached 1 billion, and by 2035 experts project that India will overtake China as the world's most populous country. But India already holds first place in another category: the country is home to the world's largest number of poor people. Today an estimated 350 million out of 1 billion Indians fall below the poverty line. This number represents enormous human suffering: while India claims self-sufficiency in production of grains, two-thirds of Indian children under age 5 are malnourished. Infant mortality is 65 per 1,000 live births, compared with 33 for China. Adult literacy rates of 65 percent for men and 38 percent for women fall far short of those in China—90 percent for men and 73 percent for women.

To be sure, India has reduced the share of its people living in poverty significantly, from 55 percent in the early 1970s to about 35 percent today, but India's record of poverty reduction pales when compared with that of other Asian countries. Indonesia, for example, slashed the proportion of its population living in poverty from 58 percent in 1970 to just 8 percent in 1993 (although the Asian economic crisis has set the country back significantly). China reduced the incidence of absolute poverty within its borders from 270 million in 1978 to 65 million in 1996.

Studies show that economic growth, particularly agricultural growth, has been the main source of poverty alleviation in India. "In the areas where growth has been strongest, poverty has fallen the most. The problem is that by itself it's not enough," says Pranab Bardhan, professor of economics at the University of California at Berkeley. G. S. Bhalla, coauthor of a forthcoming 2020 Vision discussion paper on India's food balances, says, "The underlying sources of agricultural growth during the past quarter century have largely run their course, and new sources of production growth must be found."

Can India achieve its own economic miracle, pushing back poverty and stimulating a vibrant economy with opportunities for all of its people? The task for India's policymakers is to recharge agricultural growth, enabling poor people to contribute their skills and energies to the country's economic activities and to reap the benefits of economic success.

The Record on Growth and Poverty

When India achieved independence in 1947, about half of its people lived in poverty, and for the next two decades, poverty remained entrenched. "Before the 1970s, growth did not help poverty, mainly because the rate of growth was far too slow to have any impact," says Siddiq Osmani, professor of development economics at the University of Ulster, Belfast. "After 1970 growth picked up, not by East Asian standards, but by India's own standard. And since growth was especially strong in agriculture, on which most of the rural poor depend, poverty did decline, from about 55 percent in 1973 to about 33 percent in 1993."

What was behind the falling poverty rates? The key was the Green Revolution, in which farmers used improved crop varieties, fertilizers, and irrigation to raise crop yields and accelerate agricultural growth. The government's investments in new technologies and infrastructure together with the farmers' efforts in the fields averted a predicted famine and helped pull millions out of poverty.

Poverty did not fall evenly throughout India, however. In 1990–91, less than 20 percent of the population of Punjab and Haryana was poor, compared with nearly 60 percent in Bihar. States that managed to make a sizable dent in poverty followed one of two strategies. One was rural economic growth. Punjab and Haryana, for example, benefited from the agricultural growth stimulated by the Green Revolution. As yields rose, poor farmers and even landless agricultural workers reaped the benefits. The second strategy was development of human resources, through education. Kerala stressed universal education, but its economy did not grow enough to absorb all of the skilled labor. As a result many workers migrated abroad, and their remittances helped reduce poverty in Kerala.

"No Indian state effectively combined both approaches. Research suggests that if any state had done so, it would have achieved rapid reductions in poverty, comparable to the progress made in a number of East Asian countries," says Martin

Ravallion, lead economist in the Development Research Group of the World Bank.

In the early 1990s, India experienced a balance of payments crisis. In response, the government devalued the rupee, cut government spending, and raised interest rates. Rural poverty increased temporarily and then returned to its pre-reform level, where it has remained. "Overall, the post-reform period has seen no reduction in rural poverty, unlike the decade and a half preceding the reforms, although GDP growth has been similar, and in fact better since 1992," says Abhijit Sen of the Center for Economic Studies and Planning, Jawaharlal Nehru University. According to Sen, the reasons are several. "Agricultural growth has been somewhat slower in the 1990s than in the 1980s. Cuts in public spending have slowed the extension of the Green Revolution to the poorest regions and restrained the growth of rural infrastructure and rural nonagricultural opportunities. Also, the relative price of cereals has increased considerably during the 1990s, compared to the reduction of the 1980s."

The Promise of Agricultural Growth

"The important poverty story in India is the rural sector," says Ravallion. "In terms of sheer numbers, this is where the poverty problem lies." Three out of four of India's poor live in the rural areas. "Urban poverty has fallen somewhat in recent years, but rural poverty has not," says Ravallion.

"There are still big disparities between regions," says Gaurav Datt of the World Bank, "and that speaks to a lot of potential for growth."

Given the persistence of rural poverty, many experts agree that the key to reducing poverty in India is agricultural growth, accompanied by strong nonagricultural growth that reaches the rural poor. Moreover, research conducted by Ravallion and Datt has shown that economic growth in rural areas tends to help the poor in both the countryside and the cities.

But Benoit Blarel, an economist with the World Bank, is concerned that substantial rural growth may be hard to come by. "The historical sources of growth and poverty reduction in rural India are now difficult to find. Rapid technological change, massive public investments, declining food prices, and agricultural diversification are no longer there to support rural growth, raise wages, and reduce rural poverty. These historical sources of growth have been undermined by lopsided public spending, especially on subsidies that do little for either growth or poverty. And even with 300 million poor people, much-needed reforms are politically difficult."

Peter Hazell, director of IFPRI's Environment and Production Technology Division and a coauthor with Bhalla of the forthcoming 2020 discussion paper, agrees: "Further expansion of irrigated area will be more costly, and agriculture must increasingly compete with other water users such as industry and urban households for limited water resources. The Green Revolution technologies have also already spread widely in the areas where they are most economic, so there is limited scope for further production gains from the greater use of improved varieties and fertilizer."

The potential for agricultural growth differs for different growing conditions in India, says Hazell. Irrigated areas were the source of the rapid growth during the Green Revolution, but productivity growth is stagnating in these areas, partly because the biggest gains have already been made and partly because intensive irrigated farming is leading to environmental stresses like salinity and waterlogging of soils. Use of new varieties, better crop management, and better management of irrigation water could help raise yields in irrigated areas.

Nonirrigated areas fed by rain may offer the most promise for agricultural growth. Rainfed areas can be divided into high-potential areas with good rainfall and fertile soils and low-potential areas that get little and uncertain rain. "On the whole," says Bhalla, "high-potential rainfed areas may represent India's easiest option for expanding production. Historical trends suggest that improved varieties and inputs will continue to spread to these areas, and continued improvements in infrastructure and increases in education will also help raise returns to agriculture."

In the low-potential rainfed areas, farmers produce mainly sorghum, millet, and pulses. Some higher-value activities, such as oilseeds and dairying, have expanded in those areas in recent years in response to favorable incentives, and this raises some hopes for the future. "But generally, technical solutions here are less clear than in the more favorable environments, and output growth is likely to be limited," says Hazell.

A recent IFPRI study shows that additional investment in agricultural R&D and rural infrastructure in rainfed areas, even many lower-potential areas, now offers higher returns for growth and poverty alleviation than additional investments in many irrigated areas. "These results reflect the high levels of investment that have already been made in irrigated areas, their stagnating productivity growth, and the past neglect of many rainfed areas," says Hazell, one of the coauthors of the study. Coauthor Shenggen Fan, an IFPRI senior research fellow, cautions, "Rainfed areas will need better natural resource management to avoid the same environmental problems that are contributing to stagnant yield growth in irrigated areas."

Another IFPRI study found that investing in more agricultural R&D and in more rural roads may be two of the most important steps toward raising growth and lowering rural poverty. "Our work shows that government investment in agricultural R&D is more effective than any other kind of investment at boosting agricultural growth, by producing new technologies for farmers," says Hazell. According to Fan, lead author of the study, "We found that marginal investments in roads have the biggest impact on rural poverty. This is because roads improve access to markets and reduce transport costs, they help people reach new jobs, they help kids get to school, they help farmers get access to new technologies. Lack of roads can be a big bottleneck for development."

Making the Poor Full Participants

Clearly, reaching India's millions of rural poor will require jump starting growth in the rural areas. Squeezing more productivity growth out of India's agricultural lands will be far from simple, but the task is crucial. Beyond producing more food and bringing more income to farmers and agricultural workers, agricultural growth can help revitalize the entire rural economy, including activities outside of agriculture.

"In the long run, creation of well-paying productive employment in the nonagricultural sector is the solution," says Kirit Parikh, director of the Indira Gandhi Institute of Development Research in Mumbai. "For that, human capital has to be built up through education."

Even the poorest and least-favored areas will require investment in their agricultural and nonagricultural economies, says Sen. "The poverty reduction impact of overall growth is larger if nonagricultural growth generates jobs and if the rural poor have access to them. This in turn is more likely if nonagricultural growth is regionally dispersed," he explains. The state has an important role to play in providing agricultural research, infrastructure, education, and social security. "Obviously, the ability of the state to play these essential roles depends on the resources at its disposal, and since growth eases the resource constraint, these are more likely to be undertaken if the overall GDP situation is better."

As India passes the 1 billion mark, the future of its 350 million poor people hangs in the balance, subject to the decisions of policy leaders. Whether their future will be one of increasing prosperity, food security, and improved quality of life or instead a continuing struggle against grinding poverty depends on the steps decisionmakers take now.

Chapter 28

Is Agriculture Raiding South Asia's Water Supplies?

Water Scarcity and Water Reform in South Asia

Reported by Ellen Wilson

*Across South Asia, both urban and rural water users
are provided with massive subsidies on water use;
irrigation water is essentially unpriced.*

Water is increasingly scarce around the world. In South Asia, where half of the world's poor live, international water conflicts are brewing and riots over water are taking place with increasing frequency. Many researchers, environmentalists, and others believe that agriculture is using more than its fair share of the resource. Around the world and in South Asia, agriculture, on average, uses about 80 percent of the water supply in a given country.

According to some researchers, agriculture is drinking so much water in South Asia not out of necessity, but because of poor water policies that induce excessive water use. They say that water use could be reduced without adversely affecting crop yields, and call for comprehensive reform of water policies. These reforms could save irrigation water, freeing it up for nonagricultural uses, and, at the same time, decrease irrigated water's negative effects on the environment. But others challenge the assumption that increasing water efficiency could free up a lot of water. They hold that there is simply not enough water to go around. In the future, this edginess over water will only increase as population pressures make the need to produce greater amounts of irrigated food staples even more urgent.

"There are no easy answers to water scarcity and water allocation issues," said Prabhu Pingali, senior economist at the Philippines-based International Rice Research Institute. "But what is happening all over Asia is that water scarcity is increasing. As it does increase, farmers will become more conscious about their water use. Farmers have shown the ability to organize themselves to solve certain problems in the past. I think we will see farmers organizing to create solutions to water scarcity in the future. And one of the most important solutions will be to increase water efficiency."

Water Scarcity

Researchers say there are water shortages during the dry season in parts of rural areas and in every major city in South Asia. These shortages are leading to conflicts. According to Peter Rogers, Gordon McKay Professor of Environmental Engineering at Harvard University, "The major conflict between Pakistan and India about the Indus River waters was largely diffused in the 1960s. Now there is a conflict between India and Bangladesh over the Ganges. But of even greater concern are the water conflicts between the states in India on every boundary that crosses a major flow of the Ganges. And also in the south of India, which is not in the Ganges River basin, people have been killed in riots about intrastate water conflicts.

"In Madras, there is no water in the city pipes," continued Rogers. "Mobs of desperate people must chase water delivery trucks twice a week to get their share. There is plenty of water during the monsoons. But this water is not stored properly and is mainly used for agriculture."

Many researchers believe that water is being used excessively in agriculture. "For our water-intensive crops such as rice and sugar cane, we are going deeper and deeper underground," said Ashok Gulati, a director at the National Council for Applied Economic Research in India. "In the modern part of India's Punjab, so much water is being pumped from wells, the water table is going down by one and a half feet per year."

Irrigated water in agriculture has had and continues to have negative environmental effects. "Unless there is proper drainage, bringing irrigated water onto fields can cause waterlogging and salinity buildup in soils," said Ruth Meinzen-Dick, research fellow at IFPRI. "This has become especially problematic over large areas of prime irrigated land in Pakistan and northern India."

This water-induced land degradation is leading to long-term declines in the very crops the irrigated water was supposed to be spurring into ever-increasing production. "In addition, intensively irrigated land leads to long-term declines in the soil's nitrogen supply, and this affects the ability of the soil to produce the same yields as before," said Pingali.

Declining growth in crop yields makes the prospect of decreasing the use of water on farms particularly scary. But surprisingly, researchers have found that if farmers decreased their water use on rice paddies, there would be little or no impact on yields.

"We have enough field level experiments, conducted in various countries in South Asia, which show that you can reduce irrigation water by as much as 40 percent without affecting crop yields," said Pingali. "The problem is that farmers have no incentive to reduce their water use because water is free or costs very little."

Water: A Business or a Social Program?

Across South Asia, both urban and rural water users are provided with massive subsidies on water use; irrigation water is essentially unpriced. The government also subsidizes the electricity required to draw groundwater up from wells.

"With water provided by public systems at little or no cost to the user, no one in the water allocation business, whether it's the bureaucrats, the farmers, or urban citizens, has an incentive to conserve water," said Mark Rosegrant, research fellow at IFPRI. "As a result, water is overused. Any excess water ends up going downstream or seeping into the groundwater, or is otherwise lost to the system, requiring costly pumping to recover. What is needed is an improvement in the overall, systemwide efficiency of water use on farms."

However, some believe there is no water to spare on farms. "If you're looking for more water in Asia, be careful about thinking that improved water efficiency will free up a lot of water," said Harald Frederiksen, principal engineer at the World Bank. "Farmers are short of water, just like everyone else, during the dry season because every river runs dry. When push comes to shove, South Asia, like so many other regions around the world, is out of water.

"To solve the problem, there are four choices," continued Frederiksen. "One, displace people out of urban areas by not providing water; two, displace people around reservoir sites by building new reservoirs to capture water in the wet season; three, displace people out of agriculture by turning off irrigation to the rural areas; or four, population control, the only painless solution. In the longer term, the solution must be population control, but it's getting pretty late."

Nevertheless, there is no disputing the fact that governments across South Asia seem to be foundering under the burden of water subsidies. "Water reforms will be increasingly well received because the past policies have become self-defeating," said Rosegrant. "Water costs more now because of its growing scarcity. And the costs of maintaining the subsidies and centralized control of water are skyrocketing."

One obvious solution to water overuse and escalating costs is to put a price on water. "Irrigation should be a business and not a social program," said Harvard's

Rogers. "Farmers must be required to pay a price for water that is at least as much as it is worth to them. Governments should seek to reclaim the full cost of water. No one will die of thirst. If we just increased the price from close to zero to a price that is 10 percent more, this would produce so much water, people wouldn't know what to do with it."

But Is Priced Water Feasible?

How feasible would it be to ask farmers to pay for something that was once free? "It will take great political will and institutional reform to raise the cost of water to its true cost," said Gulati. "You can't ask farmers to pay more without improving the quality of the water service in return."

Current irrigation systems do not serve many farmers' needs, making farmers ever disgruntled customers. In addition, there is wasteful leakage from current irrigation systems. According to Basawan Sinha, the former chief engineer of irrigation for Bihar State in India, the major problem with water is that the old canal and distribution systems were not planned and designed to provide water to farmers on demand, in sufficient amounts, at the right time. "And there are many hectares of land for which we have failed to provide water at all," said Sinha.

Researchers also warn that raising the price of water would not do much to conserve water unless the method of billing farmers for water use was revised. "Farmers are currently charged on a per-hectare basis," said Meinzen-Dick of IFPRI. "If you just raised the charge, farmers would likely use even more water to get more for their money. If farmers were charged for the volume of water they use, then raising the price might encourage conservation."

However, Meinzen-Dick adds that measuring and monitoring volumes of water used on farms would be an enormous logistical challenge. "If countries do not have the administrative capacity to adequately bill for electricity when the technology is fairly simple, then I have serious doubts that they can bill individual farmers for their water consumption."

Empowering Farmers with Water Rights

Researchers call for reform of water policies to help solve some of these problems, including establishing farmer water associations and granting them legal rights to water. "Strengthening the role of water user associations is one of the most promising ways to improve the quality of irrigation service while at the same time reducing the financial burden on governmental agencies of managing irrigation systems," said Meinzen-Dick. "Associations could purchase water for several hundred hectares of land, divide that water among their members, and encourage water conservation.

Many countries, ranging from the Philippines and Indonesia to Mexico and Chile, have transferred management responsibility from state agencies to farmer organizations. But for this to work, farmers have to have incentives great enough to offset the added costs of managing the irrigation systems. Improvements in water service and clear water rights for the organizations can provide such incentives."

According to Rosegrant from IFPRI, water rights could also be bartered or sold to other farmers or other farmer associations, thus encouraging farmers to use less water and sell off what they don't really need. Farmers would also approve new investments in irrigation system hardware, have more say about when and where the water is allocated, and ensure that the water reaches all who need it. It would also be necessary to make minor capital improvements in the old systems and make these systems more flexible in accommodating farmers' evolving needs. Portions of the water system would still be owned by the state; the rest would be owned by the farmers.

"In the past, turnover of water infrastructure management to farmers has often failed because it was not accompanied by secure access to water," said Rosegrant. "Reform in Chile shows that well-defined water rights provide the incentive for user groups to economize on water use and to bargain effectively with the governmental water bureaucracies for timely and efficient service."

Chile's water companies have been completely privatized. "A market solution can make a great contribution to solving water scarcity in the future and can improve the efficiency of investments in water infrastructure in the present," said Renato Gazmuri, former secretary for agriculture in Chile. "Farmers will not approve unprofitable capital improvements. Because of their increased water efficiency, Chilean farmers now irrigate 22 percent more land with the same amount of water as before."

An increase in the flexibility of water systems would also better accommodate a possible shift from rice monocultures in the dry season to less water-intensive crops, such as corn, vegetables, or fodder legumes. Such high-value crops could help farmers pay for priced water. "However, there must be a market demand for these crops or they can't be grown," said Pingali. "We have seen a tremendous shift to nonrice crops in the dry season in Thailand, driven mainly by an increasing demand from wealthier urban populations for vegetables and fruit. A large-scale shift across South Asia would have to be preceded by dramatic income growth. This won't happen overnight."

Water Marketing

In the future, farmer water rights could also free up water for nonagricultural uses through a system known as water marketing. Farmers could sell their water rights to the cities, which would be more than willing to pay for scarce water. "We've seen this work in California where the drought disappeared because of water trades between the agriculture sector and the municipalities," said Rogers. "The government in California ended up with more water than it could deal with. At the end of the year, it still had about 200,000 acre-feet left unsold." But to make this work, again, there must be a water measuring and monitoring system, and an adequate "plumbing system" between the farms and the cities, another expensive logistical challenge.

No one believes that large-scale water marketing can happen quickly in most developing countries, but some reform of water is on the horizon. "Exactly what sort of institutional reforms will take place remains to be seen," said Gulati. "India is just beginning to change in a direction that is a more bottom-up versus a top-down approach. As a result, users—the farmers—will be involved in the ownership and management of irrigation and electricity. We are trying to sell this idea to chief ministers of different states in India. We hope that some of the reforms in water will take place within the next two to three years in some of the states. Changes could take place in electricity as soon as within the next year or two."

Some have faith that the farmers may move faster than anyone expects. According to Rogers, "I met a farmer, who, on three hectares of land, was growing roses and delivering them to the airport each day to be sold around the world. He used to grow sorghum. Now he's buying color televisions and sending his kids to college. Farmers are now using subsidized irrigation water to grow citrus, table grapes, and roses. They can afford to pay for water. The farmers are ready to begin to make more rational choices about water use."

Chapter 29

Transforming the Rural Asian Economy
The Unfinished Revolution

Mark W. Rosegrant and Peter B. R. Hazell

*To complete the economic transformation in
rural Asia requires further growth, but growth
that is more equitable and environmentally
sustainable than it has been in the past.*

D eveloping Asia as a whole has taken remarkable strides since the food crises
of the 1960s. Improvements in food security, poverty reduction, and per capita income initiated by the Green Revolution have been substantial and lasting. Per capita gross domestic product increased by 190 percent between 1970 and
1995, and calories per person per day by more than 20 percent. In 1975, one out
of every two Asians lived in poverty. By 1995 this ratio fell to one in four. The incidence of rural poverty also decreased, from one in two to one in three between 1975
and 1995, and the total number of rural poor fell by 7 percent despite a substantial increase in population.

Although life has improved for most rural Asians, about 670 million still live in
poverty, and they must tolerate lower levels of health, education, and general well-
being than their urban counterparts. About 2 billion people live in rural Asia.
Another 300 million are expected to join their ranks by 2020. The vast majority of
these rural inhabitants still rely, directly or indirectly, on agriculture, forestry, or fishing for their livelihoods, a dependence that places enormous pressure on natural
resources. The continuing degradation of these resources could well cause social conflict over remaining resources and discontent about the widening gap between urban
and rural quality of life. These problems would be particularly severe in South Asia.

Meeting the Challenges of the Future

To complete the economic transformation in rural Asia requires further growth, but growth that is more equitable and environmentally sustainable than it has been in the past. Meeting this challenge will warrant more efficient application of the lessons already learned about agricultural growth, public-sector investment, rural poverty reduction, and natural resource protection. The following six emerging challenges will also need special attention.

Making Growth Pro-Poor

Because the poor live mostly in rural areas and generally depend on the farm sector for their incomes, growth that stems from agricultural productivity and that raises the incomes of small-scale farmers and landless laborers is particularly important in reducing poverty. But growth alone will not rapidly reduce poverty. Policymakers must reach the poor directly, by investing in health, nutrition, and education. In the case of particularly vulnerable or marginalized groups, policymakers can use income transfers or safety nets to help relieve short-term stress. For the poor to participate in growth, land must be distributed relatively equitably; agricultural research must focus on the problems of small farmers as well as large; new technologies must be scale-neutral and profitable for all farm sizes; efficient input, credit, and product markets must ensure that all farms have access to needed modern farm inputs and receive similar prices for their products; the labor force must be able to migrate or diversify into rural nonfarm activities; and policies must not discriminate against agriculture in general and small farms in particular.

Managing the Legacy of the Economic Crisis

The 1997 economic crisis in East and Southeast Asia caused serious drops in real income and employment. Although recovery has begun, the affected countries will need time to recover from the loss in real income and cuts in government investment in rural growth and safety nets. Governments and donors need to give high priority to restoring investment fundamentals in the crisis economies and strengthening safety nets. Good-governance reforms must seek greater transparency and accountability in public-sector activities and the regulation of financial institutions and corporations to reduce the possibility of future financial crises.

Managing Globalization

Globalization offers immense market, technological, and financial opportunities for further economic growth in Asia. Open markets and global integration have already boosted rural growth, but such processes also risk economic losses to superior competitors, instability, and worsening inequality. The solution to these problems lies in creative policies, not in withdrawal into isolation. Competition can be managed, for example, through a phased transition, as many of the Southeast Asian countries have shown. The pace of liberalization should take into account institutional capacities, competitive readiness of agriculture and industry, and the effects on social and political stability. The management of the transition to globalization should favor not only an open economy and growth, but also macroeconomic stability, human capital formation, and poverty reduction.

Revitalizing Agricultural Research and Technology Dissemination

New agricultural technologies in Asia are increasingly complex, knowledge-intensive, and location-specific. They require a more decentralized research and extension system and more information and skills for successful adoption than did Green Revolution varieties and fertilizers. Extension and research that is driven by information from the bottom up could help farmers cope with the complexity of the new technologies. The private sector could also help revitalize agricultural research, though with some risks. Governments are making it easier for the private sector to appropriate and use research results and hybrids. And biotechnology innovations are likely to increase private-sector involvement in agricultural research. But the public sector will continue to play an important role in agricultural research because corporations may not want to invest in technologies that governments consider important for equity and poverty alleviation. Moreover, the private sector has generally shown little interest in increasing the yield of key commodities such as wheat or rice varieties adapted to Asian agroclimatic zones. And it has made virtually no investments in tropical crops, fruits, and vegetables.

Managing Land and Water Scarcity and Degradation

Population pressure on the land; agricultural intensification and inappropriate farming practices; and waste disposal from a rapidly growing livestock sector all pose significant threats to the rural environment. But water scarcity and quality are probably the most severe challenges facing developing Asia and will reach crisis levels in many Asian countries in the next decade or two. Water is becoming scarce not only because of growing demand from agriculture, industry, and households, but because the potential for expanding the water supply is diminishing. Deteriorating water quality will further aggravate water shortages. Policies that can improve water management include removal of subsidies and taxes that encourage misuse of resources and establishment of secure property rights. Water users will need to have greater power to make their own decisions regarding water use, and markets will need to send correct signals about the real value of water.

Building Good Governance and Social Capital

Asian societies are changing because of rising incomes and globalization. People are demanding greater participation in policy decisions, more democratic and decentralized forms of governance, and more accountability from public agencies. At the same time, the nature of many public goods is changing. The private sector is playing a larger role in agricultural research and the supply of health and education services, and nongovernmental organizations are organizing communities for collective activity and investment. These changes require that the roles of the public and private sectors and civil society be reconfigured to provide public goods and services in a more cost-effective manner and in a way that better meets the needs of rural people. For consumers whose limited purchasing power prevents a satisfactory response from the private sector, governments inevitably will continue to play a large role in meeting basic needs.

Alternative Scenarios for Developing Asia

Even though the size of the agricultural sector has declined relative to other sectors during the course of Asia's economic transformation, agricultural output has continued to grow, as it must. Slower agricultural growth could jeopardize food security and increase child malnutrition in many countries, cause significant new unemployment and poverty (particularly in rural areas), and reduce nonagricultural growth.

If, under a pessimistic scenario, governments become even more complacent than they are today about agriculture, invest less in rural areas, and fail to make needed policy reforms, projections based on IFPRI's IMPACT model show that the number of malnourished children, a good indicator of current and future poverty, will remain virtually unchanged in 2010 from the 1993 level of 140 million. On the other hand, if government policies continue as usual, that number would drop to 113 million children. But if governments become a little less complacent about agriculture and complete economic reforms as well, the number of malnourished children would drop sharply to 76 million, 65 million less than in the pessimistic scenario. South Asian children would suffer most from government complacency. (The publication cited at the end of this brief gives details about the assumptions made in the various scenarios.)

In two decades it is feasible to virtually eradicate poverty and child malnutrition according to the IMPACT model. But to do so, most of the poorest Asian economies would have to grow at rates close to the peaks experienced by the most dynamic economies in the region, agricultural productivity would have to reach the levels achieved during the heyday of the Green Revolution, and Asian governments would have to make significant new investments in agriculture and rural areas and spend 50 percent more annually on social programs. Although, realistically, South Asia would need to take a longer view, China and Southeast Asia could reasonably eradicate child malnutrition by 2020.

Conclusions

Asian policymakers on the threshold of the 21st century must make major decisions that could delay the completion of the economic transformation in rural areas or hasten it. Although the region's economy has hit a rough spot, governments must not turn away from a market orientation if they are to carry through the transformation. Rather, they should support the private sector where possible and supplement it where its growth is not sufficiently compatible with poverty alleviation and environmental improvement. Good governance is another key to sustained growth. Transparent and responsive governments must increase the level of investment made in rural infrastructure, agricultural research and extension, education, and health, and expand the reach of social safety-net programs. Some countries could meet a significant part of these costs by reducing wasteful public expenditures in rural areas, particularly on input and credit subsidies, and by improving the efficiency of public institutions. Natural resources should be better managed as well. Completion of the rural transformation, radical reduction in poverty, and improvement in food security in rural Asia are attainable if governments resist complacency.

PART 7

Microcredit for the Rural Poor

Chapter 30

Rural Financial Services for Poverty Alleviation

The Role of Public Policy

Manfred Zeller and Manohar Sharma

*Successful financial outreach to the rural poor requires
institutional innovations that reduce the risks and
costs of lending small amounts of money.*

For poor rural families in developing countries, access to credit and savings facilities such as banks has the potential to make the difference between grinding poverty and an economically secure life. Well-managed savings facilities permit households to build up funds for future investment or consumption. Credit enables them to tap finances beyond their own resources and take advantage of profitable investment opportunities. Farmers may invest in land or in new agricultural technology that will provide higher incomes, while rural households that do not own land can establish or expand family enterprises. Credit and savings also serve as insurance for the poor. In rural areas of developing countries, short-term loans or past savings are often used to provide basic necessities when household incomes decline temporarily—after a bad harvest or between agricultural seasons, for example.

But in most developing countries, rural financial services are sadly inadequate. In countries as diverse as Ghana, Malawi, and Pakistan, access to credit and savings facilities is severely limited for small farmers, tenants, and entrepreneurs, particularly women. In many countries only about half of the loan applicants can borrow an adequate amount at the going interest rate, either from formal institutions such as banks and cooperatives or from the informal sector—friends, relatives, pawnbrokers, and moneylenders. Those who want to borrow from the formal sector are usually deterred by the strict collateral requirements and high transaction costs frequently involved in doing business with formal institutions, including time spent in travel and doing paperwork. Many potential borrowers are in such need of credit that they are willing to pay substantially higher interest rates in the informal markets—sometimes as high as 80 percent per year. But the amount of credit available through informal markets is often constrained by bottlenecks in the local supply of funds. Even households with annual incomes well above the poverty line may experience difficulty in purchasing enough food during the preharvest season when previous food stocks have been depleted.

The story on the savings side is similar. Costs involved in making small deposits at faraway banks are high. Moreover, the transaction cost per dollar of deposit rises as the size of the deposit becomes smaller, discouraging farmers and rural entrepreneurs from making a series of tiny deposits, as they prefer to do. Many rural financial institutions choose not to accept deposits; others are legally forbidden to do so to protect depositors from fraud and for other reasons. Because most credit and savings programs still depend on the urban-based banking system for depositing their clients' savings and for channeling and disbursing loans, they usually are not able to reach out to locations far away from branches of state-owned or privately owned banks.

Traditional Institutions and the Rural Poor

As important as rural finances are, the task of providing credit and saving opportunities at a reasonable cost to those who have only meager assets has been neither straightforward nor easy. Until the 1980s, in many developing countries, state-run agricultural development banks—armed with subsidized funds and eloquent pro-poor directives—took the lead in establishing formal credit markets in rural areas. However, the shortcomings of the institutional principles they were based on—collateralized lending, an organizational setup without any incentives to do business with the poor, and pervasive political patronage—severely handicapped their performance. Not only did they fail to serve the poor who could not pledge collateral, but their inefficiency made them so dependent on state subsidies that they became financially unsustainable. Since then, support for state-sponsored agricultural banks has greatly declined, and the need for financial market reforms to rectify distortions caused by past policies is almost universally acknowledged.

Now, the most basic roles of government—establishing macroeconomic stability, ensuring that financial markets are free to respond to economic incentives while following sound banking practices, and maintaining and enforcing a legal framework that ensures contract compliance—are beyond dispute. However, these actions alone cannot trigger development of rural financial institutions that serve the poor. This is because rural financial markets have inherent problems that make investments risky as well as costly, and formal financial institutions have been unable to devise profitable savings and loan services for the rural poor. Information about potential borrowers, especially in far-flung areas, is difficult to obtain, making loan applications excessively costly to evaluate, especially when loans are small. The poor also own few assets, making it infeasible for the financial institution to secure its lending with collateral. As a result, private investors either shy away from the financial sector or limit their services to financial institutions in the urban economy, where information on prospective borrowers is less costly to obtain. IFPRI studies have found private commercial banks in most rural areas of developing countries conspicuous by their absence, except in a few high-potential, densely populated areas. For example, in the rural areas of Cameroon and Pakistan, less than 10 percent of loan transactions take place in the formal sector.

This is not to say that private-sector banks will not have a role in the rural financial sector in the future. Many countries such as Bangladesh, Madagascar, Malawi, and Nepal initiated serious financial reforms only in the second half of the 1980s. Therefore, it is too early to conclude that private banks, which are just now establishing themselves in urban areas, will not gradually expand their services to rural areas as these become more developed and prosperous.

Currently, though, it is the lenders in informal markets that provide the bulk of loans to the rural poor, according to IFPRI studies in Bangladesh, Egypt, Madagascar, and Pakistan. In all these countries, informal lenders make loans without collateral, using various techniques for screening applicants and enforcing repayment. In Bangladesh, Cameroon, Madagascar, Nepal, and Pakistan, for example, more than 90 percent of the loans are not secured by physical collateral. Households or even small communities may enter into mutually beneficial risk-pooling schemes; traders disburse credit to farmers in exchange for the right to market the growing crop; shopkeepers increase sales by providing credit for food, farm inputs, and household necessities; and large landholders secure access to labor in the peak season in return for earlier loan advances to laborers. In countries like Cameroon and Egypt, informal credit and savings associations play an important role in the provision of financial services. In fact, the ingenuity of informal lenders and self-help organizations in tailoring loan products to the requirements of their clients or members makes them indispensable in both the urban and rural financial landscape of developing countries.

But innovative and useful as the informal sector may be, it frequently runs up against severe constraints. Informal credit markets, by their very nature, are segmented. A "market" typically consists of a single village community. And informal lenders seldom manage savings deposits. Hence, financial intermediation in the sense of providing a common clearinghouse for borrowers and lenders does not take place to the fullest extent possible. As a result, the supply of credit is limited, resulting in either severe credit rationing or extremely high interest rates for some lenders. It is not surprising, therefore, that in all studies conducted by IFPRI, informal sector transactions are generally small, short-term loans taken to finance the purchase of urgently needed goods for household consumption—especially food—or, to a lesser extent, inputs such as seeds and fertilizer. In Bangladesh, for example, the average size of a loan in the informal sector was about US$15 taken for about three months. Invariably, when larger projects need to be financed, such as a new enterprise, an irrigation pump, or agricultural land, people turn to institutional lenders in the formal sector. Also, especially in agricultural regions, risks arising out of droughts or floods affect both informal lenders and borrowers simultaneously, so a credit supply crunch is likely to take place just when the demand for credit peaks.

Formal institutions offer several advantages in this respect. Banks usually have a network of branches across different regions of a country and are therefore in a better position to diversify risks. And when banks are allowed to collect savings deposits, they serve the needs of savers as well as borrowers. Formal institutions can also leverage funds in other financial markets such as the bond market. But, as already noted, only a relatively few borrowers have access to formal financial institutions.

Overall, it is clear that the task of delivering financial services to the rural poor cannot be left entirely to market forces.

The Promise of Innovative Institutions

Successful financial outreach to the rural poor requires institutional innovations that reduce the risks and costs of lending small amounts of money. So far, most innovations in microfinance have come from nongovernmental organizations (NGOs) that do not have commercial profit as their principal objective. By taking fresh approaches, these new microfinance institutions have penetrated rural financial markets and serviced an underclass of borrowers in a way that was unimaginable some 20 years ago. In 1988, IFPRI published one of the most detailed studies then available of the innovations in group-based banking introduced by the Grameen Bank of Bangladesh, which has provided credit to 2.1 million women in 36,000 villages. Since then, IFPRI has examined the experiences of other institutions, including member-owned village banks in Madagascar; other large-scale, group-based credit programs in Bangladesh and Malawi; and savings and credit cooperatives in Cameroon. These innovative microfinance institutions have provided financial services to the poor, increased their welfare, and often maintained impressive repayment rates.

Far from being one-shot transfers, loans from such institutions have helped poor families make permanent positive changes in the quality of their lives. In Bangladesh, Madagascar, and Malawi, IFPRI studies show that over time poor households participating in innovative credit programs have increased their household income more than nonparticipants have. In Pakistan, access to credit was associated with greater use of improved seed, fertilizer, and other inputs to enhance crop yields. And in Malawi, profits from nonfarm businesses funded by the special credit programs were reinvested in farms, through increased expenditures on improved seed and fertilizer. By boosting farm production and overall household income, these innovative institutions enabled poor households to acquire more and better food.

Of course, lack of capital is only one factor keeping poor rural households from improving their welfare. In rural areas of developing countries, illiteracy is high, basic social and market infrastructure is lacking, and many people are in poor health. When seed or irrigation water for the farmer, market access for the rural producer, or elementary bookkeeping skills for the would-be entrepreneur are absent, the returns to financial services will be low or sometimes even wasted. It is not a coincidence, then, that in several countries the most successful NGO institutions have operated in relatively well-endowed rural areas. In other cases, innovations have offered financial services in combination with other complementary services. For example, microfinance institutions such as the Bangladesh Rural Advancement Committee (BRAC) and the Grameen Bank combine credit services with basic literacy programs, training in enterprise management, and education in health and family planning. This bundling of services has, among other things, enabled these institutions to successfully penetrate into high poverty areas and to achieve repayment rates in excess of 95 percent.

Public Policy for the Future

It would be unwise to conclude that the new microfinance institutions such as the Grameen Bank have found the right formula and all that is needed now is replication. One lesson is becoming increasingly clear: there is no single blueprint for success. Recent experience has shown that programs must be designed to harness a community's particular strengths—based, for example, on local resources, historical and cultural experiences, ethnicity, and occupational patterns—in order to reduce costs of screening participants, monitoring financial activity, and enforcing contractual obligations. The group-based system has worked well in Bangladesh, whereas several programs in Indonesia successfully use local agents to assess borrowers' creditworthiness. Institutional design varies even for similar target groups within the same country. In Bangladesh, for example, the Association for Social Advancement and BRAC give loans to clients themselves, while Rangpur-Dinajpur Rural Services forms and trains groups, which then obtain agricultural loans from banks.

Designing, experimenting with, and building financial institutions for the poor require economic resources and adequate consideration of longer-term social returns. By itself, the market has not been able to stimulate much institutional innovation. In the last two decades, NGOs have taken the lead partly because the subsidies they receive from donors and government organizations make it feasible for them to invest in innovations. Just as public policy should play a role in promoting technological innovations that generate social benefits, it should also help promote institutional innovations that assist the disadvantaged or address intrinsic market failures. As policymakers seek to make rational policy choices, they must weigh the social costs of designing and building financial institutions for the poor against their social benefits. Well-directed support, including initial subsidies, to promising microfinance institutions is likely to have payoffs in both equity (services to the poor) and long-term efficiency (reduced cost of services). This is a point of view that those who argue for a complete removal of subsidies should not ignore.

Of course, some experiments in institutional innovations will succeed, while others will fail. Public policy will need to support and evaluate this experimentation process and nurture those designs or institutions that hold promise of future success. Governments, donors, practitioners, and research institutions must work together closely to pinpoint the costs, benefits, and future potential of emerging financial institutions.

In the long run, the payoff to public investment in institutional innovations will lie in the transformation of now nascent microfinance institutions into full-fledged, financial intermediaries that offer savings and credit services to smallholders, tenant farmers, and rural entrepreneurs, thus alleviating poverty. Evidence of this transformation is already emerging in countries such as Bangladesh, Indonesia, and Thailand. The payoff will also come from the development of viable lending methodologies that private commercial banks can readily adopt to profitably provide savings and loan services to the poor. This is already happening in some parts of the world: in urban Latin America, for example, private commercial banks have started to adopt group-based lending methods developed and tested by nonprofit organizations that initially depended on public support. With the right combination of public policy, private initiative, and objective research, public investments in financial institutions designed to serve the poor in other rural areas of Africa, Asia, and Latin America will bear fruit as well.

Chapter 31

Microfinance

Reaching Poor Rural Women

Manohar Sharma

Microfinance programs provide a handy, potentially cost-effective, and politically feasible tool for moving toward gender equality.

Promises and Ambiguities

Among financial institutions serving poor households around the world, microfinance programs have emerged as important players. These programs typically make small loans—sometimes as small as $50 to $100, and sometimes as large as several thousand dollars—to households lacking access to formal-sector banks. One important achievement of the microfinance movement has been its relative success in deliberately reaching out to poor women living in diverse socioeconomic environments. Of the nearly 90,000 village bank members worldwide that have received loans from the Foundation for International Community Assistance (FINCA), 95 percent are women. The Association for Social Advancement (ASA), one of the most prominent microfinance institutions in Bangladesh, has provided US$200 million exclusively to women borrowers. In Malawi, 95 percent of loans provided by the Malawi Muzdi Fund go to women borrowers. Since 1979, Women's World Banking has made more than 200,000 loans to low-income women around the world. Literally hundreds of similar examples can be found in Asia, Africa, and Latin America.

The premises behind such targeting are twofold: (1) that microfinance is an effective tool in improving women's status, and (2) that overall household welfare is likely to be higher when microfinance is provided to women rather than men. Women's status, household welfare, and microfinance interact in the following ways:

- A woman's status in a household is linked to how well she can enforce command over available resources. Increased ability to tap financial resources independently enhances her control, and, therefore, her influence in household decisionmaking processes.

- Newly financed microenterprises open up an important social platform for women to interact with markets and other social institutions outside the household, enabling them to gain useful knowledge and social capital. Many microfinance programs organize women into groups, not just to reduce transactions costs in credit delivery, but also to assist women in building and making effective use of these opportunities.

- Women's preferences regarding household business management and household consumption goals differ from men's, particularly in societies with severe gender bias. In such situations, placing additional resources in the hands of women is not a mere equalizer: it also materially affects both the quality of investments financed by the microfinance programs and how extra income is spent. IFPRI studies have underlined the importance of women's control of resources in achieving better welfare outcomes in food, nutrition, education, and other health statuses of children and their families.

- Women are thought to make better borrowers than men: timely repayment of loans is more likely to take place when women borrow. An IFPRI study in 1997, for example, shows that Bangladeshi groups with a higher proportion of women had significantly better repayment rates.

- Loans are not simple handouts. If microfinance programs are designed to cover all costs, a potential win-win situation emerges. Development goals related to women's empowerment and improved household welfare are self-financing and no subsidies are required.

Unfortunately, positive empowerment effects cannot be unconditionally guaranteed. In some male-dominated societies, men may use the agency of the woman to gain access to microfinance funds, diminishing women's role to being mere conduits of cash. Even if women can maintain autonomy in how they access and use microfinance services, their management of newly financed enterprises and shouldering of all attendant risks may alter interhousehold dynamics. Since loans have to be repaid even if the project fails, new activities may increase exposure to financial risks and may impose additional pressures on the already overburdened woman. Finally, in societies following the practice of female seclusion, the new pressures to interact in the marketplace may initially involve a difficult learning period and trigger negative responses. Project failures may lead to serious reprimand and additional negative sanctions against the woman, especially if household resources have to be diverted to repay outstanding debt.

Emerging Evidence

If the arguments presented thus far about the impact of microfinance on women's empowerment are ambiguous, then does empirical evidence resolve the ambiguities? While the record on outreach has been quite impressive, evidence on impact is not yet conclusive. Part of the problem is methodological. First, "empowerment" is not readily observable, necessitating the use of proxy indicators. Empowerment is most strongly manifested in the decisionmaking process; but when outcome variables—such as changes in income and education levels—are used as proxies, not much light is shed on either the decisionmaking dynamics or the mechanism of impact. Second, "empowerment" is a cultural and personal concept; the informant and the researcher may frequently have differing notions of what empowerment means and how it is expressed. Third, there is the perennial problem of bias arising out of self-selection in programs. If microfinance programs tend to attract already-empowered women, ignoring this fact will overestimate the empowerment effect. Similarly, an underestimate of the empowerment effect will result if programs attract or seek out relatively more oppressed women.

Despite these shortcomings, what does the empirical evidence on impact show? Much of the completed research on empowerment effects of microfinance comes from Bangladesh, where the campaign to use microfinance as a vehicle for women's empowerment has been most aggressively pursued. However, policymakers must be careful not to generalize findings from Bangladesh to other sociocultural settings.

The most widely cited series of studies on gender-differentiated impacts of microfinance, and one that takes special care to control for selection bias, was recently completed by the World Bank based on data collected during 1991–92 from 87 villages in Bangladesh. The study found that welfare impacts on the household were significantly better when borrowers were women. For every Bangladeshi taka lent to women, the increase in household consumption was 0.18 taka, compared to 0.11 taka when borrowers were men. Only when women borrowed was there a large and important effect on the nutritional status of both sons and daughters. Assets other than land also increased substantially when women borrowed—

but not when men borrowed. Similarly, it was only when women borrowed that education of girls (rather than just boys) increased. Men, on the other hand, tended to take more leisure as a result of borrowing.

Other studies have more directly attempted to assess impact on empowerment. One widely cited study that made special efforts to construct measures of empowerment incorporating client perspectives is based on a 1996 survey of 1,300 married Bangladeshi women members of the leading microfinance institutions, Grameen Bank and the Bangladesh Rural Advancement Committee (BRAC). The study found that married women participating in these credit programs scored higher than nonparticipating women on a number of empowerment indicators such as involvement in major family decisionmaking, participation in public action, physical mobility, political and legal awareness, and the ability to make small and large purchases. An IFPRI study in Bangladesh similarly indicated significant positive impacts on physical mobility of women and increased social interactions in the community.

However, empirical studies point out that positive gender effects cannot always be taken for granted. Many women, lacking skills and confidence, lean on their husbands to make use of their loans. A 1995 study in Bangladesh indicated that while 94 percent of Grameen Bank's borrowers are female, only 37 percent of them are able to exercise control over loan use. Another survey in Bangladesh in 1998 indicated that only 3 percent of the 150 women borrowers surveyed used the money on their own. The others gave it to their husbands or other male relatives. In fact, some conclude that women's lack of empowerment is what makes it easier for program managers to enforce loan conditions, therefore making women preferred borrowers. Microfinance institutions tend to downplay this plausible but not yet widely accepted conclusion.

Directions for the Future

This short review calls for a positive but cautionary assessment. Microfinance programs targeting women obviously have a strong potential to empower women whose daily lives are constrained by a pitiful lack of command over household and societal resources. Targeting does not mean simply requiring women to sign off on loan papers, since there is no automatic guarantee that this will allow women to retain control over the use of the loan. For the empowerment effect to be significant and lasting, financial products and institutional packages need to be tailored to the specific local preference and skill-base of women.

Hard-nosed market research is required to identify microenterprises in which women have a strong niche and stand to gain good financial returns. This will considerably reduce incentives for powerful male relatives to commandeer the newly available resource to their own benefit. Saving services should provide women the freedom to manage cash flow productively and safely. Women's property rights on the newly financed assets should be clearly established and enforced. The Grameen Bank in Bangladesh, for example, requires homes financed through their loans to be legally registered in the borrower's name.

Finally, the institutions used to draw women into microfinance programs have to respond to pre-existing social and cultural constraints. In Bangladesh, women's credit groups have been particularly successful in strengthening social capital and providing traditionally secluded women a non-intimidating and socially acceptable platform from which to learn and conduct business outside the house. They have also provided a critical launching pad for women to increase and exchange knowledge and assert themselves as visible and important partners in the community. Success in other sociocultural settings will require making equivalent adaptations. Innovations must also focus on reducing costs of service delivery to maintain the popular support that microfinance has so far received.

Ultimately, women's empowerment requires fundamental changes in society that call for more direct policy instruments. New policies should renegotiate property rights, replace rules sustaining gender inequality, and improve access to and quality of education. Fundamental change of this scale can hardly be worked out easily or quickly, especially in countries where gender bias has been a norm for centuries. Over the short run, microfinance programs provide a handy, potentially cost-effective, and politically feasible tool for moving toward gender equality. Group-based activities by women have served as important catalysts of change in Asia and Africa. The scale of change they ultimately catalyze will depend, however, on how seriously other social reforms bearing on women's empowerment are pursued.

PART 8

Gender and Education Issues: Women and Food Security

Chapter 32

Generating Food Security in the Year 2020

Women as Producers, Gatekeepers, and Shock Absorbers

Lynn R. Brown, Hilary Feldstein, Lawrence Haddad, Christine Peña, and Agnes Quisumbing

Women could achieve much more in food production, provision, and utilization if agricultural researchers, plant scientists, extension agents, and policymakers would level the agricultural playing field.

M eeting world food needs in the year 2020 will depend even more than it does now on the capabilities and resources of women. Women are responsible for generating food security for their families in many developing countries, particularly in Sub-Saharan Africa. Women not only process, purchase, and prepare food, but they also play a significant role in national agricultural production, producing both food and cash crops. Population growth, urbanization, and the limited potential for increasing production through the expansion of cultivated area imply that, for food needs to be met in the future, yields will have to increase. Agricultural research continues to develop new varieties with higher yields and increased tolerance to unfavorable environmental conditions, but an untapped source of productivity gains could lie in addressing gender disparities in agriculture. This brief examines the key roles that women play in maintaining the three pillars of food security—food production, food access, and food utilization—and it looks at how strengthening these pillars through policies that enhance women's abilities and resources provides a solution to meeting world food needs in the year 2020.

Women as Food Producers

The sustainable production of food is the first pillar of food security. Millions of women work as farmers, farm workers, and natural resource managers. In doing so they contribute to national agricultural output, maintenance of the environment, and family food security. Women account for 70 to 80 percent of household food production in Sub-Saharan Africa, 65 percent in Asia, and 45 percent in Latin America and the Caribbean. They achieve this despite unequal access to land, to inputs such as improved seeds and fertilizer, and to information.

Women farmers have shown that they can be experts in their own domain. For example, scientists at the Rwandan Agricultural Research Institute (ISAR) and the International Center for Tropical Agriculture (CIAT) in Colombia collaborated with local women farmers in an attempt to breed improved bean varieties. Formerly, the breeders' success at predicting the 2 or 3 bean varieties that displayed most potential under actual growing conditions resulted in mildly successful increases in bean productivity. In this collaboration, the women farmers were invited to examine more than 20 bean varieties at the research station and take home and grow the 2 or 3 they thought most promising. The selections of the women farmers substantially outperformed the selections of the bean breeders. Similar results have come from India and the Philippines, demonstrating that a vast reservoir of expert human capital remains largely untapped: few women are agricultural extension agents, and agricultural research and extension institutions rarely seek the expertise of local women farmers.

Studies that demonstrate lower yields from plots of land controlled by women than from those controlled by men may contribute to the idea that women lack farming expertise. Other studies, however, show that these lower yields are usually the result of lower use of labor and fertilizer per acre rather than managerial and technical inefficiency. Unequal rights and obligations within the household, as well as limited time and financial resources, pose a greater constraint to women. Given equal access to resources and human capital, women farmers can achieve equal or even, as some studies show, significantly higher yields than men. Including women in the evaluation of new technologies is an excellent way of efficiently diffusing technology since women are likely to share their knowledge with other women farmers, whereas male farmers are reluctant to impart such information to women.

Laws governing women's rights to land vary widely. Some religious laws forbid female landownership. Even when civil law gives women the right to inherit land, local custom may rule otherwise. In Sub-Saharan Africa, where women have prime responsibility for food production, they are generally limited to user (or usufruct) rights to land, and then only with the consent of a male relative. Women tend to be allocated poorer land, whose quality deteriorates even further as it is intensively cultivated. Some resettlement and irrigation projects have actually eroded women's rights to land by providing formal titles only to men. This insecurity of tenure reduces the likelihood that women will invest much time and many resources in usufruct land or adopt environmentally sustainable farming practices.

The weakness of women's land rights also results in an inability to use land as collateral to obtain access to credit, which is often critical to the timely purchase of productivity-enhancing inputs such as improved seed varieties and fertilizer. The absence of credit limits women's ability to adopt new technology, to hire labor when it is needed, to grow crops that require large outlays of cash up front, to purchase their own land where women do have legal rights to land, or to purchase capital goods. Yet, the evidence indicates that when women are able to overcome these constraints they are equally if not more likely than men to be innovators. In Zambia, a recent study found that wealthier farm households headed by females were more likely than households headed by males to adopt improved maize varieties.

Agricultural extension agents are a critically important source of information for women farmers, given that women generally have lower levels of education than men. Yet in 1988 the United Nations Environment Programme reported that less than 1 percent of government-employed agricultural advisers in Asia and the Middle East are women. The corresponding figures for Africa and Latin America are 3.0 percent and 8.5 percent respectively. Even in Sub-Saharan Africa, despite the long tradition of female farming, male farmers have far greater contact with extension services. Employing female agricultural extension workers is particularly important in societies that forbid the interaction of female farmers with male agricultural extension agents. But employing female agents is not sufficient. They must be trained in agricultural subjects rather than home economics, so that they can deliver agricultural extension messages effectively.

Women as Gatekeepers

The second pillar of food security is making sure that household members, particularly the children, receive an adequate share of the food that is potentially available. Women act as the "gatekeepers" of their households' food security through the allocation of their own time and income.

Real income is one of the key determinants of household food consumption. However, a growing number of studies now suggest that it is not simply the level of household income but who earns that income that influences food security. Evidence suggests that men spend a higher proportion of their incremental income on goods for their personal consumption. By contrast, women are more likely to purchase goods for their children and for general household consumption.

An increasing body of evidence from Asia, Africa, and Latin America confirms the positive impact of female control of income on household food expenditure, calorie intake, and anthropometric indicators. At similar levels of overall income, households where women control a larger share of income are more likely to meet calorie requirements. One of the most careful studies of this issue finds that the positive effect on the probability that a child will survive in urban Brazil is almost 20 times greater when certain income sources accrue to women rather than men.

Given the positive nutritional outcomes associated with increasing women's incomes, the growing percentage of female-headed households is a cause for concern, for recent evidence suggests that women are overrepresented among the poor. Poverty is a major threat to the food security both of the family and of particular individuals within the family, and the combination of poverty and gender inequality is an even greater one. Lower levels of education and other resources can severely limit earning potential for the growing number of women who are the sole income earners for their families.

The third pillar of food security—food utilization—means ensuring that the food consumed contributes to good physical and cognitive development. This entails the provision of "care," namely, paying adequate time and attention to meeting the physical, mental, and social needs of growing children and other household members. Care affects food security in two broad ways: first, through feeding practices such as breast-feeding and the preparation of nutritious foods for weaned infants and others in the family, and second, through health and hygiene practices such as the bathing of children and the washing of hands before food preparation. These caring behaviors are time-intensive. Given women's roles in agricultural production, domestic production, and reproduction, women in developing countries are relatively short of time, compared with men. The time constraint is especially acute for female heads of households.

In addition, in many regions of the world, women spend up to five hours a day collecting fuelwood and water and up to four hours a day preparing food. This does not leave much time for child care. Indeed, the rapid pace of urbanization and increased female participation in the labor force imply even greater demands on women's time. Women turn to processed foods and "street foods" to save time. Development of technology that relieves women's time burdens in agricultural production and household maintenance without sacrificing their ability to earn independent incomes is therefore critical.

Women as Shock Absorbers

During times of economic hardship, it is assumed (often by women themselves) that women will act to absorb shocks to household welfare by expanding their already tightly stretched working day. This behavior stems from an undervaluation of women's time (by both men and women), due in large part to the invisibility of women's economic contribution inside and outside the home. Even when women participate in the labor force, it is often assumed that they are secondary income earners. Yet this additional income is important, and is the only income source for female heads of households. A less well documented observation is that women may act as shock absorbers through the liquidation of their own nutritional status. Studies of the seasonality of maternal and preschooler nutrition status have shown that in times of food surplus women's nutrition status returns to normal more quickly than that of preschoolers, but in the lean season female nutrition status is depleted more rapidly than that of preschoolers. Policymakers need to establish safety nets to protect vulnerable groups—the poor, women, and children—from income shocks.

Conclusions

Women are major contributors to agriculture and play a prime role in ensuring the food security and nutrition status of their household members. Yet women could achieve much more in food production, provision, and utilization if agricultural researchers, plant scientists, extension agents, and policymakers would level the agricultural playing field. Women face an uphill struggle as a result of weak land tenure rights; exclusion from an active role in seed development and selection; neglect by agricultural extension services; and barriers to access to complementary inputs such as fertilizer, improved seeds, and credit. These impediments are likely to result in forgone economic growth through lower crop yields, delayed adoption of new technology and plant varieties, and environmental degradation.

Reductions in asymmetries between men and women in access to agricultural and other resources, the use of women's expertise in the early evaluation of new technologies, and the development of technologies that relieve women's time constraints are essential if the three pillars of household and national food security are to be strengthened by the year 2020.

Chapter 33

Urban Women

Balancing Work and Childcare

Patrice L. Engle

*Urban women now are more likely to work for
income when their children are very young and to stay
in the labor force longer than they previously did.*

As the urban population in all developing regions grows over the next 20 years, governments and families will face unique challenges in their efforts to ensure the well-being of millions of children. They will have to take into account changes in women's roles, in strategies for childcare, and in the means of obtaining food security. All these changes will have major implications for the livelihoods of people residing in the new urban megacities.

Extent of Labor-Force Participation

Many studies in developing countries show that women contribute as much or more than men do to family food security and children's nutritional status when unpaid work is included in the estimation. Nowadays more women also work for income than ever before. Globally women's rates of participation in the labor force were 54 percent in 1950 and 66 percent in 1990 and are projected to reach almost 70 percent in 2010. Urban women now are more likely to work for income when their children are very young and to stay in the labor force longer than they previously did. Worldwide they enter the labor market at high rates in their 20s, increase labor force participation through their 30s and 40s, and leave work only after age 50.

The percent of households that rely on women's financial contribution for food security is also increasing. Women provide the main source of income in more than

20 percent of households in Latin America, Sub-Saharan Africa, and most of Asia. Even in dual-parent families, women are contributing a higher percentage of income than before.

The forces that have increased women's labor force participation—urbanization and globalization—have pulled women into jobs that are of lower quality (low-skilled jobs with no security or protection), part-time, home-based, or all of these. More than 80 percent of women work in largely gender-segregated occupations, and women on average still earn less than 70 percent of what men earn. Since women are in lower-skilled and temporary jobs, they are more likely to lose jobs than are men during financial crises. Women also still lag far behind men in having the skills to handle new technologies, making them less likely to get higher-paying jobs that require these skills.

Consequences of Labor-Force Participation

Urban residence can have mixed consequences for women and children. On the one hand, women workers in an urban economy can potentially earn a higher percentage of the family income. Since percentage of income earned has been shown to relate to decisionmaking in the family, these women might be less tied to traditional restrictions, such as food taboos during pregnancy. According to a recent United Nations study, urban women also have fewer children, and they and their children are much more likely to be literate than rural women and theirs. Services such as family planning may be more available in urban areas, and women's increased independence may lead to higher self-esteem and recognition of rights.

On the other hand, urban women who work may be more vulnerable to violence and harassment at the workplace than rural women and may be forced into informal work such as street vending that offers few protections. Many women with little income must raise their children surrounded by the inadequate infrastructure of urban slums. For new migrants to urban squatter settlements, support systems may be weak, leading to stress and family dysfunction. Poor or sporadic job opportunities for men, as well as the need to obtain food with cash, may result in a decline in male support for families and less food security.

Women are now much more likely to work when their children are under 12 months old, a period of time when children have the greatest need of intensive care for good growth and development. Workers in the formal sector, for example, are limited to 12 weeks of maternity leave in most countries, even though about 6 months of exclusive breastfeeding is recommended. For women working in the informal sector, any leave at all is taken at the risk of losing income and job opportunities.

Although in some countries working mothers breastfeed less, work itself does not necessarily limit breastfeeding, nor does mothers' work seem to affect children's nutritional status in some developing countries. In two studies in urban Latin America, income earned by the mother when the child was at least 12 months of age was positively associated with the child's nutritional status when income levels were controlled for. Women's income had a stronger positive association with children's nutrition than men's income. However, when women did not have the power to decide how to spend their income on children, wage work led to negative effects on children's nutritional status.

Adequate childcare is essential for working mothers. In urban Ghana, women's strategies for providing childcare were more important for children's nutritional status than family income. In urban Guatemala, maternal employment did not increase children's chances of malnutrition unless they were cared for by a preteen. Work at home, however, often considered to be a positive option, has been associated with poorer nutritional status for children if demands of the work are intense and time-bound (for example, piecework).

In sum, when mothers are poor—with time-intensive, low-paid, and inflexible work; no control over earnings; and no good alternative caregivers—infants are at risk of poor growth. Some women who work during their child's first year of life have no other sources of support. For these women, work is a survival strategy; the alternative is starvation for mother and child.

Current Limits of Childcare

Day care in the urban slums of developing countries, particularly for children under three, is usually woefully inadequate in coverage and quality. The most common day-care centers are run by governments or private voluntary organizations. These centers are likely to be attended only by children over three and have extremely limited coverage because of the large investment needed in buildings and equipment. Yet childcare is clearly necessary. United Nations data from 23 countries in Africa, Asia, and Latin America show that a majority of working women with children under five work away from home.

Some innovative approaches to childcare include family day-care homes, in which one mother watches five or six neighbor children in her home; or mobile crèches, which involve childcare facilities set up near the employment site of working mothers. In lieu of day-care options, families use older female siblings (much more than male siblings), thus keeping girls out of school; other family members; and neighbors. There are cases of families resorting to drastic strategies, such as giving children a dose of opium so that they will sleep during the day.

Improving Working Mothers' Ability to Provide Care

More women will work for earnings in the next 20 years, particularly when their children are young. Although the smaller family sizes associated with urbanization should decrease the time needed for childcare, this may turn out not to be the case. Many urban parents will want their children to be schooled in order to attain the best opportunities for a successful life. The consequent focus on developing children's language and social skills may increase rather than decrease time commitments for care.

Three factors have been shown to reduce the negative effects of maternal work on young children: helping mothers not to work when their children are very young, providing an adequate wage rate and flexible working hours, and providing reasonable alternative childcare. Ensuring these will be necessary for the health and well-being of an urbanizing society.

Policies are also needed that provide women protection against returning to work too soon after giving birth. Maternity protection legislation is woefully inadequate. Whereas 192 countries have ratified the Convention on the Rights of the Child, only 38 have ratified the International Labour Organization's 1952 Maternity Protection Convention. Even if signed, the latter's provisions apply to only a small proportion of the population.

Cultural and social attitudes also need to reflect women's equality in the work force. For example, although girls are attending school at much higher rates and are performing as well as or better than boys in many countries, these gains have not been translated into correspondingly equal employment and training opportunities, according to the International Labour Organization's 1999 World Employment Report.

Policies can go a long way toward improving women's income by, for example, implementing gender-blind minimum wage rates, organizing informal or self-employed labor, and supporting urban development projects. To improve outcomes for children, governments can legalize squatter settlements after a period of time to allow people living in them access to services, and they can invest in health, day care, and infrastructure. Training women for skilled jobs is also a key component for raising incomes and thereby improving child health. Outside pressures, such as the Beijing Conference on Women, and efforts of United Nations and bilateral agencies, can help, but sustained efforts are needed within countries to implement and monitor good policies.

Caring adequately for urban children will be essential for their nutritional status and the health of urban society. Providing alternative childcare means that women's work in childcare, which was traditionally unpaid, must now be paid for. Model urban programs, such as Child Friendly Cities Programs, do invest in childcare for working women, but these efforts are not enough. Innovative approaches are needed to provide good childcare, especially for the youngest age group. These approaches must rely on partnerships between employers, workers, and government to provide adequate care. Innovative strategies could include support for parental childcare cooperatives, social insurance to enable mothers or fathers to stay home after the birth of a child, childcare linked to schools, and even the involvement of elders in childcare. Good childcare is not cheap, but the investments made at this age are perhaps the most important for the next generation and for working women themselves.

Chapter 34

The Fruits of Girls' Education

Reported by Heidi Fritschel and Uday Mohan

*"Educating girls yields a higher rate of return than any
other investment available in the developing world."*
—*Lawrence Summers*

For millions of women around the globe, lack of education is a handicap for which they pay a heavy price. Some 565 million women are illiterate, mainly in poor rural areas. These women cannot sign their names, decipher simple instructions, or fill out an application form. Their lack of education limits their ability to earn money and get credit, to participate in decisionmaking in their families and communities, to delay childbearing, and to offer their children the best life chances. The failure to educate these women when they were girls is the result of a range of factors, including the need for girls' labor in the home, attitudes that devalue education for girls, fears about girls' security outside the home, and lack of resources to pay for education.

Research has shown that educating girls offers a multitude of benefits for girls themselves, their current and future families, and their societies. Many of the benefits of educating girls are the same as those of educating boys: education helps create more productive workers and thereby improves income equity. It helps people participate more meaningfully in political and civic life. It improves overall economic growth and leads to greater care of the environment. And it helps people adapt to the demands of globalization and to shape it. Other benefits are particular to educating girls, such as the improvements in quality of life both for educated girls and for their future children. In 1992, Lawrence Summers, then vice president and chief economist of the World Bank and now U.S. treasury secretary, said, "When one takes into account all its benefits, educating girls yields a higher rate of return than any other investment available in the developing world."

The barriers to girls' education, however, are complex and persistent. Although national governments, local communities, and development organizations around the world now recognize the need to educate girls and are implementing programs for doing so, 73 million girls of primary school age are still without access to basic education, according to the United Nations Children's Fund (UNICEF). But if the world is to make a sizable dent in poverty and hunger in the next two decades, getting these girls into school will clearly have to be part of the equation.

Education for a Better Life

Evidence is irrefutable that education improves girls' own lives now and in the future. "Women understand this quite acutely themselves," says Michelle Adato, a research fellow at IFPRI who has examined the effects of a Mexican antipoverty program that gives cash and in-kind benefits to poor rural mothers whose children attend school and visit health clinics. "Rural Mexican women we interviewed emphasized the importance of girls' education. Most of them stated that it led to some or better employment. Others simply said that education led to a better life. And still others told us that it enabled girls and women to improve their standing in relationships, that it allowed them to better defend themselves and to take care of themselves and their children if their marriage did not work out." Here, for example, is how one rural woman put it: "In my case I didn't study, so I didn't know anything. If I had a daughter, I would say it would be better for her to study so she wouldn't be the same as I was."

One of the strongest nonmarket effects of girls' education—one that nonetheless reverberates across households and national economies—is the reduction in fertility. Better-educated females marry later and have fewer unwanted pregnancies. And their higher earning power may lower the number of children parents want as income earners. Moreover, educated females reduce the infant mortality rate through better childcare, thus reducing the number of replacement babies they have. A 1992 World Bank paper showed that one additional year of female education reduces fertility by 5 to 10 percent.

"Educating boys does not have noticeable effects on fertility rates," says Beryl Levinger, senior director for global learning at the U.S.-based Education Development Center and distinguished professor at the Monterey Institute of International Studies. "Schooling for girls, on the other hand, is a potent population intervention. And these girls will pass down what they learn to their children.

The policy some countries have of expelling pregnant girls from school is extremely counterproductive."

A dramatic example of reduced fertility is provided by a girls' education project in rural Zimbabwe run by the Cambridge Female Education Trust (CamFed). Ann Cotton, CamFed's executive director, says that only 5 percent of the 387 girls who graduated from secondary school with the help of CamFed became mothers between the ages of 18 and 24. This represents a sharp turn away from the national average of 47 percent of girls aged 20–24, many of them with little education, who gave birth by the time they turned 20. "The social safety net we provide, in conjunction with the community committees that we've helped set up, provide the vital support a girl may need to complete the education she desires," says Cotton. "The value of education is so strong that girls do want to continue it if they are given the chance. Moreover, they want to secure their economic situation before starting a family," she adds. There are now 79 growing businesses run by young women in the CamFed project areas in rural Zimbabwe, where there were none before.

The income-earning benefits that girls' education confers can hardly be in dispute. But its advantages relative to other means of acquiring wealth are less well known. A study by Agnes Quisumbing, a senior IFPRI research fellow, and two colleagues from Tokyo Metropolitan University shows that of the two key means of transferring wealth to the next generation in the Philippines—bequeathing land and investing in schooling—the latter carries far larger effects. "We found that sons inherit 0.19 hectare of land more than daughters, on average, while daughters stay in school for 1.5 years more than sons. Because of higher rates of return to education in nonfarm jobs, the average additional lifetime income of daughters is 10 to 100 percent higher than the additional lifetime income of sons. For other countries this finding implies that as jobs and wages for women increase, parents may close the education gap and invest more in their daughters' education."

According to a recent World Bank study by David Dollar and Roberta Gatti, closing the education gap would help not only women, their families, and their communities, but also the economies of the countries they live in. They report that "girls' access to education creates a better environment for economic growth and that the result is particularly strong for middle-income countries. Thus, societies that have a preference for not investing in girls pay a price for it in terms of slower growth and reduced income."

Girls' education also has effects that cannot be quantified but are powerful nonetheless. It can transform consciousness, not only of women but of men as well. Peggy McIntosh, associate director of the Center for Research on Women at Wellesley College, says that as girls get educated they begin to see themselves as decisionmakers beyond the household and as carriers and makers of knowledge. A whole new political, social, and economic narrative comes into view. "And boys," says McIntosh, "are better for it because they begin to take girls seriously."

A Boon for the Next Generation

Besides improving the lives of girls themselves, education makes them better caregivers when they have children of their own. A forthcoming 2020 Vision discussion paper by IFPRI researchers Lisa Smith and Lawrence Haddad examines the factors contributing to reduced child malnutrition in 63 developing countries. They found that female education was by far the most important reason why child malnutrition decreased by 15.5 percent between 1970 and 1995—much more important than, for instance, improved health environments or food availability.

"The fundamental importance of female education for raising children's nutrition levels is beyond question," says Haddad. "Partly because a mother uses her new knowledge and the additional income she earns from it to improve diets, care, and sanitation for her children, female education is probably the strongest instrument we have for reducing infant mortality and child malnutrition." Indeed, the 1993 World Development Report notes that a 10 percent increase in female literacy reduced child mortality by the same amount in 13 African countries between 1975 and 1985. An increase in male literacy had little effect. The report also notes that infant mortality drops with more maternal schooling. In the late 1980s in Peru, for example, 4–6 years of maternal schooling reduced the risk of infant mortality by almost 40 percent; 7 or more years reduced it by 75 percent.

Growing evidence shows that girls' education also leads to better education for their future children. "Children of educated mothers," says John Hoddinott, an IFPRI research fellow, "do better in school because children are healthier, mothers can help them with their homework, educated mothers can be role models, especially for girls, and mothers may be less intimidated by their children's teachers, so if a teacher says, 'Your child won't amount to anything,' the mother is more likely to argue back."

A recent study by Jere Behrman, professor of economics at the University of Pennsylvania, and his colleagues shows that children of literate mothers in rural India spent 1.8 hours more a day on their studies than similar children of illiterate mothers. "The data also show," says Behrman, "that in rural India a woman's dowry is almost three-fourths lower if she has a few years of education, probably because her prospective husband thinks she will participate more in the education of their children."

What Keeps Girls out of School?

Evidence on the benefits of girls' education is overwhelming. So why are so many girls still not being educated? The obstacles are many and complex. Some are common to many different geographic areas, while others are specific to a particular country or village.

Parents often perceive that education is not as necessary for their daughters as for their sons. According to Sudhanshu Handa, an IFPRI research fellow who has studied education issues in Mozambique and Mexico, "Parents may say, 'Girls are going to stay home, so there's no point in educating them.'"

The positive link between mothers' education and children's health and well-being may not be obvious to parents. May Rihani of the Academy for Educational Development, who is now in charge of AED's girls' education programs in Pakistan, India, Guinea, and Mali, recalls a community meeting in Mali where she was explaining that educated mothers tend to have healthier children. She was soon challenged by a man from the village. "He said, outraged, 'Do you mean to say that uneducated women love their children less than educated women?' 'You're right,' I said, 'it has nothing to do with love. It has to do with mothers' ability to read and write. Educated mothers can, for example, read instructions on medications.' He said, 'If what you are saying is right, we may have to think about that.'"

A perceived lack of job opportunities for women may also keep parents from sending their daughters to school. But the logic about keeping girls out of school can become a vicious circle: girls do not get educated because there is a lack of wage-earning opportunities for women, and women who are uneducated cannot get wage-earning employment. Parents may also perceive that their sons will be the ones to support them in their old age and that any economic gain that results from educating a girl will go to her future husband and his family.

Handa's work shows that in rural areas in particular, lack of education among parents is a sizable obstacle, for parents' decisions about whether to educate girls often depends on their own education levels. "In Mozambique, the difference in boys' and girls' enrollment rates is much less in urban areas—something that is true for most countries. That's because in urban areas parental education is higher, and there are more job opportunities for women and girls."

Security is another big concern of parents. In rural areas, schools can be far from home. "If a girl has to walk a long way to school, parents don't want that for security reasons," says Rihani. "Parents don't want girls walking home in seasons when school continues until dark. If these conditions are not dealt with, girls' education won't happen."

Inadequate school facilities can also keep girls away. "Some school facilities can actually make it difficult for girls to go to school," says Levinger. "For example, when a girl reaches puberty and there are no sanitary facilities, that becomes a problem. Also, the presence or absence of facilities to care for siblings can affect girls' attendance, because they often take care of their siblings."

In Pakistan, says Rihani, it is taboo for male teachers to instruct girls, but female teachers are hard to find. "For girls, mingling with men and boys is unacceptable," she explains. "There are government schools for girls and these have women teachers, but they are too few to serve everyone. And if a school is in a remote area, it is hard to get female teachers because there isn't a big pool of educated women." To overcome this situation, leaders of a project in Pakistan decided to recruit less-educated women to teach in remote rural schools. "One of our biggest successes," says Rihani, "was convincing the government that the criteria for teachers in this project could be different and that attendance and quality wouldn't suffer."

The cost of educating girls is a deterrent to many families. Even when schooling itself is free, other costs may arise. In Pakistan, government books are free, but families may have to travel some distance to pick them up, thereby incurring transportation costs, explains Rihani. In other areas, the loss of the girl's time is counted as a significant cost. Families often rely on girls to help care for younger siblings and perform other household chores and even, in some cases, to earn income. They simply cannot afford to lose the household labor that girls represent.

Chipping Away at the Barriers

Although the barriers to girls' education may be many and complex, they are not insurmountable. The cultural and economic barriers will probably continue to weaken as economies grow, priorities get reordered, and cultures come under pressure to adapt to new realities. Knowledge about the benefits of educating girls may also help transform attitudes and priorities.

Countries worldwide are overcoming education barriers for girls by developing innovative programs that lower costs, offer stipends, involve communities in identifying problems, and building infrastructure. Mexico's PROGRESA program, for instance, gives families higher cash payments for girls in secondary school than for boys.

To get girls into school, Malawi has eliminated school tuition fees for girls (and later for boys as well), and relaxed the requirement that girls wear uniforms to school. And to spread the message about the importance of girls' education, they borrowed a technique first used in Latin America: "social mobilization" through theater performances designed to initiate dialog at the village level. University drama and music students travel to Malawian communities, where they listen to villagers and then perform skits on the role of girls in the community. The skits address fears and expectations regarding girls' schooling and stimulate discussion on how to help girls become educated.

Surveys show that pregnancy is the most common reason girls drop out of school in Malawi. So in 1993 the country changed its policies to allow girls to resume their education after giving birth. According to John Hatch of the U.S. Agency for International Development's Girls' and Women's Education Project,

"Girls return to school after one year. The girls do go to a different school from the one they attended before, and they must show that the child is being well cared for."

Ironically, successful campaigns to increase enrollment can exacerbate another problem faced by many developing countries: overcrowded schools. Colombia is confronting the problem by offering poor children vouchers they can use to enroll in private schools. "The government could build more public schools," says Elizabeth King, principal economist at the World Bank, "but there's already excess capacity in the private schools, so they're using that capacity." The vouchers have had a greater effect on girls' enrollment than on boys', she points out, because "girls' enrollment is more sensitive to price."

In Guinea, a national effort to raise girls' enrollment helps local communities identify constraints and seek solutions. In one remote northern village, for example, girls who completed primary school had to go to a school in Mali to continue their studies, according to Aly Badara Doukoure, the girls' education administrator of Guinea. "This was very difficult for them. In 1998 the community identified having a school nearby as a solution, and now, in 1999, they have already built a three-classroom school for their girls," says Doukoure. Similarly, another village identified the expense and inconvenience of procuring school materials as a barrier to girls' education. "So they set up a community store where all families can buy school materials at a reduced price," Doukoure says.

Bangladesh has also made a massive push to educate more girls. Part of the government's strategy is to offer girls a stipend for secondary schooling, in the hope that this will lead to increased enrollment in primary school. Bangladesh also benefits from a well-known partnership with the Bangladesh Rural Advancement Committee. BRAC, a nongovernmental organization (NGO), runs some 30,000 primary schools serving about 900,000 students. The BRAC schools aim to have each school made up of at least 75 percent girls. These schools, which have longer school years and lower student-teacher ratios than public schools, attract many girls who have either dropped out of public school or never attended.

Government Cannot Go It Alone

In most developing countries, the task of getting girls into school, especially poor girls in rural areas, is simply too large for government to accomplish alone. Partnerships between governments, communities, donors, businesses, and NGOs appear to be the solution. Support from these partners for girls' education may be financial, in-kind services, or just leadership, expertise, and time. "In Morocco, NGOs successfully petitioned for funds to make improvements to schools that communities had identified as necessary to attract and keep girls, and local businesspeople have helped with the improvements," says Hatch. "Peru and Guatemala have had good interest and support from business groups. In some communities, religious organizations have set up babysitting co-ops for younger siblings of students so that girls can attend school. In Guinea parent groups monitor attendance of both students and teachers."

"We're trying to make a revolutionary change in how people think about education," says Rihani. "We want to change the idea that education can be offered as a service only if the government offers it. The private sector can also do it. The community can do it. They can build a school and pay a teacher."

Obviously, the moral imperative that sees education as a critical individual and public good extends to everyone, including girls. Besides this moral rationale, the economic and social benefits offer convincing arguments in favor of stepping up efforts to educate all girls. Few development investments can match the overwhelming evidence on the returns to girls' education, yet too few resources are still being devoted to this effort. In a recent report called Education Now, Oxfam calculates the additional cost of universal primary education worldwide as $8 billion per year for 10 years—the equivalent of four days' worth of global military spending. By paying this relatively small price now, governments, communities, and their partners can lay the groundwork for rewards that will extend into the future for many generations.

PART 9

What Will Globalization Bring?

Chapter 35

Globalization, Trade Reform, and the Developing Countries

Eugenio Díaz-Bonilla and Sherman Robinson

*Globalization, particularly trade expansion and
capital flows, offers new opportunities but also
raises new challenges for developing countries.*

Since the first round of trade negotiations under the General Agreement on
Tariffs and Trade (GATT) after World War II, multilateral trade liberalization has progressed at a fairly steady pace, mostly among the developed countries. But the Millennium Round of trade negotiations, if it proceeds, will look
somewhat different. Of the 134 members of the World Trade Organization (WTO)
in February 1999, some 70 percent are developing countries. This growing developing-country involvement in the WTO, as well as in regional trading blocs and
other trade arrangements, represents a distinct break with the past.

While there were relatively few developing-country members of GATT, they
did take a more active role in the Uruguay Round of negotiations (which were completed in 1993) than they had in earlier rounds. This round saw some substantive
progress toward adoption of issues of importance to developing countries. One such
area was agriculture, where the Uruguay Round established a new framework for
international trade rules encompassing export subsidies, domestic subsidies, and
market access, while related agreements covered other issues of importance for agricultural production such as sanitary and phytosanitary measures.

Still, recognizing that the new rules agreed upon were only the beginning of
the reform process, the participating countries decided to resume the negotiations
in the year 1999. Therefore, with or without a Millennium Round, agricultural
negotiations will recommence sometime at the end of this year.

This essay looks at the evolution of agricultural markets leading to the Uruguay Round negotiations and places them in the context of an increasingly global world economy, focusing on developing countries. The essay then considers, also from the perspective of the developing countries, several issues that are likely to arise in the coming negotiations.

Moving toward a Global Economy

The Forces of Globalization

Globalization refers mainly to the recent trends toward stronger economic, political, and cultural ties among many of the world's nations. One of its most important manifestations is the expansion of international trade, but it also encompasses increased international flows of capital, technology, and labor around the world, along with tendencies toward universal application of some institutional, legal, political, and cultural practices.

Within that context, some developing countries have had a strong growth performance, while others have fallen behind, both relative to other countries and, in some unfortunate cases, in absolute terms. Increased participation by countries in global markets has also been uneven. The expansion of trade has been driven by a number of forces that have affected developed and developing countries in different ways. An important factor has been the progressive dismantling of trade barriers for goods and services between countries through both successive rounds of GATT negotiations and unilateral liberalization in many countries.

A separate influence has been rapid technological change. Investment in transportation, communications, and information processing systems has skyrocketed. Major changes in production technology in many sectors, combined with improved transportation and communications, have allowed producers to separate stages of the production process geographically, sending raw materials far away from where they are grown to be processed and packaged. Producers can also pursue economies of scale and specialize by making large quantities of a single item to be sold throughout the world. Within manufacturing, the process of specialization has accelerated trade in the components that go into finished products. While these trends have been most evident in developed countries, a number of semi-industrial countries have participated and benefited from growth based on increased trade in manufactures. The early pioneers, such as the Asian "gang of four" (Hong Kong, Korea, Singapore, and Taiwan), achieved spectacular growth during the 1970s and 1980s. Following the lead of the Asian countries, many developing countries have shifted from inward-looking to outward-oriented development strategies, deepening their links to world markets.

Yet globalization involves more than just commodity markets. Increasing integration of world capital markets has greatly expanded international flows of both short-term and long-term private financial capital, with important effects on investment and growth. However, the poorest countries, with undeveloped capital markets and high risk premiums, have largely been left out of this growing international financial market. Also, some countries, as a consequence of global economic developments beyond their control as well as inappropriate domestic policies, have faced damaging episodes of macroeconomic instability, requiring "structural adjustment" to restore growth and stability.

Globalization of world financial markets has also led to problems. The recent Asian financial crisis revealed weaknesses in both the international financial system and the financial systems of a number of developing countries. Many developing countries are simply unable to absorb or efficiently manage the kinds of large short-term capital flows that have become more common.

Globalization, particularly trade expansion and capital flows, offers new opportunities but also raises new challenges for developing countries. As they approach the Millennium Round, these countries should evaluate their current development strategies and domestic macroeconomic policies, as well as their stance at the negotiating table, in order to gain the greatest benefits from the new global economy.

Changing Agricultural Markets

In addition to the obvious influences of population, weather, and wars, growth in world agricultural production and trade in the postwar era has been affected by changes in three main areas: macroeconomic policies, trade and agricultural policies, and technology.

At the macroeconomic level, expansionary monetary and fiscal policies during the 1960s and 1970s led to faster economic growth, but also eventually to higher inflation and negative real interest rates, which hurt growth. The macroeconomic environment changed radically during the 1980s, when tight monetary policies lowered real growth and inflation rates and turned real interest rates strongly positive for the entire decade. By the second half of the 1990s, inflation had fallen to levels similar to the 1960s. What has been labeled the "rise and fall of inflation" had an important impact on agriculture. In the 1970s high real commodity prices combined with negative real interest rates led farmers to expand their productive capacity, but prices fell steeply in the 1980s when macroeconomic policies were changed and farmers faced weak demand for their expanded supplies of agricultural goods.

Second, trade and agricultural policies in different countries and regions have gone through dramatic changes in recent decades. The Soviet Union went from being an important component of world demand in agricultural markets since the mid-1970s to collapsing as a political entity by the end of the 1980s. China sizably increased its agricultural production thanks to sweeping policy changes instituted at the end of the 1970s that emphasized decentralization and price incentives for farmers. The European Union (EU), driven by large production and export subsidies under the Common Agricultural Policy (CAP), moved from being a net importer of grains, meat, and sugar in the 1960s and 1970s to becoming a net exporter. Also, the United States pursued farm support policies that led to large surpluses in production and increased exports, some of which were sold with subsidies in world markets starting in the mid-1980s.

A variety of developing and emerging economies have shifted from inward-oriented development strategies in the 1960s and 1970s to greater reliance on free markets and international trade, particularly since the late 1980s. These new strategies have led policymakers to undertake major domestic agricultural policy reforms. In the past, IFPRI research found that a combination of overvalued exchange rates, protection of domestic industry, and explicit taxation of agricultural exports led to economic biases against agriculture, especially in very poor countries in Africa. After the policy changes of recent years, research at IFPRI and elsewhere suggests that such reforms have greatly reduced and in some cases eliminated the bias against agriculture in many developing countries. Although further improvements in domestic trade and macroeconomic policies are still needed in various developing countries, the reforms already undertaken provide a better framework for traditional investment policies and projects in the agricultural sector, focusing on human capital, land, water, property rights, management, technology, and infrastructure. These agricultural policies had been largely abandoned during the period when redirection of the overall macroeconomic and trade framework appeared central.

Third, changes in agricultural technology, such as mechanization, use of chemicals, and improvements in biology, have been continuous, as the Green Revolution emerged and spread in developing countries. The development of new seeds and more recent advances in genetic engineering have already provided dramatic productivity increases and will likely be the basis for continuing growth in the next century. Likewise, existing technologies disseminated from the developed to the developing countries provide a major impetus to their agricultural growth and are expected to do so for some time.

All in all, these macroeconomic, trade, and technological factors contributed to a phase of high growth in world agricultural production during the 1970s and later to a period of weaker demand and growth in the 1980s and early 1990s. By the end of the 1980s, the high and rising fiscal costs of the EU and U.S. policies were becoming politically unsupportable. These policies also led to instability in world markets, causing concern among other agricultural producers. For a few developed countries with large agricultural sectors (such as Australia, Canada, and New Zealand) and for a few developing countries (such as Argentina, Brazil, and

Thailand), agricultural exports have always been extremely important. The major agricultural exporters outside the European Union and the United States organized themselves into a negotiating bloc called the Cairns Group, which effectively represented their interests in the Uruguay Round negotiations. After much effort, the combination of concerns about distorted world markets, fiscal constraints in the United States and the European Union, and diplomatic pressure from agricultural exporting countries, led to the successful conclusion of the Uruguay Round negotiations in 1994. The result was probably less reform than was hoped for when the negotiations began but more than was expected by the end. There is still much to do.

Agricultural producers in all countries now operate in less distorted domestic and international environments where they are subject to more market discipline and where international trade plays a greater role. Policymakers must adjust their domestic policies to the new conditions and have a stake in shaping that environment through trade negotiations. This is particularly important for developing countries that have already made significant domestic policy changes but still have to contend with developed-country agricultural policies that have negative welfare effects for the whole world.

Getting Ready for New Trade Negotiations

Bringing agricultural policies under international scrutiny was an important accomplishment of the Uruguay Round, but the reform process has not finished. Agricultural negotiations, alone or as part of a new round, will resume during 1999.

The world economy and the trade policy environment have changed substantially since the completion of the Uruguay Round negotiations. The European Union is expanding its membership and is considering further reforms to its Common Agricultural Policy to accommodate new members. The North American Free Trade Agreement (NAFTA) and the Southern Cone Common Market (MERCOSUR) are up and running, and regional institutions such as the Asia-Pacific Economic Cooperation (APEC) forum and the Free Trade Area of the Americas (FTAA), which were embryonic at the time of the Uruguay Round, have become more prominent. Subregional trade agreements in Africa, Asia, and Latin America are expanding and consolidating.

New problems have also appeared. Asia, the largest source of net demand for world agricultural products, has seen income and demand fall, as the countries cut their trade deficits in the wake of the Asian financial crisis. Partly resulting from that crisis, the U.S. trade deficit has already started to increase dramatically, leading to renewed protectionist pressures. Low world agricultural prices and fiscal surpluses have led to increased demands to abandon the market-oriented reforms of the

1995 Farm Bill. President Clinton has yet to secure "fast-track" negotiating authority, considered necessary for serious trade negotiations. In Europe recent changes in agricultural policy do not appear enough to restrain growing agricultural surpluses that hurt agricultural producers in other countries.

The international financial crisis points to the complexity of international financial transactions and could pose a long-run threat to greater market openness. Therefore, coordinating macroeconomic policies and designing more resilient international financial architecture may be at least as important as WTO negotiations for expanding international trade.

Completing the Unfinished Agenda of the Uruguay Round
While many developing countries have significantly reduced distortionary domestic agricultural policies, the benefits these countries and the world can enjoy are thwarted by the subsidies of developed countries. In future negotiations developing countries should seek to eliminate developed-country export subsidies, strengthen surveillance of state trading enterprises, and establish an integrated framework for food aid and export credits. As for domestic subsidies, developing countries should seek further limits on developed countries' trade-distorting payments to farmers. Least developed and developing countries are allowed "special and differential" treatment on these issues, which is desirable if they use their flexibility wisely, smoothing rather than fighting needed adjustment and structural change.

If the developing countries are to succeed in diversifying their agricultural sectors, they must have expanded access to markets in developed countries. The developed countries must increase the volume of imports allowed under the current regime of tariffs and quotas, make the administration of tariffs and quotas more transparent and equitable, further reduce high tariffs on some key products, and complete the process of tariffication where exemptions were granted. Also, eliminating or at least reducing tariff escalation in nonagricultural products is important for developing countries. Rising tariffs undermine the production and export of processed goods that use agricultural inputs.

Considering the Needs of the Most Vulnerable
Upon completion of the Uruguay Round, participating trade ministers agreed on a declaration recognizing the special concerns of the least-developed and net-food-importing countries. These concerns include the preservation of adequate food aid, the provision of technical assistance and financial support to develop agriculture in those countries, and the expansion of financial facilities to help with structural adjustment and short-term difficulties in financing food imports. If prices in world markets become more volatile or if agricultural policies in the developed countries are not further reformed, these poorer countries may lose secure access to food sup-

plies at reasonable prices. Because world grain stocks have been declining as a share of consumption, officials must monitor volatility in agricultural prices carefully. Negotiating countries should also work on improving mechanisms to give early warning of potential food shortages, lowering food transportation and storage costs, and providing better-targeted food aid programs and financial facilities for emergencies.

The impact of changes in trade and agricultural policy on poorer consumers and producers is a matter of debate. Certainly the goals of development and poverty alleviation will not be served by trade-distorting interventions that operate as taxes on food consumers (with the greater burden falling on the poor) or by subsidies that allocate scarce fiscal revenues to wasteful programs. Under the agreements reached in the Uruguay Round, unfair competition that hurts poor farmers, such as subsidized (or dumped) agricultural exports, are being disciplined. At the same time, the agreement allows developing countries to continue most agricultural and social policies linked to poverty alleviation and agricultural development.

Other Trade-Related Issues

Genetically modified agricultural products present a special challenge. The public may block the development of important new technologies to feed the world in coming decades if policymakers do not handle the issues surrounding genetically altered food sensitively, particularly through rigorous analysis of the risks to human health and biodiversity.

Debates over links between trade, labor, and the environment will continue to require scrutiny of the different claims regarding the impact of low wages and environmental standards on agricultural trade.

New WTO Members

Although the issue of WTO accession of new members is not part of the upcoming agricultural negotiations—those discussions proceed on different tracks—the way it is handled can have important consequences for world agricultural markets. Particularly important is China, the world's largest agricultural producer, representing about 20 percent of world production. The list of eventual members of WTO also includes countries such as Russia, Taiwan, Ukraine, and Viet Nam, all important players on both the supply and demand sides of world agricultural markets.

The Political Economy of Trade Negotiations

During the Uruguay Round agriculture was part of a wider negotiation that allowed negotiators to consider trade-offs between agricultural and nonagricultural interest groups within countries. The United States and the European Union were under pressure to reduce the fiscal cost of agricultural support; world agricultural markets were badly distorted; and the U.S.-EU subsidy war was disrupting world markets. Now negotiators face different issues. The fiscal position of the United States has improved significantly, and the European Union has reduced its fiscal deficits, although the cost of EU support for agriculture remains high. Some of the distortions in world agricultural markets have been reduced, and export subsidies for several products have declined below the levels required by the Uruguay Round agreement. Also, if the negotiations on agriculture are conducted apart from other issues, the leverage of countries interested in further reforms will be reduced. In any case, as in the past, the new WTO agricultural negotiations may well be defined by the pace and shape of the reform of the EU's Common Agricultural Policy, currently under discussion.

The Role of Developing Countries in New Trade Talks

Results from the IMPACT global projection model developed at IFPRI show that past trends in agricultural growth will continue into the next century, with world trade in agricultural goods becoming more important. The projections also indicate that countries that pursue comparative advantage will benefit from increasing specialization in agricultural production. In that context, developing countries, as small players in the global arena, should be active participants in designing and implementing international rules that limit larger countries' ability to resort to power politics and unilateral action. Developing countries may overcome some of the constraints to participation by resorting to collective action. For instance, they could consider creating alliances based on shared policy concerns, like the Cairns Group. This approach could reduce the fixed costs of negotiations by spreading them over groups of countries, allow better use of scarce technical expertise, and improve their bargaining position.

It is clearly in the interest of the developing countries to be active and informed participants in general trade and financial talks, as well as in agricultural trade negotiations. IFPRI's research on global trade and macroeconomic issues will continue to produce data and policy analysis to try to clarify the different commercial and financial scenarios and analyze their likely effects on developing nations, looking particularly at low-income countries and the poorer producers and consumers within them. In the final analysis, the developing countries as a group have much to gain from continued progress toward a transparent, rule-based trading system in agriculture as an integral part of a more solid and balanced world trade and financial system.

Chapter 36

Globalization and Nutrition

Julie Babinard and Per Pinstrup-Andersen

*Despite its potential for improving nutrition, several
aspects of the globalization process may worsen
human nutrition in developing countries.*

Of the world's 6 billion people, about 800 million do not have enough to eat. Globally, nutrition has improved in recent decades, but malnutrition—including deficiencies in micronutrients—is still widespread. Hunger, combined with low intake of important micronutrients such as vitamin A, zinc, iron, and iodine, contributes to low birth weight, infections, and increased risk of death. In developing countries, close to 24 percent of all newborns have impaired growth due to poor nutrition during fetal development. About 33 percent of all children under the age of five are stunted. Because of iron deficiencies, about 2 billion people worldwide suffer from anemia, and 9 out of 10 of them live in developing countries.

Improving nutrition will continue to be a challenge, and the current move toward accelerated globalization can play either a positive or a negative role in reducing malnutrition and hunger. Policies that reduce the negative and enhance the positive effects of globalization on nutrition and groups most at risk will be needed, at both the international and national levels.

The Positive Impact of Globalization on Nutrition

Global expansion of agricultural trade and finance can prevent fluctuations in food supply, thereby enabling developing countries to import food at adequate and stable prices. Three-fourths of the world's poor live in rural areas and depend—directly and indirectly—on agriculture. In about 25 percent of developing countries more than two-thirds of total exports are agricultural commodities. Improved market access for these countries can increase agricultural exports, thereby increasing foreign exchange earnings and imports of food (and capital goods). Raising the level of income and employment among low-income rural families also increases the amount of food poor people can afford and protects them from higher food prices in the event of shortages in domestic markets.

The globalization of advances in technology and transport can improve traditional methods of agricultural production and marketing, contributing to the achievement of food security and providing access to better nutrition in the long run. Poor populations often lack access to markets, information, and communication technologies, putting them at a competitive disadvantage in world markets. However, recently developed technologies could be adapted to the constraints faced by developing countries and the poor. For example, wireless phones require a lower capital investment to set up and are particularly suited to remote locations.

Improved access to information and data via the Internet can allow researchers and policymakers to learn about new nutrition initiatives, share information, obtain best practices, and map food production and undernutrition by country and by regions within countries. Information networks can provide a forum for debate on nutrition-related issues, increasing global awareness.

The integration of labor markets gives the poor and malnourished a greater variety of employment possibilities and opportunities to acquire and diversify their income. The growth in relatively labor-intensive, long-distance services—data processing, software programming, clerical and professional services—could increase the commercial service exports of developing countries. These opportunities indirectly offer potential improvements in nutrition, but there is also the risk that malnourished and unhealthy individuals may not be able to capture these jobs.

Nutritional Risks and Emerging Dietary Challenges

Despite its potential for improving nutrition, several aspects of the globalization process may worsen human nutrition in developing countries. Increasing trade could create a major shift in the structure of diets, resulting in a growing epidemic of the so-called "diseases of affluence." Traditional, low-cost diets, rich in fiber and grain, are likely to be replaced by high-cost diets that include greater proportions of sugars, oils, and animal fats, giving rise to higher food costs and an increase in weight gain, obesity, and associated chronic diseases that affect children and adults alike. Aggressive promotion of such goods by producers and distributors can further accelerate adverse changes in diet. In China, for example, the number of overweight adults jumped by more than half—from 9 to 15 percent—between 1989 and 1992. These problems are no longer limited to the well-off. A recent IFPRI study found that a large share of poor Asian households have at least one obese member.

In addition to potentially harmful dietary changes, huge cross-border capital flows leave developing countries particularly vulnerable to international economic fluctuations. For example, recent evidence from Indonesia, whose economy was badly hit during the East Asian financial crisis of 1997 and 1998, shows an increase in poverty and nutritional deficiencies for that period.

The impact of globalization on nutrition also depends on the domestic policies of industrialized countries. While efforts have been made over the years to improve market access, developed countries are still reluctant to open up their domestic markets. Distorting policies and high tariffs, sometimes 100 percent or higher, set for meat, dairy, and other products in the U.S., Europe, and Japan, restrict trade in products of particular importance to poor farmers in developing countries—a situation that denies them the benefits of trade liberalization and increasing globalization.

As globalization proceeds, food safety standards are becoming more uniform across countries. For groups already at risk nutritionally, elevating these standards could mean a trade-off between food safety and food security. The safety concerns of developed countries may further restrict market access for food products from developing countries. Farmers in developing countries may not be able to meet the standards because they lack the adequate institutions and infrastructure. In addition, imposing these standards on developing countries could result in higher food prices for poor consumers.

Shaping Globalization to Improve Nutrition

An urgent task for the international community is to help developing countries become better integrated into the world economy. This can be done by helping them build up needed supporting institutions and policies, by helping them adjust to and comply with international agreements and terms of trade, and by enhancing their access to world markets.

Reducing the high, trade-distorting barriers that are in place in most industrialized countries would facilitate developing countries' market access and create a favorable environment for agricultural development in these countries. Progress has been made in reducing tariff barriers on unprocessed tropical products like coffee, tea, and cocoa. Many more developing countries would benefit if similar improvements in market access were granted for other agricultural products, such as temperate-zone horticultural products, sugar, cereals, and meat, as well as for processed agricultural products. Multilateral liberalization would also substantially increase world prices for these commodities, thus benefiting producers.

The nutrition and health communities must respond to problems of unhealthy diets and overnutrition. While the stigma against obesity is absent in most developing countries, people affected by these trends will be hurt in the long run if measures to address them are not taken. Through cost-effective nutrition interventions, education programs, and dissemination strategies, an infrastructure must be set up to help foster a balanced and low-cost diet that will limit the risks of obesity and coronary disease. New policies should encourage the production and marketing of vegetables, fruits, legumes, and a variety of other foods of plant origin, along with decreasing support for the production of fat, sugar, and fatty, sugary foods and drinks.

Modern science and new technologies in information, biology, and communications can provide the poor and malnourished with a voice in policymaking and the tools to become more effective at facing the competitive forces and risks brought about by globalization. For such opportunities to materialize, innovations must be specifically targeted to solving the nutritional and agricultural problems of these groups. For example, while science based on molecular biology is moving at great speed, its application to small-scale agriculture in developing countries has thus far been limited to cotton in China. If focused on reducing hunger and malnutrition, biotechnology could help combat widespread nutritional problems such as iron and vitamin A deficiencies.

Improvements in health care and access to drugs must also be facilitated. The World Health Organization estimates that only eight percent of the $50 to $60 billion in health research worldwide goes to diseases that afflict people in developing counties. Given the synergy between nutrition and health, targeted research and health interventions can contribute significantly to the promotion of nutritional well-being. A health infrastructure capable of delivering comprehensive care and adequate follow-up can help identify and rehabilitate people who are malnourished. At the same time, the access of poor people to essential medications at affordable prices must be protected.

In countries exposed to globalization, the role of the public sector in many areas of food security and nutrition appears to be shrinking, while the involvement of civil society and the private sector is increasing. Such a shift may be appropriate, but globalization should not substitute for appropriate national policies. Recent research and experience shows how important an effective public sector is in areas related to nutrition and food security. Access to land, primary education, primary health care, and other pro-poor policies become even more important as the at-risk groups are exposed to the competitive forces, risks, and opportunities brought by globalization. Governments should assess how globalization will affect at-risk populations, determine whether they can limit the negative impact, and design and implement compensatory schemes and safety nets where needed.

Good governance is needed to guide the transformation of the agricultural sector in a direction beneficial to the poor. Inadequate domestic policies and lack of access to resources and markets are presently making it difficult for the poor to gain from globalization. Governments should ensure that markets remain competitive. They need to implement the appropriate policies and make the necessary changes that will reduce marketing costs and price distortions and allow the agricultural sector to benefit from new technological opportunities.

PART 10

Biotechnology and Information Technology: How Can the Poor Benefit?

Chapter 37

Biotechnology for Developing-Country Agriculture

Problems and Opportunities

Gabrielle J. Persley and John J. Doyle

*Modern biotechnology will not solve all the problems
of food insecurity and poverty. But it could provide a
key component to a solution if given the chance.*

Today, almost a billion people live in absolute poverty and suffer from chronic hunger. Seventy percent of these individuals are farmers—men, women, and children—who eke out a living from small plots of poor soils, mainly in tropical environments that are increasingly prone to drought, flood, bushfires, and hurricanes. Crop yields in these areas are stagnant and epidemics of pests and weeds often ruin crops. Livestock suffer from parasitic diseases, some of which also affect humans. Inputs such as chemical fertilizers and pesticides are expensive, and the latter can affect the health of farm families, destroy wildlife, and contaminate water courses when used in excess. The only way families can grow more food and have a surplus for sale seems to be to clear more forest. Older children move to the city, where they, too, find it difficult to earn enough money to buy the food and medicine they need for themselves and their young children.

As these detrimental social and environmental changes are occurring in the developing world, a revolution in biotechnology and associated information technology is improving the health, well-being, and lifestyle of the privileged and creating more wealth in a few rich countries. Can this revolution also be harnessed to serve the food and nutrition needs of the world's poor? What are the opportunities, problems, and risks involved with the new technologies and can they be managed? The last question is particularly pressing in light of the current controversy between the United States and the European Union over genetically modified foods. The benefits and risks of biotechnology weigh differently for food in areas of food surplus than they do for life-threatening diseases in those same areas.

Opportunities

In 1998 the global market for biotechnology products (see box for definition of terms) totaled at least US$13 billion. About 80 products, most of them medically related, are on the market or nearly ready for it. In recent years, the fruits of two decades of intensive and expensive research and development (R&D) in agricultural biotechnology has begun to pay off. Approximately 28 million hectares of land were planted with 40 transgenic crops in 1998. Most of these crops were new varieties of cotton, corn, soybean, and rapeseed. Developing countries held 15 percent of the area planted with the transgenic varieties.

Most biotechnology-based solutions for agriculture are likely to be delivered in the form of new plant seeds or new strains of livestock. These solutions continue the tradition of selection and improvement of cultivated crops and livestock developed over the centuries. The difference is that new gene technology identifies desirable traits more quickly and accurately than conventional plant and livestock breeding. Modern biotechnology can also introduce the genes that control desirable traits into plant and animal strains with far greater precision and control than can conventional methods.

Biotechnology applications in agriculture are in their infancy. The first generation of genetically engineered plant varieties have been modified only for a single trait, such as herbicide tolerance or pest resistance. The rapid progress being made in genomics will transform plant, tree, and livestock breeding as the functions of more genes are identified. Breeding for complex traits such as drought tolerance, which is controlled by many genes, should then become common. This is an area of great potential benefit for tropical crops, which are often grown in harsh environments and on poor soils.

To determine if modern biotechnology can benefit the poor in developing countries, policymakers at the national, regional, and international levels need to analyze the problems that are currently constraining agricultural productivity or damaging the environment, assess whether these problems may be solved by integrating modern biotechnology with conventional R&D, and prioritize solutions. This may seem self-evident, but such strategic analyses are indispensable for anticipating the potential benefits and risks that may arise while using modern biotechnology to solve specific problems. In addition to analyses, both public and private resources for R&D need to be mobilized if the poor in developing countries are to profit from the genetic revolution.

Definitions of Biotechnology and
Its Component Technologies

Biotechnology is any technique that uses living organisms or substances from those organisms to make or modify a product, improve plants or animals, or develop microorganisms for specific uses. The key components of modern biotechnology are

- Genomics: the molecular characterization of all species;

- Bioinfomatics: the assembly of data from genomic analysis into accessible forms;

- Transformation: the introduction of single genes conferring potentially useful traits into plant, livestock, fish, and tree species;

- Molecular breeding: the identification and evaluation of desirable traits in breeding programs with the use of marker-assisted selection;

- Diagnostics: the use of molecular characterization to provide more accurate and quicker identification of pathogens;

- Vaccine technology: use of modern immunology to develop recombinant DNA vaccines for improving control of lethal diseases.

Policy Framework

Modern biotechnology will not solve all the problems of food insecurity and poverty. But it could provide a key component to a solution if given the chance, and if steered by a set of appropriate policies. These policies should guide (1) increased public investments in R&D, including that in modern biotechnology; (2) regulatory arrangements that inform and protect the public from any risks arising from the release of genetically modified organisms (GMOs); (3) intellectual property management to encourage greater private-sector investment; and (4) regulation of the private seed and agricultural research sector to protect the interests of small farmers and poor consumers in developing countries.

Public-Sector R&D

Pro-poor policies can help expand agricultural R&D, including traditional and modern biotechnological research, in order to solve problems of particular importance to the poor. The problems of orphan commodities (important subsistence food and/or tropical export commodities that hold little commercial interest for the private sector) require particular attention. Given the high rates of return, more public support for agricultural R&D should be encouraged in most developing countries. Additional public financial support for R&D at the national, regional, and international levels would help to develop public goods the poor can afford.

Biosafety

The term biosafety describes a set of measures used to assess and manage any risks associated with GMOs. Such risks may transcend or be inherent in the technology and need to be managed accordingly. Technology-transcending risks emanate from the political and social context in which the technology is used. They include concerns that biotechnology may increase the prosperity gap between the rich and the poor, and may contribute to a loss of biodiversity. Ethical concerns about patenting living organisms and moving genes between species also fall into this category.

The principles and practices for assessing and managing technology-inherent risks are well established in several countries. They take into account the nature of the organism, the familiarity of the product, any distinguishing features of the process by which a product was produced, and the environment into which it will be introduced. A science-based assessment of these factors on a case by case basis, and identification of any concerns expressed by stakeholders, enable regulators to find out what risks may be associated with a particular product and to make appropriate recommendations. A regulatory system that enjoys the confidence of the public and the business and farming communities is essential for the effective use of biotechnology. The current and proposed international agreements that govern movements of GMOs also contribute to biosafety.

Intellectual Property Management

The purpose of intellectual property management is to protect local inventions and enable access to technologies developed elsewhere. Trade-related intellectual property rights (TRIPs) are a matter of ongoing concern within the World Trade Organization. The present patent system favors those countries that have a strong innovation base. Despite much effort, no satisfactory system exists to recompense traditional owners and improvers of germplasm. The lack of intellectual property protection also constrains private-sector investment in developing countries.

The Private Sector

The participation of the private sector is critical to the development and delivery of new biotechnology products. The enabling environment to encourage private-sector participation includes a regulatory system that accurately informs the public of the benefits and risks involved in the use of new technologies; a legal framework for protecting intellectual property; adequate infrastructure for power, transport, and telecommunications; a fair tax system and investment incentives; a skilled workforce, including a well-supported university sector; public funding for R&D; and incentives to establish innovative public-private collaboration and joint ventures at the national and international levels.

Delivering Solutions for the Poor

The successful application of modern biotechnology to the problems that cause undernourishment and poverty could be called a biosolution. The delivery of new biosolutions to the problems of food security and poverty will require continual policy development and actions at the national, regional, and international levels. These efforts will involve the following five areas: (1) determining priorities and assessing relative risks and benefits in consultation with the poor, who are often overlooked while others decide what is best for them; (2) setting policies that benefit the poor and that minimize technology-transcending risks that adversely affect the poor; (3) establishing an environment that facilitates the safe use of biotechnology through investment, regulation, intellectual property protection, and good governance; (4) actively linking biotechnology and information technology so that new scientific discoveries worldwide can be assessed and applied to the problems of food insecurity and poverty in a timely manner; and (5) determining what investments governments and the international development community will have to make in human and financial resources in order to ensure that biosolutions to the problems of food security reach the poor.

Chapter 38

Developing Appropriate Biotechnology Policies for Developing-Country Agriculture

Per Pinstrup-Andersen

Modern biotechnology research may help reduce poverty, improve food security and nutrition, and make the use of natural resources more sustainable, only if it focuses on the problems and opportunities poor people in developing countries face and only if appropriate policies accompany it.

Modern biotechnology can enhance agricultural productivity in developing countries in a way that further reduces poverty, improves food security and nutrition, and promotes sustainable use of natural resources. But such benefits from biotechnology require policy action on a number of fronts. The small farmer in developing countries faces a variety of problems and constraints. Crop losses due to insects, diseases, weeds, and drought threaten income and food availability. Acid soils, low soil fertility and lack of access to reasonably priced plant nutrients, and other biotic and abiotic factors also contribute to low yields. Poor infrastructure and dysfunctional markets for inputs and outputs, along with lack of access to credit and technical assistance, add to the problems plaguing the small farmer. Solutions to these problems will benefit both farmers and consumers. Although modern biotechnology cannot solve all these problems, it can provide a critical component to the solution if it is guided by appropriate policies. Four sets of policies are particularly important. Each of these is briefly discussed below.

Policies to Guide Research for the Poor

Policies must expand and guide research and technology development to solve the problems of particular importance to the poor. These problems include diets with inadequate levels of energy, protein, and micronutrients, and crop losses due to biotic and abiotic factors. Research should focus on the crops of particular importance to small farmers and poor consumers in developing countries. Bananas, cassava, yams, sweet potatoes, rice, maize, wheat, and millet, along with livestock products, feature most prominently in the diets and production activities of the poor. Except for limited work on rice, bananas, and cassava, little biotechnology research currently focuses on helping the small farmer and poor consumer solve their productivity and nutrition problems. The prediction so often heard that the poor in developing countries are unlikely to benefit from modern agricultural biotechnology in the foreseeable future could well come true—not because the technology has little to offer but because it will not be given a chance.

Allocate Additional Public Resources to Agricultural Research

There are three ways to expand biotechnology research for the benefit of the poor. First, allocate additional public resources to agricultural research, including biotechnology research, that promises large social benefits. Existing national and international agricultural research systems have to be strengthened or new ones built. Low-income developing countries currently invest less than 0.5 percent of the value of agricultural production in agricultural research, compared to about 2 percent in developed countries. Underinvestment is widespread despite high annual economic rates of return from investments in agricultural research. A recent assessment of more than 1,000 research projects and programs found an average annual rate of return of 88 percent. Investments by the private sector are limited to research that permits a large enough profit from the returns. Nonetheless, privately funded research can still generate large benefits to farmers and consumers, as illustrated by a recent study of the distribution of benefits from the use of genetically modified (GM) soybeans in the United States. The private patent holders and private seed companies captured one-third of the total economic benefits, farmers and consumers gained two-thirds. While private-sector agricultural research has increased rapidly in the industrialized countries during the last 10 to 15 years, it currently accounts for a small share of agricultural research in most developing countries.

Convert Some Social Benefits to Private Benefits

Second, expand private-sector research for the poor by converting some of the social benefits of research to private benefits for the private sector. The public sector can entice the private sector to develop technologies for the poor by offering up front to buy the exclusive rights to newly developed technology and make it available either for free or for a nominal charge to small farmers. The amount of the offer could be determined on the basis of expected social benefits, using an annual rate of return normally expected from agricultural research, for example, 60–80 percent.

The risk of failing to develop the specified technology would rest with the research agency, just as it does when technology is developed for the market. The public sector offer would come due to the research agency that first develops the technology, but only when the technology is developed, tested, and made available. Both private- and public-sector agencies could participate in this research. Opportunities for collaboration between multinational life science companies and public-sector agricultural research agencies in both developing and developed countries might increase the probability of success. With necessary refinements, the arrangement proposed here should be of interest to international development assistance agencies. This proposal builds on a similar idea that Jeffrey Sachs of Harvard University proposed for developing vaccines for tropical diseases.

Protect Intellectual Property Rights

The third way to expand biotechnology research to help the poor is to protect the intellectual property rights of a private research agency that develops a particular technology, for example, seed with infertile offspring, or that contracts directly with the farmer, in both cases forcing the farmer to buy new seed every season. This would make it easier for the private sector to recuperate the incomes needed to justify the research. But seeds with infertile offspring may be inappropriate for small farmers in developing countries because they pose large risks to food security. Existing infrastructure and production processes may not be able to keep fertile and infertile seeds apart. Small farmers could face severe consequences if they planted infertile seeds by mistake. Monitoring and enforcing contracts that prohibit large numbers of small farmers from using the crops they produce as seed would be expensive and difficult to do.

Policies to Protect against Health Risks

GM foods are not intrinsically good or bad for human health. Their health effect depends on their specific content. GM foods with a higher content of digestible iron are likely to benefit consumers with iron deficiencies. But the transfer of genes from one species to another may also transfer characteristics that cause allergic reactions. Thus, GM foods need to be tested for allergy transfers before they are commercialized. It was precisely such testing that avoided the commercialization of maize with a Brazil nut gene. GM foods with possible allergy risks should be fully labeled. Labeling may also be needed to identify content for cultural and religious reasons or simply because consumers want to know. Finally, labeling may be required to identify the production process itself when that, rather than any specific health risk, interests consumers.

Failure to remove antibiotic-resistant marker genes used in research before a GM food is commercialized presents a potential although unproven health risk.

Recent legislation in the European Union requires that such marker genes be removed before a GM food is deemed safe for consumers. Risks and opportunities associated with GM foods should be integrated into the general food safety regulations of a country.

Policies to Address Ecological Risks

Effective national biosafety regulations should be in place before modern biotechnology is introduced into a country's agriculture. Such regulations should be country-specific and reflect relevant risk factors. The ecological risks policymakers need to assess include the spread of traits such as herbicide resistance from genetically modified plants to plants (including weeds) that are not modified, and the buildup of resistance in insect populations. Seeds that produce infertile offspring may be an effective solution to the risk associated with cross pollination but, as mentioned earlier, they may be inappropriate for small farmers. The approach used to develop terminator seeds, however, offers great promise for the development of a seed that will avoid the spread of new traits through cross-pollination. The seed would contain the desired traits, such as pest resistance or drought tolerance, but each trait would be activated only after treatment with a particular chemical. Without treatment, the seed would maintain its normal characteristics. Thus, if a farmer planted an improved seed, the offspring would not be sterile; rather they would revert back to being normal seeds (before improved traits were introduced). The farmer would then have the choice of planting the normal seed or bringing back the improved traits by applying a particular chemical. Contrary to the terminator gene, this approach complies with the principle of doing no harm.

Both food safety and biosafety regulations should reflect international agreements and a society's acceptable risk levels, including the risks associated with not using modern biotechnology to achieve desired goals. The poor should be included directly in the debate and decisionmaking about their desire for technological change, the risks of that change, and the consequences of no or alternative kinds of change.

Policies to Regulate the Private Sector

Recent mergers and acquisitions have resulted in increasing concentration among companies engaged in biotechnology research. The outcome of this growing concentration may be reduced competition, monopoly or oligopoly profits, exploitation of small farmers and consumers, and successful efforts to gain special favors from governments. Effective antitrust legislation and institutions to enforce the legislation are needed, particularly in small developing countries where one or only a few seed distribution companies operate. Effective legislation is also required to enforce intellectual property rights, including those of farmers to germplasm, along the lines agreed to within the frameworks of the World Trade Organization and the Convention on Biological Diversity.

Conclusions

Modern biotechnology research may help reduce poverty, improve food security and nutrition, and make the use of natural resources more sustainable, only if it focuses on the problems and opportunities poor people in developing countries face and only if appropriate policies accompany it. Modern biotechnology is not a silver bullet, but it may be a powerful tool in the fight against poverty and should be made available to poor farmers and consumers.

Chapter 39

Governing the GM Crop Revolution

Policy Choices for Developing Countries

Robert L. Paarlberg

The inclination of developing countries to promote
or block the spread of GM crops can be judged
by the policy choices they make.

Will developing countries adopt policies that promote the planting of genetically modified (GM) crops, or will they select policies that slow the spread of the GM crop revolution? The evidence so far is mixed. In some prominent countries such as China, policies are in place that encourage the independent development and planting of GM crops. Yet in a number of other equally prominent countries the planting of GM crops is not yet officially approved.

The inclination of developing countries to promote or block the spread of GM crops can be judged by the policy choices they make in five separate areas: intellectual property rights (IPR) policy, biosafety policy, trade policy, food safety policy, and public research investments (Table 39.1).

Policy Options toward GM Crops

Intellectual Property Rights

If developing countries want to bring GM crop technologies into their farming systems, they may have to recognize some of the intellectual property rights claims of the private companies that have been developing GM crops. At one extreme, they

Table 39.1 Policy Options toward GM crops

	Promotional	Permissive	Precautionary	Preventive
Intellectual property rights	Full patent protection, plus plant breeders' rights under UPOV 1991	PBRs under UPOV 1991	PBRs under UPOV 1978, which preserves farmers' privilege	No IPRs for plants or animals, or IPRs on paper that are not enforced
Biosafety	No careful screening, only token screening, or approval based on approvals in other countries	Case-by-case screening for demonstrated risk, depending on intended use of product	Case-by-case screening also for scientific uncertainties owing to novelty of GM process	No careful case-by-case screening; risk assumed because of GM process
Trade	GM crops promoted to lower commodity production costs and boost exports; no restrictions on imports of GM seeds of plant materials	GM crops neither promoted nor prevented; imports of GM commodities limited in same way as non-GM in accordance with science-based WTO standards	Imports of GM seeds and materials screened or restrained separately and more tightly than non-GM; labeling requirements imposed on import of GM foods or commodities	GM seed and plant imports blocked; GM-free status maintained in hopes of capturing export market premiums
Food safety and consumer choice	No regulatory distinction drawn between GM and non-GM foods when testing or labeling for food safety	Distinction made between GM and non-GM foods on some existing food labels but not so as to require segregation of market channels	Comprehensive positive labeling of all GM foods required and enforced with segregated market channels	GM food sales banned, or warning labels that stigmatize GM foods as unsafe to consumers required
Public research investment	Treasury resources spent on both development and local adaptations of GM crop technologies	Treasury resources spent on local adaptations of GM crop technologies but not on development of new transgenes	No significant treasury resources spent on GM crop research or adaptation; donors allowed to finance local adaptations of GM crops	Neither treasury nor donor funds spent on any adaptation or development of GM crop technology

Note: UPOV = International Convention for the Protection of New Varieties of Plants; PBRs = plant breeders' rights; WTO = World Trade Organization.

might even adopt the U.S. approach and provide full patent protection. A somewhat less promotional policy could offer only plant breeders' rights as IPR guarantees, which entitle breeders to use protected varieties as an initial source of variation for the creation of new varieties as in the 1991 agreement of the International Union for the Protection of New Varieties of Plants (UPOV). A still weaker approach would be to embrace an earlier 1978 version of UPOV, which preserves the privilege of farmers to replant seeds from protected varieties on their own farms. Weaker still would be to provide no IPRs at all for plant breeders.

Biosafety

In the area of biological safety, the most promotional policy toward GM crops would be to approve the use of these crops without any careful case-by-case screening for unwanted geneflow or damage to nontarget species. A less promotional approach would be to screen GM crops case by case but only for risks that can be scientifically demonstrated. A more cautious approach would be to hold crops off the market case by case even without proof of risk so long as some scientific uncertainties remained. The most cautious approach would be to assume risk in all cases because of the novelty of the GM process.

Trade

Consumer acceptance of GM crops in major importing countries continues to evolve. Assuming adequate consumer acceptance, a promotional trade policy toward GM crops would be to seek the import of GM plant materials and seeds without restriction and promote the planting of GM crops in hopes of cutting farm production costs and becoming a more competitive exporter. A more neutral approach would be to neither promote nor prevent the planting of GM crops and to treat GM seed and commodity imports the same way as non-GM imports. A more cautious trade policy approach would be to develop and implement a separate and more restrictive method for regulating and labeling the import of GM seeds or commodities compared with non-GM. A preventive trade policy choice would be to ban GM imports and block the planting of GM crops. If consumer acceptance of GM crops in international markets continues to weaken, such a ban on planting GM crops could be defended on trade grounds as a way to seek price premiums on the world market as a "GM-free" exporter.

Food Safety and Consumer Choice

In this area a promotional policy would be to conclude that GM crops currently on the market pose no new hazards to human health and to impose no additional inspection or labeling burdens on them. A less promotional approach would be to require labeling of some GM foods in the interest of a consumer's right to know but to make the labeling standards lenient enough so that a complete segregation of GM from non-GM commodities is not required. A still more cautious approach would be to impose mandatory comprehensive labeling for all GM foods in a manner that would require market segregation. A fully preventive approach would be to ban all GM foods or to label them in ways intended to stigmatize and prevent their use.

Public Research Investments

Developing countries must also make a range of agricultural research investment choices toward GM crops. At one extreme they might spend treasury resources to develop their own GM crops. As a second option they could invest only in the more limited goal of backcrossing GM traits developed by others into their own domestic germplasm. As a still more limited option they could allow their scientists to pursue backcrossing of transgenes into local varieties only if donors were willing to pay for it. At a preventive extreme they could decide not to spend any money, even donor money, on GM crop research.

Policy Choices in Four Developing Countries

This system can be used to classify the actual policy choices toward GM crops that were made by governments in Brazil, China, India, and Kenya in 1999–2000 (Table 39.2). Whereas China opted for relatively permissive policies toward GM crops, Brazil, India, and Kenya have in most respects been more precautionary.

In Brazil, India, and Kenya biosafety approval has emerged as the principal point of resistance against moving the GM crop revolution forward. This is a surprising discovery given the fact that biosafety approvals for GM crops have not been such a strong sticking point in the industrial world, given the traditionally weak agricultural biosafety policies of most developing countries, and given the potential biosafety benefits of some GM crop applications (those that permit fewer and less toxic chemical sprays). It is particularly surprising that Brazil and India have moved so slowly on biosafety approvals for GM crops, given the significant state investments that are simultaneously being made in both countries to develop GM crops.

Table 39.2 Policies toward GM Crops in Brazil, China, India, and Kenya, 1999–2000

	Promotional	Permissive	Precautionary	Preventive
Intellectual property rights		Brazil	Kenya	India
			Chna	
Biosafety		China	Kenya	
			Brazil	
			India	
Trade		China	Kenya	India
			Brazil	
Food safety and consumer choice	Kenya	Brazil		
	China	India		
Public research investment	Brazil		Kenya	
	India			
	China			

International pressures of four kinds help explain this pattern of caution in the developing world: (1) environmental groups based in Europe and North America have used media campaigns, lawsuits, and direct actions to project into the developing world a tone of extreme caution toward GM crops; (2) consumer doubts in Europe and Japan regarding GM crops have discouraged planting of those crops by developing-country exporters; (3) the precautionary tone of the 2000 Biosafety Protocol governing transboundary movements of GM crops is reinforcing biosafety caution in the developing world; and (4) donor assistance to developing countries in the area of agribiotechnology has often focused more on the possible biosafety risks of the new technology than on its possible agronomic or economic advantages. One reason for China's more permissive biosafety policy is its greater insulation from some of these international influences promoting caution elsewhere.

A further spread of GM crops into the developing world will therefore depend on more than just the availability of suitable technologies. It will also depend upon the future willingness of biosafety authorities in developing countries to give farmers permission to plant GM crops. This willingness, in turn, will likely depend as much on the external pressures and influences faced by these regulators as upon actual documented threats to biosafety from GM crops.

Chapter 40

Bridging the Digital Divide

Reported by Uday Mohan

*Expensive, potentially disruptive, and extraordinarily
beneficial, ICTs are here to stay, and developing
countries can ill afford to sit on the sidelines.*

B efore the Internet came to Veerampattinam, a coastal village in southern
India, the local fisher folk went to get their daily catch without knowing sea
conditions or the location of fish shoals. Lives were sometimes lost because
of particularly high waves and rough seas. But in late 1998, the M.S. Swaminathan
Research Foundation (MSSRF), an Indian research center, installed a computer in
a "village information shop" with financial assistance from the International
Development Research Centre, Canada.

Through a wireless local-area network based on radio frequencies, the computer
makes available daily data on wave height and wind forecasts from a U.S. Navy website. This information is broadcast to the villagers in the early morning via loud-
speakers on the roof of the information shop.

Armed with this knowledge as well as with details about fish location, the fishermen now ply the seas in greater safety and with more efficiency. Not only has the
Internet-enabled computer made the main work of the village easier, but it has also
made information about prices, health and transportation facilities, and entitlement
schemes accessible. Indeed, before the computer arrived, villagers were unaware of
housing loans that they were entitled to. Most fishermen in the village have now
benefited from these low-cost loans.

Veerampattinam is one of many recent examples of the way the Internet has
reached and benefited the poor in developing countries. Although small in scale,

these examples have posed a challenge to the view that the Internet belongs to the technologically advanced and that it would be out of place in poor rural areas. As M.S. Swaminathan, MSSRF's chairman of the board, says, "The technological empowerment of the poor adds value to their work and lives. Just as with the Green Revolution, information technology in the hands of small producers, particularly women, benefits everyone, whereas information technology in the hands only of the rich does not."

Without doubt the Internet and other information and communication technologies (ICTs), such as faxes, video, digital radio, mobile phones, and satellite technologies, have helped people gain access to, process, respond to, and distribute information in a faster and more far-reaching way than ever before. This ongoing shift toward a more information-intensive society gives both added weight and new meaning to the old maxim, "information is power."

ICTs at a minimum can enhance the livelihoods of the poor and improve market efficiency. As development tools in their own right, ICTs can also help lead to higher literacy rates through distance learning; gender equality through the empowerment of women who gain greater access to economic opportunities and civil society; sustainable development through easier dissemination of appropriate information; more balanced social relations through the greater accountability imposed on the powerful by the marginalized; and other global goods. Hans d'Orville, former director of the Information Technology for Development Programme at the United Nations Development Programme (UNDP), puts it this way: "Information technology has a place alongside adequate food, health care, education, and other fundamentals. By taking this place it has broadened our definition of poverty. Those people or countries who cannot or will not participate fully in the new information economy will find it all the more difficult to climb out of poverty."

The Digital Divide

The importance of ICTs is precisely why concern has escalated over the "digital divide"—the gap in information and communication technologies that exists between technologically advanced and developing countries, poor and rich, men and women, and urban and rural areas. Recent high-level international meetings, such as the Global Knowledge II conference this past March in Malaysia and the July G-8 summit in Japan, have pressed for solutions to the divide.

An array of numbers illustrates the vast gap that has to be bridged: Nua Internet Surveys estimates that about 333 million people worldwide were online as of June of this year, but as many as 72 percent of them resided in North America and Europe. Africa claimed only 2.8 million Internet subscribers, Asia/Pacific 75.5 million, Middle East 1.9 million, and South America 13.2 million. In 1998, according to the International Telecommunications Union (ITU), low-income countries had 6.2 personal computers and 45 fixed-line and mobile phones per 1,000 people, whereas high-income countries had 311 and 832, respectively.

The digital divide is not only enormous—dwarfing even the per capita income gap ratio between high- and low-income countries—but it is increasing, according to a recent World Bank study. The authors of the study, Francisco Rodriguez and Ernest Wilson III, estimate that even East Asia, which is adopting ICTs at a rapid pace, will take another 40 years to catch up with the developed world. Inevitably, access varies widely among and within developing countries as well. Only 11 of 53 African countries for which there are data have 10,000 or more Internet users; 17 have fewer than 1,000. Gender, income, age, and other disparities also abound. In Ethiopia, for example, 98 percent of Internet users in 1998 were university graduates and 86 percent were male.

As the Internet becomes the norm for commerce and information exchange in the developed world, the poorer countries will have little choice but to try to bridge the digital divide in all its forms. They will go online to become competitive in the new economy or forgo significant growth. The stakes involve not only social development and productivity growth, but also the burgeoning e-commerce sector, which is expected to reach between US$2 and 3 trillion in transactions in the next three years.

Connecting the Poor

The last few years have witnessed a flurry of activity as the development community has put forward position papers and proposals and launched pilot projects to include the poor in the information revolution. Projects have ranged from providing price information to farmers to boosting microcredit-based sales via the web.

The hallmarks of this activity have been diversity and innovation in organization, technology, and funding. Results are trickling in, and no formula has emerged, though some ingredients appear to be critical. According to Roger Noll, professor of economics and director of the Public Policy Program at Stanford University, "Technological change has greatly affected the optimal strategy for starting ICT service. In many cases, fixed wireless is better for new networks because of its lower cost and quicker availability. And because economies of scale are not very important in wireless, competition is often feasible right from the start. Another common ingredient is that western-style universal service is not a practical reality in developing countries, where much of the population is too poor to afford individual access. The focus instead should be on convenient access through sharing, such as with telecenters and pay phones."

Meeting Community Needs with ICTs

This need to minimize cost but maximize rural access drives most ICT projects in developing countries. Not surprisingly, the Internet still often plays a lesser role than other technologies in the distribution of information in rural areas. Most farmers, for example, are years away from getting price information through the Internet because of cost and lack of human resources and adequate phone infrastructure in rural areas. But because a farmer's decisions about where, when, and how much to sell depend on the signals sent by national and international market prices, ICT proponents see the delivery of timely price information as one of the key benefits farmers can receive from the new information technologies. Consequently a number of ICT projects focus on making it easier for agricultural producers to access prices.

"Price information helps connect farmers to markets," says Mike Weber, professor and codirector of a food security program run by the Department of Agricultural Economics at Michigan State University (MSU), "and the more up-to-date the price information, the better for the farmer and the market." Weber's own group uses both low- and high-tech means to distribute prices. For the past ten years, the food security project has delivered weekly agricultural prices by newspaper and fax to government offices, the private sector, and nongovernmental organizations (NGOs) in Mozambique. MediaFax, a fax-based newspaper, provides the same information each week to a wider audience. NGOs make copies of the weekly price lists and distribute the information to farmers.

"Our first line of defense for the farmer is the fax and newspaper because they are inexpensive, and we also use the radio where possible," says Weber, "but the Internet plays a role too for those who can afford it. Our department at MSU hosts a website that provides comprehensive links to global market information, including the weekly price lists for Mozambique, but more than 50 percent of the hits right now come from U.S. farmers, traders, and analysts."

The Internet need not remain elusive, of course, as MSSRF has shown. Veerampattinam, the village in India, is actually one of five now hooked to the Internet as part of MSSRF's village information project. One of the villages serves as the information hub, with full access to the Internet. The others have wireless access only to the hub, to which they send information and requests for information. The hub searches the web and electronically delivers the requested information to the other centers, along with standard information in an email newsletter. This hub-and-spoke model avoids the cost of providing full Internet access to all villages and also creates a network for information sharing across the villages. MSSRF and its granters fund the project, asking only that the villagers house and operate the technology.

Some projects are devised to pay for themselves while providing developing-country poor with access to ICTs for socioeconomic development. Such is the case with the projects facilitated by the International Institute for Communication and Development (IICD), which was established by the Dutch Ministry for Development Cooperation in 1997. In Jamaica, for example, IICD and its partners are helping to put in place a comprehensive agribusiness information system that will enable small farmers, who are losing ground in the global marketplace, to get both print- and web-based information about markets, products, registration requirements, and technical assistance.

This demand-driven system makes information available through a continually updated database on domestic agricultural production and marketing and through the Internet. Extension agents collect the information from producers and traders using palm-top computers. The information is then downloaded to PCs located in primary extension offices. These PCs are linked to the central database at the headquarters of the Rural Agricultural Development Authority. The system is currently being tested with 80 small farmers and traders in two regions in Jamaica.

The method for delivering information is still evolving. Currently large farmers and traders with access to the Internet get the information easily. Smaller farmers and traders generally visit the extension offices, where they can obtain standardized and customized reports in hard copy. If literacy is a problem, extension officers help interpret documents. A small subscription fee makes the project sustainable, and small farmers can pool their resources and subscribe as a group.

The project will eventually extend throughout Jamaica and is expected to reach 50,000 direct users and 150,000 indirect users. Ingrid Hagen, IICD's manager of Private and Public Sector Partnerships, observes, "Access is giving these Jamaican farmers a chance to compete seriously with imports that are crowding them out of markets, even for the main domestic products. The technical, regulatory, and market demands increasingly in force due to globalization can be met only with the help of ICTs."

The belief that ICTs have a role to play in the lives of small farmers has led to their introduction in many rural areas. But most projects remain relatively small-scale and not widely replicated because of cost, the multitude of approaches and local needs, and lack of interest from the private sector.

These factors, and the fact that ICT introduction is still at an early stage in developing countries, make the impact of projects hard to judge. "Undoubtedly ICTs are very useful for the people who have an opportunity to use them, but there is also a lot of hype about what computers and the Internet can do for rural people," says Cynthia Hewitt de Alcántara, deputy director of the United Nations Research Institute for Social Development and coordinator of its program on Information Technologies and Social Development. "Some serious social science research is needed to understand the institutional context that can make these technologies really useful and sustainable in specific rural settings," she adds, "and it is not the Internet that is always most important. Older technologies too, such as community radio, are opening up societies and allowing people to talk to each other. The telephone, of course, remains vital to people's well-being."

Using Mobile Phones

Perhaps the best-known example of bringing telephones to the poor is GrameenPhone, the Grameen Bank's rapidly growing cellular phone business in Bangladesh. A little more than three years old, the venture has already put mobile phones in the hands of women in more than 1,200 Bangladeshi villages. At the same time, GrameenPhone has secured more than 50 percent of the national, primarily urban, mobile phone market in Bangladesh, thus helping to assure both its financial ability to serve rural areas and its technical ability to create a reliable urban network with which to link the rural population.

In the villages, GrameenPhone works on the same principle as the Grameen Bank's microloan program, giving rural women from landless households access to credit. A woman who has already established good credit with the Bank, whose house is located in a fairly central part of the village, and whose family has one member familiar with the English letters and numbers on a phone, can borrow the roughly $350 needed to purchase a solar-powered mobile phone. After a day's training, the woman is set to provide phone service to other villagers for a price. This access to technology not only generates substantial income for the "telephone woman," who on average earns $450 a year after expenses, but also provides villagers with access to information and services that would otherwise remain far outside their reach.

The villagers, for example, can contact medical help immediately; get prevailing market prices for the crops they grow, thus avoiding underpayment by opportunistic traders; engage in commercial activities that require quick or frequent access to timetables, regulations, or other market-related information; and easily keep in touch with family members living in the cities or abroad. The arrival of the cell phone has also, for once, turned the social pecking order on its head as the relatively wealthy rely on the poor to keep in touch with the outside world.

"Money, the old saying goes, speaks loudest, but it is user-friendly technology that begets money in the first place," says Nuimuddin Chowdhury, an IFPRI consultant on ICTs. "The GrameenPhone project has shown once again that the rural poor are among the most eager to innovate, and they could significantly improve their income if given access to ICTs, which are, moreover, environmentally clean technologies."

Using Satellites

For developing countries, bridging the digital divide generally means bridging the gap between super-sophisticated technology on the one hand and local logistics and financial ability to pay on the other. Because satellites can bring ICTs to rural areas at a relatively low cost, some NGOs promote them to help fill the information and communication needs in developing countries. Volunteers in Technical Assistance (VITA), a U.S.-based NGO, for example, links its satellite with ground terminals that enable users to send and receive stored emails four to six times a day as the satellite passes overhead.

Kept in a community center or some other central location, each terminal is estimated to serve an area of roughly 10,000 people via the email access it gives to schools, clinics, NGOs, business people, and individual users. VITA's planned services include continually updated web indexes designed to meet the information needs of remote communities and a research service to maximize the impact of the 50-page limit that can be downloaded each day by each terminal. Costs for these services and for supporting the system will be defrayed by a relatively small annual fee per terminal and by proposed private-sector use of a portion of VITA's satellite bandwidth in exchange for technological production and support.

Currently at the experimental stage, the project serves 25 terminals. VITA plans to deploy 2,500 terminals throughout the developing world. "Basically we're trying to push the envelope to give the poor access to a culture of information," says George Scharffenberger, president of VITA. "Instant access to the Internet is exciting, but for a third to a half of humanity affordable access is still several years away. In the meantime, satellites can provide low-cost communication and information services to poor and remote areas while building critical information skills among teachers, health workers, people in small businesses, women, and youth."

VITA's other partner in this venture, SATELLIFE, also runs a health information system, HealthNet, which works through a satellite-terminal system similar to VITA's and through modem-to-modem telephone links. One of Africa's first sources for email, HealthNet also provides electronic publications, access to the web, and discussion groups, including one on AIDS, to about 10,000 health professionals worldwide. Locally owned and operated, HealthNet has been helpful in dramatic cases, such as containment of an Ebola virus outbreak in Gabon, as well as in more routine health care. It has succeeded in those countries where an adequate institutional structure exists or can be built to support ICTs, where training of technical staff matches investments in technology, and where a successful business model has been implemented to offset operating expenses.

"Once familiarity with a computer-based information culture has taken root and the medical benefits have become evident," says Rebecca Riccio, SATELLIFE's director of programs, "we've routinely seen health professionals further develop that culture and demand a wider array of ICT applications, not only from us but from others."

After training at SATELLIFE's Regional Information Technology Training Centre in Kenya, for example, one participant, a medical director of a charitable dispensary in Tanzania, became a telemedicine enthusiast, setting up a mailing list for his fellow trainees and seeking out how to transmit electrocardiograms and heart and lung sounds via the Internet to specialists for interpretation. "He also convinced management to provide two computers and set up an ICT training facility for his colleagues at the dispensary," says Eliazar Karan, project manager of HealthNet Kenya.

Improving Women's Access to ICTs

As ICTs begin to play a greater role in development, concerns are growing that women will be left out of the picture. Available data show that women account for 25 percent of ICT users in Brazil, 17 percent in South Africa, 7 percent in China, and 4 percent in Arab states. All the gender faultlines are present in ICT access, with poor, uneducated, and older women particularly affected.

To address these concerns, the United Nations Development Fund for Women (UNIFEM), ITU, and UNDP recently signed an agreement guaranteeing the inclusion of gender issues in their policy dialogue and decisionmaking about ICTs. Going further, Noeleen Heyzer, UNIFEM's executive director, has advocated that UN bodies that are developing programs to promote ICTs should consider allocating 50 percent of these program funds and program activities to women and girls until the digital divide closes.

"ICTs give us a new opportunity to build a confident, skilled, and participatory knowledge community that includes women," says Heyzer, "and failure to do this will only worsen the existing gender-related gaps. We should be striving for 'e-quality.' Women and girls must receive the training and preparation to become users and producers of ICT technologies and to understand and shape the regulations and policies associated with these technologies."

Overcoming the Barriers to Universal Access

The success of some local-level projects says little yet about what should be the method and timetable for delivering universal access. Even the dilemma about whether to focus first on building a national infrastructure for instant access or on building ICTs around specific development problems remains unresolved.

Some developing countries, such as Malaysia, have made commitments to rapid and widespread ICT introduction. Others may move forward, at least in the near future, on two tracks: partnering with the private sector to install ICTs in urban areas and looking to donors, lowest-cost methods, and innovative schemes for subsidizing subscription fees to connect rural areas, with the two tracks sometimes overlapping.

"The countries that have been most successful in promoting ICT-based development," says Carlos Primo Braga, program manager at infoDev (the World Bank's Information for Development Program), "are those that have created a broad framework for fostering both competition and universal access. They've focused on expansion of the capacity to connect to ICTs, education to use that connectivity, appropriate content in the local language to make that connectivity useful, and competition to lower prices and increase market growth."

Perhaps the most neglected component of this framework is a well-developed legal system to facilitate effective regulatory policy. "Developing countries repeatedly treat this issue cavalierly," says Noll, "as if constructing an independent, effective, and efficient administrative system is something that can be set up casually over a long weekend."

As if these systemic hurdles were not enough, some governments are wary of the power of information and the political and economic uses it can be put to, or simply skeptical about its importance. They show reluctance to embrace the ICT revolution.

But the most pressing and universal barrier remains money. D'Orville estimates that a telecenter that serves 2,000–6,000 people costs roughly $60,000–$80,000, a sum that includes provisions for training, content development, operations, maintenance, and management. Even so, the picture may not be so daunting because costs are decreasing and new technical devices are emerging. "Medium-developed countries already have high TV penetration, and devices to access the Internet are going to fall below the cost of TVs," says Josh Calder senior associate at Coates & Jarratt, Inc., a Washington, D.C.-based consulting firm that analyzes and forecasts ICT applications. "More people are expected to access the Web via mobile devices than through PCs in a few years, and mobile phones already have extensive penetration even in quite poor countries. High-tech systems tend to go where they are demanded—note the ubiquitous presence of sonogram clinics in the poorest neighborhoods of India."

Expensive, potentially disruptive, and extraordinarily beneficial, ICTs are here to stay, and developing countries can ill afford to sit on the sidelines. As Richard Heeks, senior lecturer in information systems and development at the University of Manchester, puts it, "Information and communication technology is a runaway horse, and the choice for the world's poorer nations is stark: stand by and watch it carry the richer nations forward, or jump on and hope to steer it as best they can."

PART 11

Conclusion

Chapter 41

Putting the Knowledge to Work for the Poor

Required Policy Action

Per Pinstrup-Andersen and Rajul Pandya-Lorch

T he vision of a world where nobody needs to go hungry and where natural resources are managed sustainably can be achieved by 2020. But achieving it will require policy action of a nature and magnitude not currently pursued by most governments. Governments must decide that creating such a world is of paramount importance and give it the highest priority. Decisionmakers in the public and private sector must join forces with civil society around the common goal of facilitating sustainable food security for all and together take the necessary steps. Agreeing that access to sufficient food to live a healthy and productive life is a basic human right for all, rings hollow if those in power do not make every effort to assist individuals and communities in getting access.

What specific actions should be taken and who should take them will vary across communities, countries, and regions and over time. This chapter identifies the policy actions that we believe developing countries and aid agencies should consider. We suggest that local and national actions be tailored and implemented in a participatory way that includes the intended beneficiaries.

International Driving Forces

Two overriding forces—globalization and technological change—may help or hinder efforts to achieve sustainable food security for all. Globalization, in the form of trade liberalization, reduced national protection and taxation of agriculture and industry, more integrated international capital markets, and a freer flow of labor, information, and technology across national borders, is likely to continue and even accelerate. Technological change is driven by rapid scientific progress in biology and information and communications technologies. Relying exclusively on the market to direct these forces will result in a distribution of benefits and costs incompatible with the vision of sustainable global food security. It is increasingly clear that international, national, and local policies and institutions must guide globalization and technology to assure an acceptable distribution of benefits and losses.

At the international level, existing institutions such as the World Trade Organization should work closely with civil society and national governments to identify and remove factors that harm the poor. Such factors include ineffective competition and price distortions in international trade, intellectual property right regimes that are adverse to the poor, barriers to access to appropriate technology by developing countries, barriers to labor movement across national borders, and import barriers by industrialized countries to goods and services that generate income among the poor in developing countries and for which these countries are or could become competitive.

At the national level, countries should consider six sets of policy action, described here.

Policies to Improve the Human Resource

It is generally recognized that good health and nutrition are important indicators of well-being and should be pursued in their own right. But the important role of health and nutrition as inputs in the development process is still poorly understood. Sick and undernourished people will not escape poverty and associated human misery. Thus good health and nutrition are means to eradicating poverty and achieving broad-based development, as well as the ends.

Policy action to improve health and nutrition must deal with diseases affecting the poor such as HIV/AIDS, tuberculosis, and malaria as well as access to clean drinking water and safe food. Poor nutrition can be a vicious circle in which underweight babies, born of poor and malnourished mothers, grow up in an environment with unclean drinking water and insufficient and unsafe food to become underweight poor parents giving birth to underweight babies. Policies should be designed and implemented to intervene in this cycle. The most cost-effective intervention point will vary across population groups and over time.

In addition to the nutrition problems caused by food shortage, policy action is needed to alleviate widespread micronutrient deficiencies through better-balanced diets, plant breeding, fortification, and supplementation. Previously thought of as rich people's diseases, obesity and related chronic diseases are rapidly becoming a serious health problem among the poor in many developing countries. Preventive policy action such as nutrition education and food price interventions is needed along with curative measures. The dietary transition accelerating in many developing countries is resulting in the coexistence of a double burden of undernutrition and "overnutrition," placing additional demands on the public sector and civil society.

In addition to publicly funded health, water, and nutrition programs and direct transfers of income in cash and kind to the poor, policy action should focus on generating pro-poor economic growth. Primary education has shown to be particularly effective in helping people out of poverty, and emphasis should be placed on policies promoting primary education, particularly among the poor. Food for Education programs, including both school feeding and take-home food, have shown great promise as a way of expanding school enrollment of poor children and simultaneously improving the food security of participating families. Education of girls from poor families has been neglected in many societies and should be improved, not only for equity reasons but also because it improves the well-being of families and contributes to poverty alleviation in general. Improving the status of women within households and societies has also been shown to contribute not only to equity but also to general improvements in food security and economic growth. The design and implementation of policies to help the poor and food insecure should recognize the importance of social capital and build on it rather than trying to replace it.

Access to Productive Resources and Employment

If pro-poor economic growth is to succeed, the poor must have access to productive resources and employment. Between 70 and 75 percent of the world's poor people live in rural areas of developing countries. Some have access to small plots of land, most do not. Among those who have access to land, many live in areas with poor soils, irregular rainfall, and very little appropriate infrastructure such as roads and markets. While outmigration to urban or peri-urban areas may be the best solution for some, these areas can absorb only a small fraction of the rural poor every year. Thus, in the short to medium term, policy action to achieve the 2020 Vision must focus on the environments where the majority of the poor are.

Secure access to land by poor families through individual or community ownership, long-term user rights, or some other means is of paramount importance. Governments may need to intervene in existing land tenure arrangements either to redistribute land or to assure secure long-term access by households or communities. Clear property rights or user rights to other natural resources, such as water and forests, are also crucial for achieving the combined goals of poverty alleviation, sustainable management of natural resources, and productivity increases in agriculture.

272 PER PINSTRUP-ANDERSEN AND RAJUL PANDYA-LORCH

National policies should be balanced with community action. In some cases, market approaches may be appropriate. In others, delegating the necessary power to communities and user associations may be the way forward.

Although the majority of the rural poor depend on agriculture, many of them do so indirectly through employment in small-scale rural enterprises that provide goods and services for farm families. Credit and savings institutions for small rural enterprises as well as investment in rural infrastructure and competitive markets is needed to further enhance employment and add value to primary agricultural production on the basis of small-scale rural enterprises.

Although countries must focus on policies to deal with rural poverty and food insecurity, they also need to accommodate the rapidly increasing urban population. Such policies should focus on public and private investment in infrastructure, employment, housing, education, and primary health care.

Markets, Infrastructure, and Institutions

Without fair, well-functioning markets and access to both production inputs and consumption goods at reasonable prices, the poor cannot fully capture the benefits from improved human resources and access to productive resources. Small farmers must have access to efficient and effective competitive markets to buy the inputs they need in the production process and to sell what they produce. They must also have timely access to credit and savings institutions that offer reasonable interest rates and other conditions. While microcredit and savings schemes have been successful in many locations of the developing countries, these schemes are usually limited to very small-scale enterprises and frequently exclude farming. Policies are urgently needed to facilitate access to unsubsidized credit by small farmers producing primarily for the market. Access by women and collective repayment responsibility are important aspects to consider for equity and economic growth reasons.

Ongoing privatization of domestic agricultural input and output markets should be completed, and the new role of government, such as regulation, specification of standards for weight and measures, and enforcement of contracts, should be identified and implemented.

Globalization and increasing climatic fluctuations are likely to introduce new risks and uncertainties for the poor. Economies will be more interconnected, resulting in new risk factors, and consumers, producers, and labor will be less protected as markets are liberalized and subsidies reduced. Institutions to facilitate the management of risk among the poor, including credit and savings institutions and social and food security networks, as well as predictive tools such as timely weather and market forecasts, are currently weak in most countries and need strengthening.

Explicit and implicit capital subsidies as well as infrastructure investments in developing countries tend to be biased against small farmers. This may also be the case for access to input and output markets. Many rural regions consisting primarily of poor people, including small farmers, are often the last regions to get investments in infrastructure, and partly for that reason markets are poorly developed. There is a widespread erroneous view that small farmers are not competitive. While the relation between efficiency and farm size depends on many factors, it is important to remove the distortions currently embodied in capital subsidies, infrastructure investments, markets, and related policies to give the farm structure the opportunity to adjust according to relative efficiency. This step is particularly important to assure that the rural poor get their fair share of the benefits from globalization and the associated changes in market competition. Rural poor, whether farmers or not, will not benefit if they are excluded from participation or fair competition in the mainstream market economy.

Knowledge and Technology

Sustainable productivity increases in small-scale agriculture are of critical importance to achieve the 2020 Vision. In addition to access to inputs and other factors already mentioned, productivity increases will depend on access to appropriate knowledge and technology. While private sector research may produce some of the knowledge and technology needed by small farmers, publicly funded research is essential. This is so partly because poor farmers are not an attractive market for private sector research agencies and partly because much of the knowledge and technology poor farmers need is of a public goods nature.

Public sector agricultural research should embody all relevant approaches, such as agroecological, conventional, and molecular biology research methods. Opportunities for using modern information and communications technology in agricultural production and distribution as well as nonagricultural rural enterprises to help achieve the 2020 Vision should be pursued. The primary role of the government should be not to choose technologies for small farmers and others but rather to make available a menu of technology options from which they can choose. Because of past neglect of areas that are environmentally less favored, such a menu of technology options is particularly critical for these areas. To ensure that technologies are relevant to the ultimate users, research should involve the participation of these users.

Because of past labor surpluses in rural areas of many developing countries, researchers have focused on developing labor-using technologies. The result has often been low labor productivity. Situations of surplus labor are less common today than they were 10 years ago, particularly in areas affected by HIV/AIDS.

Seasonal labor scarcity is now very common in rural areas of developing countries. Planning for research and technology must take this situation into consideration and place a greater emphasis on increasing labor productivity.

Most developing countries must also strengthen their polices related to biotechnology, particularly in the areas of allocation of public resources for research, biosafety, intellectual property rights, health and ecological risks, antitrust legislation, and trade.

Management of Natural Resources

Population and income growth along with dietary changes will require continued increases in food production. Most of the increases will have to come from land currently under cultivation. Continuing to bring new land into agricultural production will entail large environmental costs in terms of land degradation, deforestation, and loss of biodiversity. Governments must take steps to ensure that continued expansion of yields on existing agricultural lands is sustainable, such as undertaking agricultural research and technology, enacting policies for water and land management, and establishing property rights to natural resources.

Policy action is needed in many of the least-developed countries to help farmers solve the problem of declining soil fertility through better soil management and cropping practices, effective use of organic matter, and access to reasonably priced fertilizers. Required policies include support of agricultural research aimed at better use of plant nutrients and the capture of nitrogen from the air, access to credit, investments in roads and rural transportation systems, government support and regulation to create an effective and efficient market for plant nutrients, and extension services. Policy action is also needed to mitigate negative effects of climate change and to reduce agriculture's contribution to global warming.

Macroeconomic Policies and Good Governance

An appropriate macroeconomic environment is critical for the achievement of the 2020 Vision. The impact of the policy measures discussed in this chapter will depend on existing macroeconomic policies, such as those affecting money supply, exchange rates, and trade.

The roles of the state, the market, civil society, and the for-profit private sector have changed markedly during the last 10 years in response to globalization, structural adjustment, and related market reforms. The role of the public sector is shrinking while civil society and the market are taking on additional responsibilities. Although this shift may be appropriate, it is important to recognize the limitations of the for-profit sector in providing public goods. Developing countries should maintain a strong and effective public sector to guide and support efforts to achieve the 2020 Vision and to provide public goods needed by the poor. These goods include primary health care; education; rural infrastructure in regions with many poor people; research to help small farmers and to enable sustainable management of natural resources; development and enforcement of effective and fair legal systems, including contract enforcement; and weight and measurement standards. Other public sector actions, such as poverty and nutrition programs, have already been mentioned. Civil society may carry out part of these actions and may play an increasingly important role in providing other public goods to the poor and malnourished.

No More Business As Usual

Achieving the 2020 Vision will not be easy. It will not happen with business as usual. A much higher level of dedication by those with the power to move the world closer to the 2020 Vision will be needed. A small sacrifice by the nonpoor may be called for in the short run, but in the long run we will all gain. Apart from the tremendous human misery they create, widespread poverty, food insecurity, and malnutrition constitute a huge economic waste that, if eliminated, would provide the foundation for enhanced well-being for poor and nonpoor alike.

Sources

Sources

Chapter 1: "The Unfinished Agenda—Famine and Poverty in the 21st Century," 2020 *News & Views,* August 1994. Reported by Ellen Wilson.

Chapter 2: Per Pinstrup-Andersen, Rajul Pandya-Lorch, and Mark W. Rosegrant, "Global Food Security: A Review of the Challenges," paper prepared for the conference "Reducing Poverty through Sustainable Agriculture," London, January 25, 2001.

Chapter 3: Lisa C. Smith and Lawrence Haddad, "Overcoming Child Malnutrition in Developing Countries: Past Achievements and Future Choices," 2020 Brief 64 (Washington, D.C.: International Food Policy Research Institute, 2000).

Chapter 4: Rafael Flores, "Overview," in *Health and Nutrition: Emerging and Reemerging Issues in Developing Countries,* 2020 Focus 5 (Washington, D.C.: International Food Policy Research Institute, 2001).

Chapter 5: "Fighting Hidden Hunger," 2020 *News & Views,* April 2000. Reported by Heidi Fritschel.

Chapter 6: "AIDS Mushrooms into a Development Crisis," 2020 *News & Views,* December 2000. Reported by Sara E. Wilson.

Chapter 7: Tony Barnett and Gabriel Rugalema, "HIV/AIDS," in *Health and Nutrition: Emerging and Reemerging Issues in Developing Countries,* 2020 Focus 5 (Washington, D.C.: International Food Policy Research Institute, 2001).

Chapter 8: Reynaldo Martorell, "Obesity," in *Health and Nutrition: Emerging and Reemerging Issues in Developing Countries,* 2020 Focus 5 (Washington, D.C.: International Food Policy Research Institute, 2001).

Chapter 9: "The Population Boom: What Do the Numbers Mean?" 2020 *News & Views,* October 1994. Reported by Ellen Wilson.

Chapter 10: John Bongaarts and Judith Bruce, "Population Growth and Policy Options in the Developing World," 2020 Brief 53 (Washington, D.C.: International Food Policy Research Institute, 1998).

Chapter 11: James L. Garrett, "Overview," in *Achieving Urban Food and Nutrition Security in the Developing World,* 2020 Focus 3 (Washington, D.C.: International Food Policy Research Institute, 2000).

Chapter 12: "Urbanization and Agriculture to the Year 2020," 2020 *News & Views,* April 1996. Reported by Ellen Wilson.

Chapter 13: "Are We Ready for a Meat Revolution?" 2020 *News & Views,* March 1999. Reported by Heidi Fritschel and Uday Mohan.

Chapter 14: Christopher Delgado, Mark Rosegrant, Henning Steinfeld, Simeon Ehui, and Claude Courbois, "Livestock to 2020: The Next Food Revolution," 2020 Brief 61 (Washington, D.C.: International Food Policy Research Institute, 1999).

Chapter 15: "Overfished Oceans, Booming Fisheries: What Does This Mean for World Food Security?" 2020 *News & Views,* October 1997. Reported by Ellen Wilson.

Chapter 16: "The Earth's Environmental Woes: Is Agriculture Part of the Problem or Part of the Solution?" 2020 *News & Views,* December 1994. Reported by Ellen Wilson.

Chapter 17: Per Pinstrup-Andersen and Rajul Pandya-Lorch, "Agricultural Growth is the Key to Poverty Alleviation in Low-Income Developing Countries," 2020 Brief 15 (Washington, D.C.: International Food Policy Research Institute, 1995).

Chapter 18: John Pender and Peter Hazell, "Overview," in *Promoting Sustainable Development in Less-Favored Areas,* 2020 Focus 4 (Washington, D.C.: International Food Policy Research Institute, 2000); and Peter Hazell and James L. Garrett, "Reducing Poverty and Protecting the Environment: The Overlooked Potential of Less-Favored Lands," 2020 Brief 39 (Washington, D.C.: International Food Policy Research Institute, 1996).

Chapter 19: Miguel A. Altieri, Peter Rosset, and Lori Ann Thrupp, "The Potential of Agroecology to Combat Hunger in the Developing World," 2020 Brief 55 (Washington, D.C.: International Food Policy Research Institute, 1998).

Chapter 20: Robert L. Paarlberg, "Sustainable Farming: A Political Geography," 2020 Brief 4 (Washington, D.C.: International Food Policy Research Institute, 1994).

Chapter 21: Sara J. Scherr and Satya Yadav, "Land Degradation in the Developing World: Issues and Policy Options for 2020," 2020 Brief 44 (Washington, D.C.: International Food Policy Research Institute, 1997); and Sara J. Scherr, "Soil Degradation: A Threat to Developing-Country Food Security by 2020?" 2020 Brief 58 (Washington, D.C.: International Food Policy Research Institute, 1999).

Chapter 22: Stephen Vosti, "The Role of Agriculture in Saving the Rain Forest," 2020 Brief 9 (Washington, D.C.: International Food Policy Research Institute, 1995).

Chapter 23: Mark W. Rosegrant, "Dealing with Water Scarcity in the Next Century," 2020 Brief 21 (Washington, D.C.: International Food Policy Research Institute, 1995).

Chapter 24: "Global Warming Changes the Forecast for Agriculture," 2020 News & Views, April 2001. Reported by Sara E. Wilson.

Chapter 25: Julio Henao and Carlos Baanante, "Nutrient Depletion in the Agricultural Soils of Africa," 2020 Brief 62 (Washington, D.C.: International Food Policy Research Institute, 1999).

Chapter 26: "Applying Science to Sub-Saharan Africa's Food Needs," 2020 News & Views, February 1995. Reported by Ellen Wilson.

Chapter 27: "Pushing Back Poverty in India," 2020 News & Views, September 1999. Reported by Heidi Fritschel and Uday Mohan.

Chapter 28: "Is Agriculture Raiding South Asia's Water Supplies?" 2020 News & Views, April 1995. Reported by Ellen Wilson.

Chapter 29: Mark W. Rosegrant and Peter B. R. Hazell, "Transforming the Rural Asian Economy: The Unfinished Revolution," 2020 Brief 69 (Washington, D.C.: International Food Policy Research Institute, 2001).

Chapter 30: Manfred Zeller and Manohar Sharma, "Rural Financial Services for Poverty Alleviation: The Role of Public Policy," 1996 IFPRI Annual Report (Washington, D.C.: International Food Policy Research Institute, 1997).

Chapter 31: Manohar Sharma, "Microfinance: Reaching Poor Rural Women," in Empowering Women to Achieve Food Security, 2020 Focus 6 (Washington, D.C.: International Food Policy Research Institute, 2001)

Chapter 32: Lynn R. Brown, Hilary Feldstein, Lawrence Haddad, Christine Peña, and Agnes Quisumbing, "Generating Food Security in the Year 2020: Women as Producers, Gatekeepers, and Shock Absorbers," 2020 Brief 17 (Washington, D.C.: International Food Policy Research Institute, 1995).

Chapter 33: Patrice L. Engle, "Urban Women: Balancing Work and Childcare," in *Achieving Urban Food and Nutrition Security in the Developing World,* 2020 Focus 3 (Washington, D.C.: International Food Policy Research Institute, 2000).

Chapter 34: "The Fruits of Girls' Education," 2020 *News & Views,* December 1999. Reported by Heidi Fritschel and Uday Mohan.

Chapter 35: Eugenio Díaz-Bonilla and Sherman Robinson, "Globalization, Trade Reform, and the Developing Countries," *IFPRI Annual Report 1998* (Washington, D.C.: International Food Policy Research Institute, 1999).

Chapter 36: Julie Babinard and Per Pinstrup-Andersen, "Globalization and Nutrition," in *Globalization, Poverty, and Food Security,* 2020 Focus 8 (Washington, D.C.: International Food Policy Research Institute, 2001)

Chapter 37: Gabrielle J. Persley and John J. Doyle, "Overview," in *Biotechnology for Developing-Country Agriculture: Problems and Opportunities,* 2020 Focus 2 (Washington, D.C.: International Food Policy Research Institute, 1999).

Chapter 38: Per Pinstrup-Andersen, "Developing Appropriate Policies," in *Biotechnology for Developing-Country Agriculture: Problems and Opportunities,* 2020 Focus 2 (Washington, D.C.: International Food Policy Research Institute, 1999).

Chapter 39: Robert L. Paarlberg, "Governing the GM Crop Revolution: Policy Choices for Developing Countries," 2020 Brief 68 (Washington, D.C.: International Food Policy Research Institute, 2000).

Chapter 40: "Bridging the Digital Divide," 2020 *News & Views,* September 2000. Reported by Uday Mohan.

Contributors

Miguel A. Altieri is an associate professor in the Department of Environmental Science, Policy and Management, University of California at Berkeley, USA.

Carlos Baanante was director of research and development at the International Fertilizer Development Center, Muscle Shoals, USA.

Julie Babinard was a senior research assistant in the Director General's Office at IFPRI.

Tony Barnett is professor of development studies at the School of Development Studies, University of East Anglia, U.K.

John Bongaarts is vice president of the Policy Research Division of the Population Council, New York, USA.

Lynn Brown is a rural development specialist at the World Bank, Washington, D.C., USA.

Judith Bruce is director of the Gender, Family and Development Program, International Programs Division, at the Population Council, New York, USA.

Claude Courbois is an economist at The NASDAQ Stock Market, Inc.

Christopher Delgado is a senior research fellow in the Markets and Structural Studies Division of IFPRI.

Eugenio Díaz-Bonilla is a research fellow in the Trade and Macroeconomics Division of IFPRI.

John J. Doyle worked on the application of molecular biology and immunology to tropical livestock disease in Africa for 20 years. Dr. Doyle died in 1999.

Simeon Ehui is coordinator of the Livestock Policy Analysis Programme at the International Livestock Research Institute, Addis Ababa, Ethiopia.

Patrice L. Engle is chief of child development and nutrition at UNICEF's office in India.

Hilary Feldstein is a social scientist at the International Center for Research on Women, Washington, D.C., USA.

Rafael Flores was a senior research fellow in the Food Consumption and Nutrition Division of IFPRI. He is now a research associate professor in the Department of International Health, Rollins School of Public Health, Emory University, USA.

Heidi Fritschel was a senior editor at IFPRI.

James L. Garrett is a research fellow in the Food Consumption and Nutrition Division of IFPRI.

Lawrence Haddad is director of IFPRI's Food Consumption and Nutrition Division.

Peter B. R. Hazell is director of IFPRI's Environment and Production Technology Division.

Julio Henao is senior scientist-biometrician at the International Fertilizer Development Center, USA.

Reynaldo Martorell is Robert W. Woodruff Professor of International Nutrition and Chair of the Department of International Health in the Rollins School of Public Health, Emory University, USA.

Uday Mohan is a senior editor at IFPRI.

Robert L. Paarlberg is a professor of political science at Wellesley College, Wellesley, Massachusetts, U.S.A., and an associate at the Weatherhead Center for International Affairs at Harvard University.

Rajul Pandya-Lorch is head of the 2020 Vision for Food, Agriculture, and the Environment Initiative at IFPRI.

Christine Peña is a human resources economist in the African Technical Human Development IV division at the World Bank, Washington, D.C., USA.

John Pender is a research fellow in the Environment and Production Technology Division at IFPRI.

Gabrielle J. Persley was an adviser to the World Bank on biotechnology-related issues.

Per Pinstrup-Andersen is the director general of IFPRI.

Agnes Quisumbing is a senior research fellow in IFPRI's Food Consumption and Nutrition Division.

Sherman Robinson is director of the Trade and Macroeconomics Division of IFPRI.

Mark Rosegrant is a senior research fellow in the Environment and Production Technology Division of IFPRI.

Peter Rosset is codirector of Food First/The Institute for Food and Development Policy, Oakland, USA.

Gabriel Rugalema is the senior policy advisor for the United Nations Development Programme's HIV Project for Sub-Saharan Africa.

Sara J. Scherr is a fellow of Forest Trends, a Washington, D.C.-based nonprofit organization promoting sustainable forestry, and an adjunct professor at the Agricultural and Resource Economics Department, University of Maryland, College Park, USA.

Manohar Sharma is a postdoctoral fellow in the Food Consumption and Nutrition Division of IFPRI.

Lisa C. Smith is a research fellow in IFPRI's Food Consumption and Nutrition Division.

Henning Steinfeld is chief of the Livestock Information, Sector Analysis and Policy Branch at the Food and Agriculture Organization of the United Nations, Rome, Italy.

Lori Ann Thrupp was director of sustainable agriculture at the World Resources Institute, Washington, D.C., USA, when she coauthored the brief in this volume. She is currently a life scientist at the U.S. Environmental Protection Agency.

Stephen Vosti is an adjunct professor in the Department of Agricultural and Resource Economics, University of California at Davis, USA.

Ellen Wilson is vice president of Burness Communications, Bethesda, Maryland, USA.

Sara E. Wilson is a consultant for IFPRI.

Satya Yadav was a research associate in the Department of Agricultural Economics and Rural Sociology at the University of Arkansas, USA.

Manfred Zeller was a research fellow in the Food Consumption and Nutrition Division of IFPRI from 1993 to 1999. He is now the director of the Institute of Rural Development, Faculty of Agriculture, University of Goettingen, Goettingen, Germany.

Index

Note: Page numbers followed by letters *f* and *t* refer to figures and tables, respectively.